Suicide Among Youth:
Perspectives on
Risk and Prevention

Suicide Among Youth: Perspectives on Risk and Prevention

Edited by

Cynthia R. Pfeffer, M.D.

Associate Professor of Clinical Psychiatry,
Cornell University Medical College; and
Chief, Child Psychiatry Inpatient Unit,
The New York Hospital-Cornell
University Medical Center,
Westchester Division,
White Plains, New York

1400 K Street, N.W.
Washington, DC 20005

Note: The authors have worked to ensure that all information in this book concerning drug dosages, schedules, and routes of administration is accurate as of the time of publication and consistent with standards set by the U.S. Food and Drug Administration and the general medical community. As medical research and practice advance, however, therapeutic standards may change. For this reason and because human and mechanical errors sometimes occur, we recommend that readers follow the advice of a physician who is directly involved in their care or the care of a member of their family.

Books published by the American Psychiatric Press, Inc., represent the views and opinions of the individual authors and do not necessarily represent the policies and opinions of the Press or the American Psychiatric Association.

The paper used in this publication meets the minimum requirements of American National Standard for Information Sciences—Permanence of Paper for Printed Library Materials, ANSI Z39.48-1984. ∞

Library of Congress Cataloging-in-Publication Data

Suicide among youth / [edited by] Cynthia R. Pfeffer.
    p.   cm.
    Includes bibliographies and index.
    ISBN 0-88048-167-6
    1. Youth—Suicidal behavior.   I. Pfeffer, Cynthia R.
    [DNLM: 1. Suicide—in adolescence.   2. Suicide—
prevention & control. HV 6546 S9477]
RJ506.S9S83   1989
616.85′8445—dc19
DNLM/DLC
for Library of Congress   88-36702
                                                          CIP

Contents

Contributors

Eugenia P. Broumas
Special Assistant to the Deputy Director; Office of the Director; National Institute of Mental Health; Alcohol, Drug Abuse, and Mental Health Administration; Public Health Service; U.S. Department of Health and Human Services; Rockville, Maryland

Lundie L. Carstensen, M.S.
Graduate Student, University of California at San Diego, San Diego, California

Lucy E. Davidson, M.D., Ed.S.
Clinical Assistant Professor in Psychiatry, Emory University School of Medicine, Atlanta, Georgia

Michael D. DeMeo, M.D.
Instructor of Psychiatry, Laboratory of Psychopharmacology, Department of Psychiatry, Cornell University Medical College, New York, New York

David M. Eddy, M.D., Ph.D.
Professor and Director, Center for Health Policy Research and Education, Duke University, Durham, North Carolina

Shervert H. Frazier, M.D.
Former Director, National Institute of Mental Health; and Past Chairman, Health and Human Services Secretary's Task Force on Youth Suicide; and Psychiatrist-in-Chief Emeritus, McLean Hospital, Belmont, Massachusetts

Barry D. Garfinkel, M.D., F.R.C.P.(C)
Associate Professor of Psychiatry and Director, Division of Child and Adolescent Psychiatry, University of Minnesota, Minneapolis, Minnesota

Heinz Häfner, M.D., Ph.D.
Professor of Psychiatry, University of Heidelberg; and
Director of the Central Institute of Mental Health,
Mannheim, Federal Republic of Germany

Harry M. Hoberman, Ph.D.
Assistant Professor of Psychiatry and Pediatrics; and Mental
Health Specialist with the Adolescent Health Program,
University of Minnesota, Minneapolis, Minnesota

Paul C. Holinger, M.D., M.P.H.
Associate Professor of Psychiatry, Rush-Presbyterian-St.
Luke's Medical Center, Chicago, Illinois

John G. Keilp, M.A.
Research Fellow and Staff Associate, Laboratory of
Psychopharmacology, Department of Psychiatry, Cornell
University Medical College, New York, New York

Gerald L. Klerman, M.D.
Professor of Psychiatry and Associate Chairman for
Research, Cornell University Medical College, New York,
New York

J. John Mann, M.D.
Professor of Psychiatry and Director, Laboratory of
Psychopharmacology, Department of Psychiatry, Cornell
University Medical College, New York, New York

P. Anne McBride, M.D.
Assistant Professor of Psychiatry, Laboratory of
Psychopharmacology, Department of Psychiatry, Cornell
University Medical College, New York, New York

Daniel J. Paight, B.A.
Graduate Student, University of California at San Diego,
San Diego, California

Cynthia R. Pfeffer, M.D.
Associate Professor of Clinical Psychiatry, Cornell
University Medical College; Chief, Child Psychiatry
Inpatient Unit, New York Hospital-Westchester Division,
White Plains, New York

David P. Phillips, Ph.D.
Professor of Sociology, University of California at San Diego, San Diego, California

Mark L. Rosenberg, M.D., M.P.P.
Assistant Director for Science, Division of Injury Epidemiology and Control, Center for Environmental Health and Injury Control, Centers for Disease Control, Public Health Service, U.S. Department of Health and Human Services, Atlanta, Georgia

Alec Roy, M.B.
Visiting Associate, Laboratory of Clinical Studies, National Institute on Alcohol Abuse and Alcoholism, Rockville, Maryland

Armin Schmidtke, M.D.
Head of the Unit of Clinical Psychology, Psychiatric Clinic of the University of Wuerzburg, Wuerzburg, Federal Republic of Germany

Mohammad Shafii, M.D.
Professor of Psychiatry and Director, Child Psychiatry Training Program, University of Louisville School of Medicine, Louisville, Kentucky

Robert C. Wolpert, Ph.D.
Associate Director for Analyses and Methodology, Center for Health Policy Research and Education, Duke University, Durham, North Carolina

Foreword

The prevalence of youth suicide is a national dilemma of such lethality that it has destroyed some of our most vital young people in the prime of their lives. This deadly disorder has not received the attention, research effort, or educational thrust afforded so many other mortal disorders, despite the fact that recognition of at-risk youths and interventions, including treatments, could save thousands of young lives.

Fortunately, Secretary of Health and Human Services Margaret Heckler had the foresight to establish the Secretary's Task Force on Youth Suicide to examine this phenomenon. The world's outstanding researchers, clinicians, and educators were convened in three panels to study this major societal and psychosocial problem and make recommendations for its resolution. Risk factors, preventions and interventions, and strategies for future research and education were the subjects of those panels.

The editors and authors of many of the chapters in this book were among those who studied, wrote, presented, and organized this effort. They are certainly the leaders in the United States in this worthy subject area. Their current knowledge, their search for new knowledge, and their abilities to institute research bode well for future development in the academic community to plan the interventions and preventions for those who would commit suicide.

Multidisciplinary efforts involving educators, counselors, and sociologists, as well as physicians, psychiatrists, psychologists, epidemiologists, and other professionals will bring the base of data in suicide to the critical mass so necessary for breakthroughs.

Pilot projects are urgently needed to develop an accurate data base. This includes education of medical examiners in regard to recording of suicide data at inquests and establishment of two or even three academic/university centers for suicide research, federally funded with participation by state mental health departments. Pilot intervention projects and services-evaluation research are a very high priority. Prevention research and education of students, teachers, principals, superintendents of schools, and counselors are needed to determine efficacy of suicide prevention services. Public education, including extensive campaigns by TV, radio, and print media regarding risk factors, substance abuse, and recognition of depression and impulse-control disorders, are the highest priorities.

We as a nation and as professionals need to become concerned about our ignorance regarding suicide and our denial of its tragic effects and enlist our efforts to change not only our own but also all citizens' awareness of suicide.

Shervert H. Frazier, M.D.

Introduction

This book presents divergent research that utilizes newly developed methodologies for understanding suicide among adolescents and young adults. Throughout the text, implications of these studies for preventing youth suicide are highlighted.

Recently, there has been widespread recognition of the great increase in youth suicide that has occurred in the last few decades; to the extent that suicide among 15- to 24-year-olds is the second leading cause of death in the United States. Data from many countries also suggest that there has been a recent rise in rates of youth suicide. These facts emphasize the important and immediate need to acquire objective understanding of this tragic phenomenon. Empirical data are necessary to provide a basis for designing programs and developing techniques to identify and treat young people who may be vulnerable to fatal suicidal acts.

This book discusses recent representative research that addresses the multifaceted dimensions of youth suicide risk: sociocultural, psychosocial, biological, and genetic factors. The main emphasis is on the application of epidemiological techniques to study these issues and to prevent suicide among youth. Because the field of systematic study of youth suicide is so new, there are many areas in which few or no data on suicide among the young exist now. In view of this, some of the authors have incorporated data about nonfatal suicidal behavior and about suicide among adults as a means of suggesting hypotheses and research designs that may be used to study suicide among youth.

The chapters present the work of investigators whose ongoing empirical research highlights the complex nature of risk for youth suicide. The text begins with research insights about the psychosocial characteristics of young people who committed suicide. Mohammad Shafii, the first investigator to apply the psychological autopsy method to youth suicide, describes this technique and his collaborative work with the local coroner. An aim of his research is to define features that distinguish youth suicide victims from a comparison group of nonsuicidal teenagers. Another approach to delineating factors associated with youth suicide involves review of records. An important resource is the medical examiner or coroner, whose records provide demographic profiles, descriptive data about suicide methods, associated factors at the time of death, and psychosocial information about the deceased. Harry M. Hoberman and Barry D. Garfinkel discuss their detailed investigation of medical examiners' records. Their study attempts to characterize gender, age, and temporal differences in young suicides. Specifically, they make three comparisons: male versus female suicide completers; persons 14 years old and under versus persons who were 15–19 years old versus individuals who were 20–25 years old; and suicides occurring between 1975 and 1979 versus those occurring between 1980 and 1985.

Data from studies that used large epidemiological samples offer a powerful perspective about trends in risk factors. Paul C. Holinger was among the first investigators to use national data on suicide to evaluate longitudinal trends in suicide rates. His chapter integrates epidemiologic data regarding longitudinal, demographic, cross-cultural, and high-risk groups for youth suicide. He suggests predictors of suicide among the young that are potentially valuable in planning suicide prevention efforts. Gerald L. Klerman reviews several large epidemiologic studies that focus on individuals who are depressed. Specifically, he describes the complex relationship between depression and suicide. He identifies and describes factors that may have resulted in an increase in a number of mental health problems in the cohort of individuals born since World War II. He suggests that interactions between genetic and environmental factors need to be studied as a way of better understanding the recent risk of suicide and other psychological problems in young people.

Imitation, contagion, and clustering of suicides have been observed to be risk factors among young people who commit suicide. Lucy Davidson reviews characteristics of epidemics of youth suicides, those that cluster in time and space. She emphasizes the need to define what constitutes a cluster of suicides and suggests approaches to prevent the contagious elements of suicide among young people. David P. Phillips, Lundie L. Carstensen, and Daniel J. Paight highlight another facet of the imitative effects that promote epidemics of youth suicide. They have amplified upon their previous work on adult suicides and discuss the effects of mass media news stories on fluctuations in youth suicide rates. They analyze content features of mass media news accounts of suicides among youth and suggest how they are related to subsequent increases in youth suicide. Heinz Häfner and Armin Schmidtke approach the issue of variation in youth suicide rates that are influenced by the presentation of suicidal models depicted in television fictional accounts of adolescent suicide. Their work has a powerful impact on illustrating the importance of imitation and social learning from models that produce increases in youth suicide. Their chapter describes how they were able to test repeated imitation effects in relation to the size and characteristics of the television audience.

Family factors are important components for risk of youth suicide. Cynthia R. Pfeffer reviews data from a variety of studies that suggest life event stresses and specific forms of psychopathology among relatives heighten risk for suicide among young people. Alec Roy explores the potential genetic mechanisms for suicide risk in families. He describes research involving family aggregation, twin, and adoption methodologies and integrates their findings suggestive of a genetic basis for suicide.

The results of using new technologies for investigating the relations between neurobiological factors, psychopathology, and youth suicide are discussed by J. John Mann, Michael D. DeMeo, John G. Keilp, and P. Anne McBride. They outline the advantages and disadvantages of several strategies of research into the biology of suicidal behavior involving studies of postmortem brain tissue from suicide victims and of biological indices of suicide attempters.

Future directions for the prevention of suicide among young people with perspectives on community or public health models are addressed in the chapter by Mark L. Rosenberg, David M. Eddy, Robert C. Wolpert, and Eugenia P. Broumas. They were instrumental in planning and integrating the recommendations of the Department of Health and Human Services Secretary's Task Force on Youth Suicide. Their chapter, in three parts, describes the use of a model to analyze the effectiveness of specific interventions for decreasing youth suicides, how such an analysis can be incorporated into a broad strategy for preventing suicide among youth, and the approaches that have been suggested by the Centers for Disease Control for preventing clusters of youth suicide.

Finally, this book reflects data of a recent international impetus to investigate youth suicidal behavior. There are certainly other issues pertaining to youth suicide that require immediate research attention. This book imparts the hope that research be ongoing with aims to seek answers to the myriad of current and future questions about suicide among young people.

Cynthia R. Pfeffer, M.D.

1

Completed Suicide in Children and Adolescents: Methods of Psychological Autopsy

Mohammed Shafii, M.D.

During the last three decades the number of suicides in children, adolescents, and young adults in the United States has increased significantly. Now, each year, more than 5,000 youth ages 15 to 24 years commit suicide (Centers for Disease Control 1986). After accidents, suicide is the most common cause of death in this age group. From the mid-1950s to the mid-1970s, the incidence of suicide for adolescents aged 15–19 years has tripled (Centers for Disease Control 1986). Every year, more than 170 children between the ages of 8 and 14 years kill themselves (National Center for Health Statistics 1976–1978). Many researchers and clinicians believe that because of cultural, religious, and social taboos along with a lack of systematic criteria, the number of suicides in children and youth is significantly underreported.

Over the last 14 years in the Child Psychiatric Services, University of Louisville School of Medicine, we have also noticed a significant increase in emergency referrals of children and adolescents with suicidal behavior (active suicidal ideation, suicidal plans, or actual suicidal attempts). For example, in 1973, 23 children and adolescents with sui-

The author acknowledges the continuous contribution and significant editorial help of Sharon Lee Shafii, R.N., B.S.N., throughout these studies. This chapter is based on the integration of information from several previously published studies (Shafii and Shafii 1982; Shafii et al. 1984, 1985).

cidal behavior were referred; however, by 1986 more than 180 children were referred. This was a 640% increase.

Among researchers, clinicians, and the public, whether there is a relationship between an individual who thinks about suicide or attempts suicide and one who actually commits suicide is debated. Some feel strongly that these groups are different (Seiden 1969). Others feel they might be the same population or speculate that there is at least an extensive overlap.

Other issues arise. Is there any relationship between youth suicide and the occurrence of suicidal behavior and/or completed suicide in family or friends? What is the relationship between completed suicide in youth and premorbid personality? Is it true, as one often hears from the family as well as from professionals, that the suicide victim was a "fairly well-adjusted and happy person" and that the suicide was "an outcome of an impulsive act" in reaction to personal crisis or momentary anger?

About 10 years ago, we began a systematic study of childhood and adolescent suicide in an attempt to answer some of these questions. This study can be divided into three phases. In phase I, between 1977 and 1980, the incidence and patterns of childhood and adolescent suicide in the city of Louisville and the surrounding area of Jefferson County, Kentucky, were tabulated, analyzed, and compared with national data (Shafii and Shafii 1982). In phase II, from 1980 to 1984, a research project entitled "The Psychological Autopsy of Completed Suicide in Children and Adolescents" was implemented to explore familial and environmental variables and personality characteristics of suicide victims compared with a matched-pair control group (Shafii et al. 1984, 1985). In phase III, which began in 1986, we began to look at neuroendocrine factors, specifically melatonin (a hormone of the pineal gland) and its relationship to the suicidal behavior of children and adolescents with depressive disorders. This chapter describes phases I and II.

PHASE I: INCIDENCE AND PATTERNS OF COMPLETED SUICIDE IN CHILDREN AND ADOLESCENTS

Many articles have been written about suicide attempts and threats in children and adolescents, but until recently there have been very few studies of completed suicide. Of these few articles on completed suicide most are based on national statistics (Centers for Disease Control 1986; Bakwin 1973; Frederick 1978; Holinger 1978). Review and analysis of local coroner's data regarding child and adolescent suicide are now beginning to emerge in the literature. However, major methodological problems exist concerning the definition and reporting of suicides. "There are inconsistencies in reporting, lack of unified standards, and variance in the background and training of certifying officials, such as coroners, medical examiners, community physicians, sheriffs, and others" (Shafii and Shafii 1982, p. 165).

Setting.   According to the 1980 census, the city of Louisville and surrounding Jefferson County, Kentucky, had a population of 684,793. Jefferson County, located by the falls of the Ohio River, has a mixed industrial, agricultural, and service-oriented economy. Whites comprise 83% of the population and nonwhites, mainly blacks, comprise 17%. Children and adolescents 19 years old and younger total 32.3% of the population.

Each county in Kentucky has a coroner who is an elected official, not necessarily a physician. The coroner has legal responsibility to rule whether or not deaths are caused by suicide. The present coroner of Jefferson County, elected in 1973, is a pediatrician who began systematically collecting data on suicide in 1974. Physicians must report to the coroner any unnatural deaths based on the International Classification of Diseases and Causes of Death. All other deaths not attended by a physician within the last 36 hours of life also must be reported. The coroner uses the following criteria to determine whether the cause of death was, beyond a reasonable doubt, suicide: presence of witness, blatant act of suicide, presence of suicide note, autopsy, police investigation and evidence, and medical examiner's report.

Review of coroner's data.   According to the coroner's records, there were 657 suicides between the years 1975 and 1980. Of these suicides, 60 (9.1%) were children and adolescents between the ages of 10 and 19 years. In 1975 the incidence of suicide was 1.5 per 100,000 people aged 10–14 years in Jefferson County; for ages 15–19 years the incidence was 7.1, and for ages 20 years and older the incidence was 25.8.

Between the years 1976 and 1980, with some fluctuations, we found an 83% increase in the suicide rate of children ages 10–14 years and a more than 100% increase in adolescents ages 15–19 years. At the same time, there was a 17% decline in the suicide rate in ages 20 years and older.

PATTERNS OF SUICIDE

The following patterns emerged when analyzing 60 cases of childhood and adolescent suicide.

Age.   Of the 60 cases of completed suicide, 9 (15%) were children between the ages of 10 and 14 years. In contrast to general belief, from this data it is clear that children do commit suicide. Forty-five percent of the suicides occurred in middle adolescence (ages 15–17 years), and 40% occurred in late adolescence (ages 18 and 19 years). It is important to note that in our study the most vulnerable ages for committing suicide were 17 and 18 years (49% of the suicides).

Sex.   Of all suicides, 82% were committed by males and 18% by females. We were surprised to find that almost 1 of 5 suicides were committed by females. This finding challenges the myth that adolescent females attempt but do not commit suicide.

Race.   Racial distribution in children and adolescents ages 10–19 years in this community is 77% white and 23% black. The suicide rate was 88% white and 12% black. Although the percentage of blacks who committed suicide was somewhat lower than the population percentage, the difference is not statistically significant. We need to discard the idea that black children and youth do not commit suicide.

Time.   The time at which the suicide occurred was documented in 52 cases. The breakdown was as follows: 27% between 8:00 A.M. and 4:00 P.M., 42% between 4:00 P.M. and midnight, and 31% between midnight and 8:00 A.M. Significantly, more suicides occurred from 7:00 P.M. to early morning—the darkest period of the 24-hour cycle.

Season.   To our surprise the highest percentage of suicides occurred in the springtime. The following pattern emerged: 35% in spring (March, April, May), 28% in summer (June, July, August), 23% in fall (September, October, November), and 19% in winter (December, January, February). The highest number of suicides occurred in March, and the second highest number occurred in October.

Method.   By far the highest number of suicides occurred through the use of firearms by the infliction of gunshot wounds to the head, chest, and abdomen (57%), followed by hanging (23%), chemical overdose (9%), carbon monoxide poisoning (5%), and other means (5%) such as drowning, methane inhalation, and jumping in front of a vehicle. In males, 61% used firearms whereas in females the use of firearms, hanging, and chemical overdose were evenly distributed. Previously, it was thought that females used less violent means of committing suicide, such as chemical overdose; however, in our study we found that approximately two-thirds (60–66%) of the females used violent means such as firearms and hanging.

PHASE II: PSYCHOLOGICAL AUTOPSY OF COMPLETED SUICIDE IN CHILDREN AND ADOLESCENTS

Medical historians and philosophers of science believe that the field of medicine began to grow by leaps and bounds after physicians and medical schools were able to incorporate systematic postmortem autopsies to find gross anatomical and cellular pathological factors contributing to the patient's death.

The field of psychiatry and mental health is far behind in this area. When a patient, whether adult or youth, commits suicide, exploration of contributing factors is ignored, often because of guilt, fear, anger, and concern about legal ramifications. Tendency toward minimizing, denying, and mythologizing suicide occurs in most cases of suicide but even more so in children and adolescents.

During this century, autopsies have often been performed to find the cause of death from physical illnesses. Autopsies are also routinely performed to establish the cause of death in cases of suicide. Unfortunately, until recently, no attempt has been made to use psychological, psychiatric, and behavioral science methods to explore the possible psychological factors contributing to suicide.

SYSTEMATIC STUDY OF SUICIDE IN ADULTS

Shneidman and Farberow (1961) and Litman et al. (1963) were pioneers in using the method of a "psychological autopsy" to assist the coroner of Los Angeles County, California, in cases of "equivocal death." They interviewed the survivors of the suicide victim to obtain specific information regarding the victim's habits, behavior, psychological state, and drug and alcohol use. In addition to the medical and family history, this information assisted the coroner in deciding whether the death was suicidal or accidental.

Robins et al. (1959) performed a systematic postmortem study of "134 Successful Suicides" that occurred in one year (1956–1957) in the city and county of St. Louis, Missouri. They devised a structured interview questionnaire for interviewing the victim's relatives, friends, physicians, and others to assess the victim's premorbid psychiatric, medical, and surgical illnesses along with other factors that might have contributed to the suicide. This comprehensive study was extensively documented in a book written by Robins (1981) entitled *The Final Months: A Study of the Lives of 134 Persons Who Committed Suicide*.

Barraclough et al. (1974) in England and Dorpat and Ripley (1960) in Seattle, Washington, also explored the psychiatric condition of the victims of suicide and contributed to our understanding of premorbid mental condition along with alcohol and drug behavior of adult suicide victims.

PSYCHOLOGICAL AUTOPSY OF SUICIDE IN CHILDREN AND ADOLESCENTS

Psychiatric and psychological investigation of completed suicide in children and adolescents faces more extensive obstacles than do similar investigations in adults. A number of investigators found that parents of suicide victims were not receptive and in many situations were hostile to their inquiries.

Herzog and Resnick (1968) attempted to interview the parents of adolescents who committed suicide, but had a high rate of refusal. When the parents did agree to the interview, their hostility, anger, and distrust toward the research team were extensive. The authors found that approaching these families was unproductive and futile.

Cantor (1975) sent a questionnaire to 100 families randomly selected from 500 cases of adolescent suicide that occurred during a 5-year period in New York City and in Maryland. Less than 10% of these families returned their questionnaires, and a large number of the questions were unanswered on the returned questionnaires. The longer the period of time since the suicide, the more hostile and unresponsive the parents were to the inquiries.

Shaffer (1974) reviewed medical records and the coroner's data on 31 suicides among children ages 12–14 years that occurred between 1962 and 1968 in England and Wales. He investigated the characteristics of these victims, but did not interview the family and did not have a control group for comparison.

Research Objectives

The objectives of our study were "to develop methodology for initiating contact and effective follow-up with bereaved family and friends; to explore and identify contributing factors to suicide (psychological reconstruction); and to attempt to prevent future suicides in bereaved families and friends by being available as a point of contact for support, education, and referral" (Shafii et al. 1984, pp. 273–274).

Research Methodology

Interviewing guidelines. Although one might be an experienced clinician, interviewing family and friends and significant others of suicide victims, especially in the case of children and adolescents, is not an

easy task. We have found that the following guidelines were most helpful in the initial and follow-up interviews with the survivors:

1. Being flexible in the nature, type, and length of interviews;
2. Realizing that the clinician-patient model of interviewing is usually
   ineffective, especially in the initial interviews, because the survivors
   are not patients;
3. Avoiding blame or inducing guilt directly or indirectly;
4. Allowing oneself to experience the survivor's loss and grief;
5. Being aware that interpretation, confrontation, and dynamic clari-
   fication are usually not helpful and may result in disruption and/or
   termination of the relationship;
6. Refraining from platitudes and false reassurance; and
7. Functioning as a resource person for the survivors and referring to
   other professionals when indicated.

Suicide research team (SRT). We organized a suicide research
team (SRT) comprised of an experienced child psychiatrist as the principal investigator, an experienced psychiatric social worker, an experienced psychiatric nurse clinical practitioner, and a research assistant.
The clinicians carried on their research activities in addition to clinical
service, teaching, and/or administration, spending approximately 4–6
hours weekly on this project, and the research assistant spent 16–20
hours weekly.

The SRT met weekly for 2 hours for research planning and organization and particularly for sharing their experiences interviewing the
survivors. Interviewing the survivors can be emotionally draining and
depleting. The weekly team meeting became a place for sharing information, catharsis, resolution of conflicts between team members,
and a source of renewal and reenergizing.

In most cases, two members of the research team went together for
the initial interviews. The follow-up interviews were done by one member of the team. Follow-up, whether in person or on the telephone,
occurred during the first year at 3, 6, 9, and 12 months and after that
every 6 months for 3–5 years.

Contacting the family. Based on studies by Seiden (1969) and
Cantor (1975), which found that the more time elapses from suicide, the
harder it is to obtain the families' cooperation, we decided to contact
the families as soon as we learned that the suicide had occurred. In
some cases the assistant coroner notified us immediately concerning
the suicide. In most cases, we learned about the suicide the next day by
reading the local newspaper's obituary section. We verified this notifica-

tion with the coroner's office and obtained the address and telephone number of the victim's family.

We contacted the family by telephone, offered our sympathy, and explained briefly, "We are doing a study to understand what factors contribute to untimely death, including suicide, in children and adolescents. We would appreciate your allowing us to meet with you and your family to help us with this study." Then we asked whether we could visit them in the funeral home. Most of the families were receptive and agreed to our visit. After meeting the family in the funeral home, we arranged for a home visit within a week with all members of the family and anyone else the family wanted to include.

Initial home visit.   The initial home visit set the tone for the subsequent relationship between the research team and the victim's family. In almost all cases, the home visit occurred in the evening or on the weekend. This unstructured interview usually lasted 3–4 hours. In most cases, parents, siblings, and sometimes significant others such as friends of the victim, close relatives, or neighbors attended.

The interviewers encouraged the survivors to talk about the suicide, including the method, the time, and the victim's state of mind during the previous year, month, week, and particularly the last 24 hours. The survivors had a need to talk about the untimely death over and over. Expression of feelings and the sharing of emotions, memories, and thoughts about the victim were encouraged. Often this initial extensive contact helped to develop a strong bond between the family and the interviewer.

During the first month, two or three additional interviews were required to obtain the following information regarding the victim:

1. Developmental, family, and medical history;
2. Previous suicidal behavior of not only the victim, but also the family and friends;
3. Drug and alcohol use and abuse;
4. Significant life events such as deaths, losses, breakups of relationships;
5. School and work patterns; and
6. Description of the victim's behavior and attitude during the immediate 24 hours, week, month, and year before the suicide.

These unstructured and semistructured interviews were written up in detail and were the basis for writing a comprehensive description of the victim's life. In addition to the above, we collected information in a standardized and structured format.

Standard data collection. In order to have consistency in data collection, the SRT developed the following instruments:

1. Psychological Profile of Suicide (PPS). This is a 109-item questionnaire partially based on DISCA (Diagnostic Interview Schedule for Children and Adolescents), with changes and modifications regarding suicide (Herjanic and Campbell 1977). Some of the data collected through this instrument are the following: information about those interviewed; date, method, time, and place of suicide; household composition; parental education and religion; previous psychiatric, social service, and legal history of the victim, family, and friends; psychiatric history of the victim and family with emphasis on specific symptoms and behavior such as death, loss, divorce, separation, desertion; history of destructive behavior; auto accidents; alcohol and drug use; social isolation; physical injuries and operations; and previous suicidal thoughts, threats, and attempts.
2. Psychological Profile of the Controls (PPC). A similar 100-item questionnaire was used to collect data on the psychological profile of the controls.

Reliability and validity of these instruments has not been tested.

Additionally the following instruments were completed by the parent(s) of the victims. These instruments have been tested for reliability and validity:

1. Louisville Behavioral Checklist (LBC). This 164-item true-false questionnaire filled out by the parent(s) of both the victims and controls assesses the parent(s)' perception of emotional disorders in their children and adolescents. Some of the areas covered by this questionnaire are infantile aggression, aggression, hyperactivity, antisocial behavior, social withdrawal, sensitivity, fear, inhibition, neurotic behavior, psychotic behavior, somatic behavior, and sexual behavior (Miller 1977).
2. Millon Multiaxial Clinical Inventory (MMCI). This 175-item truefalse questionnaire filled out by the parents is designed to assess adult psychopathology. This questionnaire helped to systematically assess psychiatric disorders in the parent(s) of the victims and the parent(s) of the controls (Millon 1977).

Choice of the control group. Most studies of psychological autopsies in adults do not report having a control group. In order to make meaningful comparisons, a control group is essential. The choice of a control group in a study such as this creates a dilemma for the investigators. The most obvious choice would be using a suicide attempter as a control. We think that there is a basic problem with this choice. Some authors feel that suicide attempters are a different group from the suicide completers (Seiden 1969). Some believe that suicide attempters are basically similar to completers and that a number of these attempters do eventually commit suicide. This would create a confounding variable situation and would make comparisons invalid. Also, suicide attempters have come to the attention of clinicians and usually have been hospitalized so they are a "selected and treated" population, which makes the comparison more difficult. Because of the above factors, we decided not to choose attempters as the control population.

The most similar control group would probably be the victims of multiple car accidents matched for age, sex, race, and season. Deaths from single-car accidents should be excluded because it is estimated that close to one-half of these "accidents" are a result of suicidal preoccupation and behavior in the victims.

Because children and adolescent victims of multiple car accidents were not readily available, we looked for other alternatives. After extensive review of the literature, we decided to use a friend of the suicide victim as a matched-pair control. This method has been advocated by Detre and Wyshak (1971). Use of friends as a control group helps to closely match for sex, age, race, socioeconomic status, education, and personal characteristics. After interviewing the victim's family, we requested the name of one or two of the victim's friends to see if they and their families would be willing to help in this study by serving as control subjects.

CASE HISTORIES OF SUICIDE VICTIMS

The following brief case histories provide examples of the victims' personal and family life before suicide.

The Youngest Victim: An Eleven-Year-Old Boy

Jerry H., the fourth of sixth children, was a blond, blue-eyed boy of slight build. He was the oldest child of the mother's marriage to Mr. H. (she had one daughter and two sons from a previous marriage). Mrs. H.'s pregnancy, except for occasional bleeding in the last trimester, was uneventful. Jerry was a healthy child and developed normally. He walked at 14 months and was toilet trained by age 2. He had problems with bedwetting until age 10. According to his mother, his only medical problems were some "minor scratches or stitches due to falling or playing."

The whole family lived together until it was discovered that the father had "raped his 13-year-old stepdaughter." The father was considered "a very good father and husband up to that time and the kids loved him very much. After this incident, the children all resented him and did not want him back." Afterward, Jerry's mother, Mrs. H., took all six children and left the father.

According to Mrs. H., this separation had a profound effect on Jerry. He had loved his father very much and took it extremely hard, but eventually "he got over it." Mrs. H. added, "He was never told about the nature of the incident. However, he must have heard rumors in the family or among friends."

Mrs. H. impressed the interviewer as being articulate, insightful, and intelligent. She said that she had a very high IQ, but never had had an opportunity to go beyond high school. "My father was an alcoholic who abused my mother and the children. My mother shot him to death when I was 11 years old. Later on, she married a nicer person. However, this tragic event has left a scar on me and my brothers and sisters."

Jerry was described by his family, friends, teacher, and neighbors as an athletic child who was nature oriented and loved horses and animals. He was likable, but at times would become argumentative and when upset would become violent. According to one of his brothers "he could not handle anger. He would throw things around, kick the walls, and tear the room apart."

The Louisville Behavioral Checklist (Miller 1977) completed by Mrs. H. revealed that Jerry was a very quiet, shy, introverted child. He kept everything to himself and did not share his problems with others. These characteristics were substantiated by his teachers, friends, and the school principal. According to this favorite teacher, Jerry had "a mind of his own." Although he liked to be with this teacher, he never got really close to him.

In recent months, Jerry cried easily and often whined and complained. Many felt that Jerry had become aloof, withdrawn, and at times unresponsive. A few times, he had been reprimanded for shoplifting. On one occasion, he told his mother that he "would kill himself." In a psychological autopsy interview with one of his close friends, an 11-year-old girl named Bonnie, we learned that he had told her on many occasions that he intended to kill himself.

Two months before his death, Jerry was suspended from school because he had smeared feces on a school window. A day before his death, Jerry brought home a rope and hid it in the closet. The night before he killed himself, he tied this rope on the bar in the closet. His brothers and mother saw the rope tied on the bar but "did not think anything of it, because it was ordinary for the kids of the neighborhood to play hangman and walk around with a rope around their neck." On the day he killed himself Jerry told his friend, Bonnie, that "he intended to go home, take some drugs, and kill himself." She did not take his statement seriously because he had often told her that he would kill himself.

After he came home from school, Jerry's mother reprimanded him and sent him to his room because his 10-year-old brother had told her that Jerry had crossed the freeway on foot that day—something he was not supposed to do. About one-half hour later, when his 10-year-old brother opened the door of their bedroom closet, he found Jerry kneeling on a sack of clothes with a rope around his neck, dead.

The psychological autopsy revealed that during the year and one-half before Jerry's death, he had lost two of his good friends by accidental deaths in which he was involved. One friend drowned while swimming with Jerry. The second was killed by an automobile while he and Jerry were crossing the freeway on foot. A third friend was injured by a car while he and Jerry tried to run across this same freeway (Shafii et al. 1984, pp. 284–288).

Suicide of a 16-Year-Old Boy

John B. was a tall, muscular, nice-looking, clean-cut 16-year-old white male who committed suicide by shooting himself in the head. John was the middle child in a middle-class family. Both parents had white collar jobs. Initially his parents did not have any idea why he killed himself. His mother, while crying, said, "John and I were very close. He was mommy's boy. John was in a car accident a few weeks ago. He ran into a telephone pole resulting in a small dent in his own car. He didn't call me at work, so when I got home and asked him why he didn't call me, he said that he didn't want me to worry. I told him that he was more important to me than the car or my work." Mrs. B. continued, "The day before John killed himself, he was suspended from school for one day because he was in a small fight with a guy."

In reconstructing the events, we learned that on the evening of John's suicide, he was picked up by one of his friends. Later that evening, he borrowed his friend's car and went to the home of his girlfriend, whom he had been dating for a month. According to his girlfriend he had the smell of alcohol on his breath. He only stayed a few minutes. Later he ran his friend's car into a tree and on into a ditch. The car was not badly damaged. John walked to his friend's house to get help to pull the car out of the ditch. At this time he told his friend that he was "going to kill himself." Shortly before 10:00 P.M. John returned home.

His father and brother were home but not his mother. According to his father, John went to the bathroom and then went downstairs into the basement. Shortly after that the father said, "I heard an explosion that I thought sounded like a bottle bursting. I went to the basement. I saw John hanging over a bed with his head blown off. My oldest son came down a minute later."

A few weeks before his suicide, Mrs. B. told John, "I am worried about your friend who is getting into trouble. He might kill himself in a car wreck or by an overdose. John said to me, 'Don't worry, Mom, it is not going to be him, it's going to be me.' He also told me that he had a recurring dream that he had a crash in a red car (his own car was red) and that he would get killed. I told him, 'I can't live without you. You should not pay attention to this dream.'" Later we also found that John had had two other car accidents previously.

When we inquired about the accessibility of guns and firearms, we learned that Mr. B. and his brother both collected guns. Mrs. B. said that the house is like "an artillery place." She was particularly distraught because John killed himself with the gun that she had bought for him as a gift.

We learned that John's uncle (father's brother) committed suicide by a gunshot wound when John was 4 years old. John's aunt (father's sister) talked a lot to John over the years about his uncle's suicide. Also, another uncle, this time on his mother's side, shot his wife to death the previous year. At the time of John's suicide this uncle was in jail awaiting trial. Mrs. B. said, "We (she and John) both love him (her brother) very much. We both were very upset about this terrible act of killing her like a dog."

Three years earlier, at age 16 years, John's older brother, Leo, and his girlfriend took an overdose of 14–15 capsules of Dalmane. Leo had a long history of alcohol, marijuana, and drug abuse. Also, he had been hospitalized previously for the above problems and depression.

Regarding the family constellation, both parents are middle-aged with a high school education. Fifteen years earlier, following a car accident, Mrs. B. was hospitalized at a psychiatric facility for "nerves." Mr. B. did not have a psychiatric history but was considered a "heavy drinker." Long-standing disharmony, tension, and fights existed between the parents and between the parents and the children.

John, we learned from a friend, had abused alcohol and marijuana for at least 3 years. At the time of John's autopsy, his blood alcohol level was 0.17%, and his toxicology report showed a trace of Valium.

Mrs. B.'s pregnancy was uneventful, but because she was "2 weeks overdue," labor was induced and forceps were used. Following birth, John was mildly jaundiced. John's developmental history was normal. Toilet training began at age 18 months and was completed at age 2.

From ages 2 to 5 he had severe temper tantrums. He would hold his breath and a few times, because of this, fainted. At age 6 it was found that he had nonproblematic heart murmur. Also, at age 6 he had a tonsillectomy and adenoidectomy. At age 8 he was evaluated at a local community mental health clinic for "dyslexia," but no evidence of it was found. John had to repeat third grade. He was considered a slow reader.

During the last few years, John was perceived by his friends as "very immature and insecure." They felt that he would do anything "to be funny and get attention. In some ways he didn't care what people thought. For example, if he had to pee, he would step out of the car and go on the road. He was eager to keep a macho image although he was an insecure puppy underneath. He wanted to be a leader, but in reality leaned heavily on a couple of us."

DATA ON FAMILIES INTERVIEWED

From January 1980 through the end of June 1983, the coroner documented 24 cases of childhood and adolescent suicide between the ages of 11 and 19 years. "Twenty (83%) of the families agreed to participate in the study. Of these twenty ($n = 20$), 95% were white and 5% black" (Shafii et al. 1985, pp. 1062–1063). Ninety percent of the suicide cases were male, and 10% were female.

We obtained 17 matched-pair controls for the 20 victims. Remarkable similarities existed between the victims and the controls regarding sex, race, education, religious background, family income, and father's level of education.

In this report, we are presenting the data obtained from the in-depth interviews and the psychological profiles of both victims and controls. The McNemar test, χ^2-test, and Yates correction were used to evaluate the significance of the variables between the victims and the matched-pair controls.

Significant Findings

1. *Exposure to the suicide of parent(s), adult relative(s), sibling(s) and/or friend(s).* Sixty-five percent of the victims had exposure to suicide (completed suicide, suicide attempt, threat, or ideation) as opposed to 18% of the controls (McNemar = 6.12, $p < .008$, df = 1).
2. *Parent(s)' emotional problems.* Sixty percent of the parent(s) of the victims reported having had emotional problems as opposed to 24% of the parent(s) of the controls (McNemar = 5.14, $p < .02$, df = 1).
3. *Parental absence or abuse.* Fifty-five percent of natural parent(s) of the victims were absent or physically or emotionally abusive as op-

posed to 29% of the parent(s) of the controls (McNemar = 3.2, $p < .04$, df = 1).

There were no statistically significant differences between the victims and the controls regarding the following variables: broken homes (includes divorce, death, separation, stepparents/adoptive parents, guardian, or any other arrangements where the individuals' own natural parents were not living together at the time of the incident); overcrowded family or large number of children; parental dependency on drugs or alcohol; and demanding parents.

Victims' Personality Characteristics

1. *Expressed suicidal ideation* (expressed the wish to die to family/friends/others once or more). Eighty-five percent of the suicide victims expressed suicidal ideation as opposed to 18% of the controls (McNemar = 11.07, $p < .001$, df = 1).
2. *Suicidal threat* (made a suicide threat to family/friends/others once or more). Fifty-five percent of the victims made at least one suicidal threat versus 12% of the controls (McNemar = 5.81, $p < .008$, df = 1).
3. *Suicidal attempt* (one or more attempts to kill oneself). Forty percent of the victims attempted suicide at least once as opposed to 6% of the controls (McNemar = 4, $p < .02$, df = 1).
4. *Frequent use of drugs and alcohol.* Seventy percent of the victims frequently used nonprescribed drugs and alcohol as opposed to 29% of the controls (McNemar = 4, $p < .02$, df = 1).
5. *Antisocial behavior* (involvement with legal authorities, shoplifting, firesetting, constant physical fights with others, suspension from school due to disciplinary problems, pushing drugs, or prostitution). Seventy percent of the victims had a history of antisocial behavior as opposed to 24% of the controls (McNemar = 7.11, $p < .003$, df = 1).
6. *Inhibited personality* (not sharing problems with others, very quiet, not having close friends, feeling lonely, keeping things inside, being introverted, being very sensitive). Sixty-five percent of the victims had the above characteristics as opposed to 24% of the controls ($\chi^2 = 9.28$, $p < .003$, df = 1; McNemar NS).
7. *Previous psychiatric treatment* (any contact with mental health professionals due to emotional problems). Forty-five percent of the victims had at least one previous contact with a mental health professional as opposed to 24% of the controls (McNemar = 3.57, $p < .004$, df = 1). Only one victim was under psychiatric care at the time of the suicide.

SUMMARY

Significant increase in the referral of children and adolescents with suicidal behavior to our child psychiatric facility led us to examine the incidence and patterns of completed suicide in children and youth ages 19 years and younger in Jefferson County, Kentucky.

The question of whether any relationship exists between children and adolescents who talk about or attempt suicide versus those who commit suicide stimulated us to develop a research project on the psychological autopsy of completed suicide in children and adolescents.

The methodological problems and principles regarding psychological autopsy are discussed. Data on the psychological autopsy of 20 cases of completed suicide in children and adolescents ages 11 to 19 years and 17 friends of the victims as matched-pair control subjects were presented.

In this study we found that 85% of the suicide victims expressed suicide ideation at least once to parents, relatives, and particularly friends before they killed themselves, as opposed to 18% of the controls. Also 55% of the victims versus 12% of the controls threatened suicide. Regarding previous suicide attempts 40% of the victims attempted suicide at least once as opposed to 6% of the controls. Also 65% of the victims had been exposed to completed suicide attempt and/or threats of parent(s), relative(s), sibling(s) or friend(s) versus 18% of the controls.

Suicide victims came from all socioeconomic groups. Incidence of history of alcohol and drug abuse, antisocial behavior, and having inhibited personality were significantly higher among suicide victims than among their matched-pair controls.

CONCLUSION

From our studies over the last decade on the incidence, patterns, and psychological autopsy of completed suicide in children and adolescents, we found that:

1. Long before committing suicide these children and adolescents manifested various psychopathological symptoms, such as decline in school performance; social isolation and withdrawal; intensive difficulties with parents, siblings, and peers; drug and alcohol abuse; antisocial behavior (shoplifting, running away from home, breaking and entering, and fighting with others); and reckless behavior (frequent car accidents or exposing oneself to dangerous situations).

2. More than 80% of the victims verbalized their intention to kill themselves at least once during the previous days, weeks, or months before committing suicide.
3. Forty percent of the victims had at least one previous suicide attempt.
4. Only 12% of the controls threatened and 6% attempted suicide. In a 4-year follow-up study of the controls, we found that one who previously had threatened did commit suicide. The risk of suicide in friends of suicide victims was 181 times higher than the risk of suicide in children and adolescents of the same age (Shafii 1986).
5. Exposure to suicidal behavior or completed suicide of parents, siblings, friends, and neighbors significantly increases the risk of suicide in a vulnerable child or adolescent.
6. To our surprise, 95% of the victims as opposed to 48% of the controls fulfilled DSM-III and DSM-III-R criteria for at least one and in most cases two or more psychiatric disorder(s) (Holden 1986).
7. Major depressive disorder and/or dysthymic disorder were the primary or secondary postmortem diagnosis in 76% of the victims versus 24% of the controls (Shafii et al., in press).
8. Conduct disorder and alcohol, marijuana, drug, and other substance abuse were frequently associated with depressive disorders in the suicide victims.
9. Parental neglect, abuse, and dissension were much more prevalent in the suicide victims as opposed to the controls.
10. We found that friends and peers were more aware of the victim's habits; behavior; suicidal ideation, threats, and attempts; and drug and alcohol abuse than parents, siblings, relatives, educators, or others.

From these studies, we have concluded that suicide in children and adolescents is not an impulsive act in reaction to an immediate personal crisis in an otherwise healthy individual. In most cases the "immediate personal crisis" occurring during the previous days before suicide was merely the final straw in a long history of serious, chronic emotional and behavioral problems. Unfortunately, in most cases, these problems were denied, neglected, or not recognized. In children and adolescents, suicidal ideas, messages, plans, threats, and attempts should be taken very seriously. In most cases the ones who talk about suicide often become the ones who commit suicide.

It behooves us to raise the consciousness of mental health professionals, physicians, nurses, educators, clergy, and, most importantly, children, adolescents, and parents to the signs, symptoms, and behavioral manifestations of suicidal behavior. Effective prevention begins with increased awareness of suicide risk. Friends and peers play an important role in spotting vulnerable youth and acting as a link between these suicidal youth and helping professionals. We should encourage everyone, especially friends and peers, who notice signs or symptoms of suicidal or self-destructive behavior to make certain a responsible person knows about and seeks immediate help for the vulnerable child or adolescent.

REFERENCES

Bakwin RM: Suicide in children and adolescents. J Am Med Wom Assoc 28:643, 1973

Barraclough B, Bunch J, Nelson B, et al: A hundred cases of suicide: clinical aspects. Br J Psychiatry 125:355–373, 1974

Cantor P: The effects of youthful suicide on the family. Psychiatric Opinion 12:6–11, 1975

Centers for Disease Control: Youth Suicide in the United States, 1970–1980. Atlanta, GA, Centers for Disease Control, November 1986

Detre K, Wyshak A: A matching procedure for epidemiological studies. J Chronic Dis 24:83–92, 1971

Dorpat TL, Ripley HS: A study of suicidal behavior in the United States. Compr Psychiatry 1:349–359, 1960

Frederick CJ: Current trends in suicidal behavior in the United States. Am J Psychother 32:172–200, 1978

Herjanic B, Campbell JW: Differentiating psychiatrically disturbed children on the basis of a structured interview. J Abnorm Child Psychol 5:127–134, 1977

Herzog A, Resnick HLP: A clinical study of parental response to adolescent death by suicide with recommendations for approaching survivors, in Proceedings of 4th International Conference for Suicide Prevention. Edited by Farberow NL. Los Angeles, CA, International Association for Suicide Prevention, 1968

Holden C: Youth suicide: new research focuses on a growing social problem. Science 233:829–841, 1986

Holinger PC: Adolescent suicide: an epidemiological study of recent trends. Am J Psychiatry 135:754–756, 1978

Litman RE, Curphey T, Shneidman ES, et al: Investigations of equivocal suicide. JAMA 184:924–929, 1963

Miller LC: Louisville Behavior Checklist Manual. Los Angeles, CA, Western Psychological Services, 1977

Millon T: Millon Multiaxial Clinical Inventory. Minneapolis, MN, Interpretative Scoring Systems, National Computer Systems, 1977

National Center for Health Statistics, Washington, DC, unpublished data for 1976, 1977, 1978

Robins E: The Final Months: A Study of the Lives of 134 Persons Who Committed Suicide. New York, Oxford University Press, 1981

Robins E, Murphy GE, Wilkinson RH, et al: Some clinical considerations in the prevention of suicide based on a study of 134 successful suicides. Am J Public Health 49:888–899, 1959

Seiden RH: Suicide Among Youth—A Review of the Literature, 1900–1967: Public Health Service Publication, 1971. Washington, DC, U.S. Government Printing Office, 1971

Shaffer D: Suicide in childhood and early adolescence. J Child Psychol Psychiatry 15:275–291, 1974

Shafii M: Letter to the editor. Am J Psychiatry 143:1193–1194, 1986

Shafii M, Shafii SL: Self-destructive, suicidal behavior, and completed suicide, in Pathways of Human Development: Normal Growth and Emotional Disorders in Infancy, Childhood, and Adolescence. Edited by Shafii M, Shafii SL. New York, Thieme-Stratton, 1982

Shafii M, Whittinghill JR, Dolen DC, et al: Psychological reconstruction of completed suicide in childhood and adolescence, in Suicide in the Young. Edited by Sudak HS, Ford AB, Rushforth NB. Littleton, MA, PSG Publishing, 1984

Shafii M, Carrigan S, Whittinghill JR, et al: Psychological autopsy of completed suicide in children and adolescents. Am J Psychiatry 142:1061–1064, 1985

Shafii M, Steltz-Lenarsky J, Derrick AM, et al: Postmortem diagnosis of children and adolescents who committed suicide compared with a matched-pair control group. J Affective Disord (in press)

Shneidman ES, Farberow NL: Sample investigations of equivocal deaths, in The Cry for Help. Edited by Farberow NL, Shneidman ES. New York, McGraw-Hill, 1961

2

Completed Suicide
in Youth

Harry M. Hoberman, Ph.D.
Barry D. Garfinkel, M.D., F.R.C.P.(C)

Recently, pressure has increased for communities and public schools to develop intervention and prevention programs for youth at risk for completed suicide; this necessarily raises the question "What are the relevant characteristics of young people who take their lives?" Based on what features should clinicians and members of the community heighten their vigilance and take action? In 1974, Haim noted that knowledge of the factors associated with youth who commit suicide was quite limited. Petzel and Cline (1978) and Berman and Cohen-Sandler (1982) noted the scarcity of research on suicide completers. Currently, despite the well-documented increases in the rates of completed suicide among adolescents and young adults (Centers for Disease Control 1986) and the accompanying degree of interest on the part of the general public as well as health care professionals, relatively little information yet exists that describes characteristics of youth who commit suicide. To make matters worse, misconceptions by the public and professionals regarding young people who commit suicide are frequently made, given the limited knowledge we have about younger suicide victims. Consequently, in attempting to monitor youth potentially at risk for suicide, individuals may be applying the wrong criteria for what constitutes a person at risk. Thus, those young people most in need of early interven-

This chapter is essentially the same as the article "Completed suicide in youth" (Can J Psychiatry 33:494–504, 1988); the Introduction, Methods, and Discussion sections are essentially the same as those that appeared in the article "Completed suicide in children and adolescents" (J Am Acad Child Adolesc Psychiatry 27:689–695, 1988). The material is reprinted with permission from both the Canadian Journal of Psychiatry and the Journal of the American Academy of Child and Adolescent Psychiatry.

tion may pass unnoticed by the community of concerned parents and professionals.

Beyond Jan-Tausch's (1964) initial study of 41 child and adolescent suicides, only six studies have carefully attempted to delineate factors associated with self-inflicted death among younger people in Western societies (Shaffer 1974; Pettifor et al. 1983; Garfinkel and Golombek 1983; Shafii et al. 1985; Thompson 1987; Poteet 1987). Shaffer (1974) studied children 14 years and under who had committed suicide in England and Wales between 1962 and 1968 ($n = 31$). Pettifor and colleagues (1983) described differences between 40 adolescents seen at a mental health clinic in Alberta, Canada, between 1946 and 1980 who eventually committed suicide (between 1956 and 1979) and a matched group of nonsuicidal clinic outpatients. Garfinkel and Golombek (1983) examined coroners' and police reports and collected information on 1,554 suicides by persons aged 10 to 24 in Ontario, Canada. Poteet (1987) studied medical examiners' reports for 87 suicides (ages 13–19) that occurred between 1970 and 1985 in Shelby County, Tennessee. Shafii and associates (1985) have described the results of "psychological autopsies" conducted on 20 persons aged 19 and under. Finally, Thompson (1987) reported on 190 suicides by persons aged less than 20 in Manitoba from 1970 to 1982. Although each of these studies has contributed significantly to our understanding of youth suicide, each study possesses certain limitations. Several involve relatively small numbers of subjects. One study focuses on a potentially idiosyncratic group of patients (e.g., help-seeking persons). Several studies include persons who committed suicide a number of years ago (Shaffer 1974; Pettifor et al. 1983; Garfinkel and Golombek 1983; Shafii et al. 1985; Thompson 1987; Poteet 1987), which raises the question of potential cohort differences. Given the continuing increase in youth suicide rates over the last 30–40 years, it is quite possible that the characteristics of the youth who has recently taken his or her life may be quite different from one who committed suicide several decades ago. In short, a variety of methodological issues may compromise the application of the limited knowledge available concerning younger suicides.

Complicating the state of our knowledge is the finding that numerous writers in the area of suicide among the young describe characteristics of "suicidal youth," but have consistently failed to distinguish between suicide attempts and completions. Petzel and Riddle (1981) explain that "Suicide attempters rather than those successfully completing suicide have been the focus of efforts to piece together factors that lead to suicide" (p. 379); writers have attempted to generalize findings regarding attempted suicide to completed suicides. Suicide attempts and completions among the young do overlap to a certain extent. However, as Murphy (1986) notes regarding suicide attempts, approximately 90% of attempters never commit suicide. Moreover, Murphy's estimate was based on a presumed prevalence of suicide attempts of 1.2% (p. 577). Recent community-based surveys of adolescents demonstrated high rates of self-reported suicide attempts (e.g., 3% in the last month; Garfinkel et al. 1986). Consequently, given that many more suicide attempts occur in adolescents than Murphy estimated, there may be an even smaller relationship between attempts and completions in this population. Moreover, youthful suicide attempters and completers differ on some obvious demographic variables; e.g., females predominate in the former and males in the latter group. As Murphy observed, "The persistent confusion of suicide attempt with suicide in this literature is both frustrating and misleading. Incautious statements about suicide that have only, or principally to do with suicide attempters are one result" (p. 574). Suicide attempters constitute a group at somewhat elevated risk for completed suicide relative to the general population (Herjanic and Weiner 1980). It remains to be seen to what degree those youth who attempt and complete suicide resemble each other. At present, however, it would be incorrect and unfortunate to generalize about adolescent suicide completions based on characteristics of those who attempted suicide.

It seems obvious that relatively little information is now available regarding the nature of suicide completions among young people. At the same time, suicide prevention programs are rapidly proliferating but often with a questionable understanding of the very nature of adolescent suicide. This chapter describes a study undertaken in an attempt to provide a description of completed suicide among young persons. Following the lead of Jan-Tausch (1964) and Shaffer (1974), we examined the medical examiner's records of a consecutive group of deceased children, adolescents, and young adults. We did not conduct a detailed psychological autopsy (e.g., interviewing the decedent's family and friends) described by Shafii and colleagues (1985). Instead, we were interested in examining a larger number of youth suicide victims over a number of years in order to examine differences between subgroups of those who died. In particular, the study attempted to characterize gender, age, and temporal differences in young suicide victims.

SUBJECTS AND METHODS

Subjects for this study consisted of individuals 25 years and under whose deaths occurred between January 1, 1975, and December 31, 1985. Decedents included in the study were those whose deaths were investigated by either the Hennepin or Ramsey County, Minnesota, medical examiner's office and whose deaths were ruled to be the result of non-natural causes. Hennepin and Ramsey Counties contain the cities of Minneapolis and St. Paul, respectively; although they are predominantly urban and suburban, they include some more rural areas as well. Thus, subjects were those persons whose deaths were determined by the medical examiners to be suicides, accidents, homicides, or of undetermined cause. Each of the decedent records was reviewed by one of three research assistants, and information was obtained according to a structured format. The medical examiner's records contained a varied amount of information regarding the decedent, depending on the availability and cooperation of informants. Basic information found in the records of almost all decedents included demographic information concerning the decedent and information on the circumstances and means of death. Data concerning the psychosocial or behavioral aspects of the decedent were less consistently available. Regarding the possibility of underreporting, all deaths not ruled suicides were carefully reviewed. Ninety deaths, which the medical examiners had determined to be accidental, homicides, or undetermined, were considered by the investigators to be suicides; these constituted 14% of the total group of youth suicides. Deaths were reclassified based on criteria derived from previous studies of completed suicide among youth (e.g., Garfinkel and Golombek 1983); characteristics of male gender, evidence of a depressive disorder, a stressor involving loss or conflict, and circumstances of the death were all applied in the decision making. All such reclassifications were based on unanimous agreement between the two investigators who each rated the decedent separately. Later, two research assistants reviewed these records and coded the data into categories derived largely from those described in the Completed Suicide Informant Interview (Shaffer 1985). This interview specifies a coding scheme for the classification of variables of interest regarding completed suicides (e.g., types of precipitants, relevant circumstances surrounding suicides). A select number of cases ($n = 30$) were coded twice. Disagreements in coding were resolved through discussion. All recorded information was reviewed by both a clinical psychologist and a child psychiatrist.

In particular, information abstracted from the medical examiners' records was evaluated according to diagnostic criteria based on Family History Research Diagnostic Criteria (Andreasen et al. 1977). All diagnostic decisions were made by both research assistants, and any disagreements were resolved through discussion with a clinical psychologist and a child psychiatrist. Additionally, ratings of blood alcohol based on toxicology tests were available for selected decedents; other decedents were rated for the likelihood of being under the influence of alcohol or other illegal substances.

Three comparisons were determined for the youth suicides. First, male and female completers were compared. Second, comparisons were made on the basis of age at the time of death; the groups were persons 14 years old and under, persons between the ages of 15 and 19 years, and persons between the ages of 20 and 25 years. Lastly, to examine the possibility of temporal changes in the characteristics of youth suicide, comparisons were made of suicides occurring between 1975 and 1979 and those occurring between 1980 and 1985. When differences between the various groups attained statistical significance, they are reported; conversely, if no difference is noted, the groups obtained similar values on the variable in question. In general, percentages reported are absolute figures and reflect positive evidence for a particular variable. For most of the variables described, information was available for the entire sample. Given the variability of the information contained in the records of the medical examiners, missing data might constitute either true or false negatives. In any case, these findings should be regarded as conservative estimates.

RESULTS

Demographics

Table 1 shows the prevalence of the groups of suicides being studied. As expected, males predominated among youthful suicide victims (77%); the ratio of males to females was 3:1. Older adolescents (ages 15–19, 32%) and young adults (ages 20–25, 65%) constituted the overwhelming number of cases studied; persons under age 15 made up only 3% of the decedents. Ninety-three percent of the suicide victims were white, 4% were black, and the remainder were members of other minority groups. Regarding occupation, 39% of the suicide victims were students, 29% were laborers, 23% were otherwise employed, and 8% were

Table 1. Age, Sex, and Cohort Differences for Suicides

	n	Percentage
Age (years)		
< 15	21	3.2
15–19	208	31.7
20–24	427	65.1
Sex		
Male	508	77.4
Female	148	22.6
Cohort		
1975–1979	313	47.7
1980–1985	343	52.3

unemployed. Only 7% were married, and 8% were separated or divorced; thus 85% of the victims were single at the time of their deaths. A majority (57%) of the youthful suicide victims were living with their parents, with another 11% living with a spouse; only 9% lived alone.

Male and female suicide completers did not differ in terms of age, race, or religion. More male decedents were likely to be employed as laborers, whereas females were more likely to be working in sales or clerical positions ($\chi^2 = 110.4$, df = 7, $p < .0000$). More female suicide completers were likely to be married or separated, whereas males were more likly to be divorced ($\chi^2 = 13.10$, df = 4, $p < .01$).

Age groups accounted for a number of differences on demographic variables. As would be expected, all of the young suicide victims were students, as were 70% of those aged 15 to 19. However, 18% of this latter group were either laborers or unemployed at the time of their deaths. Similarly, virtually all of the two youngest groups of decedents were single at the time of their suicides.

No cohort differences were identified for age, gender, or marital status of the decedents. Such differences were identified for the occupation of the decedent ($\chi^2 = 23.29$, df = 7, $p < .002$); recent suicide victims were twice as likely to be unemployed.

Method of Death

Table 2 shows the methods of death for the total group, males and females. The predominant cause of death was firearms; 39% of the suicides resulted from weapons, with rifles and shotguns used more frequently than handguns. Carbon monoxide poisoning (17%), hanging (15%), ingestion (13%), and falls (8%) were the other leading causes of deaths. Only 1% of the suicides involved motor vehicle accidents. It is worth noting that 36% of the fatal overdoses were from antidepressants, nearly three-quarters of which had been prescribed for the decedent.

Females differed from males regarding the method of death

Table 2.   Gender Differences in Means of Suicide

	Males (n = 490)	Females (n = 144)
Firearms	45%	17%
Hanging	16%	10%
Carbon monoxide poisoning	15%	22%
Ingestion	8%	31%
Jumping	6%	12%
Suffocation	1%	1%
Other	8%	6%

($\chi^2 = 82.50$, df $= 7$, $p < .0000$); this is shown in Table 2. Whereas males were more likely to use firearms and hanging, females were more likely to choose ingestions, carbon monoxide poisoning, and jumping.

Age differences were evident in the method of suicide ($\chi^2 = 33.73$, df $= 14$, $p < .002$). Over one-half (52%) of the suicides of the youngest group involved hanging. The rate of carbon monoxide poisoning for the two older groups (17%) was triple that of the younger group. The use of firearms was highest for the middle group (44%), relative to the younger group (24%) or older group (38%).

Variations in method of death were noted for the two cohorts ($\chi^2 = 27.69$, df $= 7$, $p < .0003$). Deaths from ingestion have decreased over time, while those from firearms, hanging, and carbon monoxide poisoning increased. For those youth who died from self-poisoning, deaths from analgesic ingestion decreased (20% to 8%), and deaths from antidepressants increased markedly (18% to 60%) ($\chi^2 = 17.43$, df $= 6$, $p < .008$).

Circumstances of the Suicide

Slightly more than one-half (57.8%) of the suicides took place in the afternoon or evening. Interestingly, there was no seasonal difference in rate. The great majority of suicides occurred at the decedent's home (63.1%), with most of the remainder taking place outdoors (22%). In 27% of the cases, someone else was present at the time of the death; in another 27%, someone was likely to contact the decedent. Only 33% of the suicide victims took active precautions to avoid discovery.

In 29% of the cases, the individuals had made some remark about suicide before their deaths; however, only 3% of the suicide cases showed evidence of definite preparation for death. Approximately one-third of the suicide victims left a note. Nearly one-half of the suicide completers were rated as sad or despairing on the day of their suicide; another 33% were rated as angry immediately before the act. Thirty-four percent of the decedents had used recreational drugs or alcohol (unrelated to the cause of death) within 12 hours of their death; blood alcohol levels ranged as high as .42. There were no gender differences identified for alcohol or drug consumption at the time of death, nor were such differences found regarding time or place of death, preparation for death, or leaving a suicide note. More females had made repeated remarks about suicide before their deaths ($\chi^2 = 9.54$, df $= 3$, $p < .02$).

There were no age-related differences in the month or time of day of the suicide. Nearly all victims in the youngest group committed suicide at home (85%) ($\chi^2 = 26.76$, df $= 12$, $p < .02$). For those for whom data were available, 71% ($n = 60$) of the ages 15–19 group and

81% ($n = 137$) of the ages 20–24 group had consumed alcohol before their suicide ($\chi^2 = 25.26$, df = 14, $p < .03$). Both older groups were more likely to be rated as either sad or despairing on the day of their death, whereas the youngest group was more likely to be rated as angry ($\chi^2 = 24.18$, df = 14, $p < .04$).

Several cohort differences emerged concerning the circumstances of the suicides. Recent suicides were more likely to have occurred in the fall and less likely to have occurred in the spring. Recent suicide victims were more likely to have died at home ($\chi^2 = 13.21$, df = 6, $p < .04$), appeared more likely to take no precautions against discovery ($\chi^2 = 18.30$, df = 2, $p < .001$), and were less likely to be discovered alive ($\chi^2 = 13.51$, df = 2, $p < .001$). Earlier suicide victims were more likely to have left suicide notes ($\chi^2 = 5.97$, df = 2, $p < .05$) and were more likely to show credible evidence of having planned their suicides ($\chi^2 = 8.62$, df = 2, $p < .02$), whereas later suicide completers were considerably more likely to be rated as committing impulsive or unplanned acts ($\chi^2 = 22.36$, df = 5, $p < .0004$). More recent suicide completers had been rated as more sad, more anxious, and less angry than the earlier cohorts ($\chi^2 = 19.04$, df = 7, $p < .008$).

Psychiatric History

At the time of the deaths, 30% of the suicide victims were rated as suffering from depressive disorders, another 13% were alcoholic, and 15% were characterized as having some type of substance abuse problem. Eight percent of the suicide victims were schizophrenic, 3% had bipolar affective disorder, and 5% were characterized as antisocial personality disorder. Overall, 57% of the decedents showed clear evidence of some type of psychiatric disorder. For 43% of the subjects, no diagnosis was assigned either because the evidence did not support such a determination or because insufficient evidence was available.

The suicide victims were also evaluated for a past history of psychiatric disorders. As many as 19% of the decedents showed evidence of previous depressive disorders; past alcoholism and substance abuse characterized 12% and 16% of the suicides, respectively.

Male and female completers differed in the types of present ($\chi^2 = 21.79$, df = 7, $p < .003$) and past ($\chi^2 = 26.81$, df = 7, $p < .0004$) psychiatric disorders. In terms of the former, females were nearly twice as likely to be rated as having an affective disorder, whereas males were more likely to be rated as having alcohol or substance abuse and antisocial personality. Similar but more robust differences characterized these gender differences for past psychiatric diagnoses.

Age differences were found for present psychiatric disorders

($\chi^2 = 27.99$, df $= 14$, $p < .01$). More affective disorders were noted for the two older groups, whereas more antisocial behavior was evident in the youngest group. Additionally, the rate of alcohol and substance abuse was highest in the 15- to 19-year-old group.

No cohort differences were noted for diagnostic status at the time of suicide; however, significant differences were noted for past psychiatric history ($\chi^2 = 14.63$, df $= 7$, $p < .04$). The proportion of depressed and antisocial youths increased, and the proportion of decedents judged schizophrenic decreased. Rates of alcohol abuse increased, and rates of other substance abuse decreased. Concerning previous suicidal behavior, 21% of the decedents were known to have made prior suicide attempts. The majority of these were drug overdoses or lacerations. Of those who had previously attempted suicide, one-half had been hospitalized or received outpatient psychotherapy as a consequence of the attempt. Female suicide completers had made nearly twice as many known previous suicide attempts ($\chi^2 = 15.25$, df $= 5$, $p < .009$).

Earlier suicide completers were more likely to show definite evidence of having ever talked about suicide ($\chi^2 = 8.39$, df $= 3$, $p < .04$). More recent suicide completers showed higher rates of previous suicide attempts ($\chi^2 = 14.44$, df $= 5$, $p < .01$); this seemed particularly true for a time period proximal to the eventual suicide. Additionally, single (versus multiple) attempts seemed to characterize the recent suicides.

Precipitants

The occurrence of a variety of stressful situations in the 3 days preceding the suicide was rated for each decedent. Results are described in Table 3. As can be seen, arguments and relationship breakups were the most common precipitants. When they occurred, arguments were most likely to take place with a spouse or significant other, followed by arguments with one or both parents. Arguments that preceded suicides were most likely to occur within 24 hours of the suicides.

Table 3. Precipitants ($n = 644$)

	Percentage
Arguments	15
Relationship breakups	9
Problems with the law	9
Disappointments	9
Work problems	8
School problems	6
Threats of separation	5
Victims of assault	2

Several gender differences concerning precipitants emerged in the 3 days before the suicide. Males were five times as likely to have experienced a relationship breakup ($\chi^2 = 10.07$, df $= 1$, $p < .002$), three times as likely to have school problems ($\chi^2 = 4.73$, df $= 1$, $p < .03$), and two times as likely to have problems with the police ($\chi^2 = 5.06$, df $= 1$, $p < .02$). Generally speaking, males were at least twice as likely to have experienced a precipitant in the 24 hours preceding the suicides compared with females ($\chi^2 = 11.42$, df $= .02$, $p < .02$). Beyond the 3-day period before the suicide, males had more problems with the police ($\chi^2 = 5.91$, df $= 1$, $p < .02$); females were more likely to have been assaulted ($\chi^2 = 6.60$, df $= 1$, $p < .01$).

Age differences were also found in the type of precipitants preceding the suicides. Arguments and school problems were highest in the youngest age group ($\chi^2 = 8.32$, df $= 1$, $p < .02$ and $\chi^2 = 48.22$, df $= 1$, $p < .000$, respectively), whereas relationship breakups were more common in the oldest group ($\chi^2 = 6.39$, df $= 2$, $p < .04$).

Several cohort differences were discovered. The rate of relationship breakups, work problems, and disappointments was twice as great for the more recent suicide victims ($\chi^2 = 9.18$, df $= 1$, $p < .002$; $\chi^2 = 5.23$, df $= 1$, $p < .02$; and $\chi^2 = 7.02$, df $= 1$, $p < .008$; respectively). The rate of suicides preceded by assaults increased by a factor of six in more recent suicide victims ($\chi^2 = 5.99$, df $= 1$, $p < .01$). Additionally, although not statistically significant, there was a clear trend for the identified precipitant to occur within 24 hours of the suicide as opposed to an earlier time.

Psychosocial Characteristics

In terms of social adjustment, only 5% of the suicide completers were characterized as loners. Generally, suicide victims were seen as having friends and/or intimate relationships. Concerning personality characteristics, decedents were rated as follows: 7% impulsive, 11% supersensitive, 16% withdrawn, 10% angry, 8% lonely, and 5% bizarre. At least 17% of the decedents had some type of illness, disability, or health problem. Only 5% had experienced a drop in academic performance; 3% had experienced discipline problems at school.

Relative to gender, males were more likely to be characterized as angry ($\chi^2 = 4.71$, df $= 1$, $p < .03$), lonely ($\chi^2 = 4.31$, df $= 1$, $p < .04$), or bizarre ($\chi^2 = 4.12$, df $= 1$, $p < .04$). More recent suicide victims were more likely to be described as angry individuals ($\chi^2 = 5.03$, df $= 1$, $p < .02$). Males were generally more likely to have been in good health, although a greater percentage were described as having a learning disability ($\chi^2 = 17.54$, df $= 5$, $p < .004$).

DISCUSSION

Our goal was to use information obtained from medical examiners' records to characterize young people who had committed suicide over a 10-year period. In addition, we were particularly interested in examining differences in suicide patterns based on the characteristics of age and gender of the decedent, as well as studying possible temporal changes in suicide. The differences identified in these comparisons are summarized in Tables 4, 5, and 6. Overall, the results of this study are in accord with those of previous investigations.

Both Hawton (1986) and Shaffer and Fisher (1981) have argued that official suicide statistics underestimate the true rate of suicide. In our study, that claim was substantiated; 14% of the deaths we classified as suicides had not been so determined by the medical examiners. The difference between the judgments of the investigators and the medical examiners showed a cohort effect ($\chi^2 = 34.44$, df $= 1$, $p < .000$). Fewer of the more recent suicides (6%) were misjudged relative to the earlier suicides (22%). This suggests that current medical examiner practices, at least in metropolitan areas, are increasingly accurate in their determination of suicides.

Concerning demographic variables, the predominance of white, young adults among the suicide victims is similar to national epidemiological data described by Shaffer and Fisher (1981) and by Poteet (1987). Shaffer (1974) found no suicides before the age of 12. Three such deaths

Table 4. Completed Suicide Survey Gender Differences

Occupation	> Male laborers, unemployed
Marital status	> Females married/separated
	> Males divorced
Method	
Males	> Firearms and hanging
Females	> Ingestions, carbon monoxide poisoning, and jumping
Circumstances of suicide	
Females	> Repeated remarks about suicide
Psychiatric History (past and present diagnoses)	
Females	> Affective disorders, > previous suicide attempt
Males	> Alcohol/substance abuse, antisocial personality
Precipitants	
Males	> Relationship breakups, school problems, and problems with police
	> Overall immediate precipitants
Females	> Assaults, pregnancy
Psychological characteristics	
Males	> Angry, lonely, bizarre

Note. > = More.

Table 5.   Completed Suicide Survey: Age Differences

Occupation	
Early and middle	> Students
Method	
Early	> Hanging
Middle	> Firearms
Middle and older	> Carbon monoxide poisoning
Circumstances	
Younger	> Angry mood
Middle and older	> Sad or despairing mood
Psychiatric history (present psychiatric disorders)	
Younger	> Antisocial behavior
Middle	> Alcohol/substance abuse
Middle and older	> Affective disorders
Precipitants	
Earlier	> Arguments and school problems
Older	> Relationship breakup

Note.   > = More.

Table 6.   Completed Suicide Survey: Cohort Differences

Occupation	
Recent	> Unemployed
Method	
Recent	< Ingestions, firearms, hanging, carbon monoxide poisoning
	> Ingestion deaths from antidepressants
Circumstances	
Recent	> Suicides in fall season
	< Precautions
	> Impulsive or unplanned suicides
Earlier	> Likely to have left a suicide note
	> Likely to have planned suicide
Psychiatric history	
Recent	> Depression, alcohol abuse, antisocial behavior, previous suicide attempts
Earlier	> Schizophrenia
	> Talk of suicide
Precipitants	
Recent	> Relationship breakup, work problems, disappointments and assaults
Psychosocial characteristics	
Recent	> Angry
	> In good health

Note.   > = More; < = Less.

were represented in our study; however, suicides were extremely infrequent in persons 14 and under. Similarly, Thompson (1987) found only 16 suicides (7%) in persons aged 14 and under. Twice the number of suicides were found for young adults than for adolescents. The rate among males of all ages was three times higher than the rate among females; the male predominance tended to be most marked (4:1) for middle adolescents and least (2:1) among younger adolescents. Males who worked as laborers or were unemployed, males who were divorced, and females who were married or currently separated appear to have been at greater risk for suicide. Unemployment posed an increased risk for more recent suicide victims.

Firearms were the major method of death for young suicide completers; this finding is in agreement with the results of Garfinkel and Golombek (1983) (40%), Poteet (1987) (74%), and Thompson (1987) (56%). However, death from carbon monoxide poisoning was twice the rate compared to the results of those studies, suggesting a possible regional or temporal idiosyncrasy. As in the studies by Garfinkel and Golombek (1983) and Thompson (1987), males were more likely to employ more violent methods (e.g., firearms). However, in Thompson's study and in one by Holinger (1978), rates of overdoses were comparable for the genders. In our study, four times the number of females compared with males were victims of self-poisoning. As in Shaffer's (1974) study of younger suicide victims, the youngest group in this study used hanging three times more frequently; carbon monoxide poisoning was much more common in the older group. That deaths from ingestions declined over time may suggest that this method allows greater opportunity for rescue or that emergency treatment is increasingly successful at preserving life. Given the high rate of depression among young suicide victims, the fact that antidepressant ingestion is becoming the leading cause of fatal self-poisoning indicates that great care must be taken in prescribing medication for depressed youth.

Certain aspects of the circumstances of the suicides in this study correspond to findings of other researchers. As in Garfinkel and Golombek's study (1983), most of the decedents committed suicide at home. Similarly, only 33% of the suicide victims left a note; in Shaffer's (1974) study, 45% left notes, whereas in Poteet's (1987) and Thompson's (1987) reports, only 29% and 21%, respectively, did so. In studies of adult suicide, approximately 33% of the decedents left notes (Robins et al. 1959; Dorpat and Ripley 1960). Although Garfinkel and Golombek's study (1983) showed that only 5% of their sample had used intoxicants before their suicide, Poteet (1987) found that 45% of her subjects showed evidence of alcohol or drug use at the time of death; at least 38% of the suicides in our study showed similar evidence. Poteet (1987) found that 33% of her subjects showed signs of depression at the time of their death; we found that 50% of our subjects were sad or despairing, and 33% were angry. Interestingly, younger suicide victims were much more likely to display anger before their suicide; Shaffer (1974) reported that 23% of his younger suicide victims left hostile suicide notes.

Whereas Garfinkel and Golombek (1983) and Thompson (1987) reported an increase in youth suicide in the fall of the year, this study showed a consistent rate of death throughout the entire year. Recent suicide victims were more likely to have been viewed as sad or despairing at the time of their deaths. It was also striking that relatively few of the suicide victims in our study showed any evidence of preparation for their suicide, which suggests the act was a result of marked impulsivity. Moreover, it was impressive that more recent suicide victims appeared to have changed in important ways; recent suicide victims were less likely to show signs of planning their suicides, to have taken precautions against being discovered, or to have left a note. All of this suggests that current youth suicides were more impulsive in nature; similarly, Shaffer (cited in Holden 1986) reported that in his most recent psychological autopsy of adolescent suicide victims, there was no evidence of a lengthy "brooding" period before the suicides.

Garfinkel and Golombek (1983) identified significant psychiatric conditions in 25% of their sample (mostly depression). Shaffer (1974) found 13% of his subjects did not show affective or antisocial symptoms. Poteet (1987) indicated that 28% of the decedents in her study showed evidence of alcohol or substance abuse, and 33% showed signs of depression or "mental problems." Shafii and associates (1985) demonstrated high rates of several psychiatric disorders in their sample: 66% were depressed, 70% were alcohol or substance abusers, and another 70% had symptoms of antisocial behavior. Shaffer (cited in Holden 1986) reported a preponderance of antisocial behavior and a limited occurrence of depression (20%) in his study of adolescent suicides. Thompson (1987) found 33% had abused alcohol, and 17% of the cases were characterized by substance abuse. In our study, the majority of young suicide victims were rated as having a psychiatric disorder, mostly depressive disorders, and alcohol or substance abuse. Most of these disorders appeared to be of a chronic nature, as opposed to more acute conditions. Affective disorders in general were much more likely to characterize females who committed suicide. Adolescent and young adult suicide victims were also relatively more likely to have affective disorders, while younger suicide victims were more likely to display antisocial behavior. Additionally, a number of studies have demonstrated that neither parents (Leon et al. 1980; Weissman et al. 1980) nor teachers (Lefkowitz and Tesiny 1980; Sacco and Graves 1985) are accurate judges of depression in children or adolescents. Consequently, medical examiners' reports, which are based on parents, teachers, or employees as sources of information, are likely to underestimate the rate of affective disorders in younger persons. It is very likely that rates of affective as well as substance abuse disorders are underestimates of the true prevalence of these disorders among youth suicide victims. Overall, the results of this and other studies of youth suicide indicate that younger suicide victims resemble older suicide victims in terms of their degree and type of psychiatric disorder. In studies by Robins et al. (1959), Dorpat and Ripley (1960), and Barraclough et al. (1974) almost all decedents had experienced psychiatric episodes, predominantly affective disorders and substance abuse.

Alcohol and substance abuse was elevated for adolescent completers. Over time, the association between affective disorders, antisocial behavior, and alcohol abuse appears to have increased. In this study, the association between drug abuse and suicide seemed to decrease. This contrasts with the finding of Rich et al. (1986) that drug abuse diagnoses were strongly associated with suicides (70%) in persons under age 30.

In this study, previous suicide attempts were identified in only 20% of the decedents; Thompson (1987) found evidence of previous attempts in 10% of his sample. These are lower figures than those found in other studies. Shaffer (1974) noted that 46% of his sample of younger suicide completers had previously discussed, threatened, or attempted suicide. Shafii and colleagues (1985) reported that 40% of their sample had made a previous attempt, and 55% had made a suicide threat. Poteet (1987) found that 29% of her sample had displayed suicidal intent or made a suicide attempt. Generally, studies based on medical examiners' records indicate lower rates of previous suicidal behavior, and those based on more extensive "psychological autopsies" demonstrate higher rates. It is very likely that our study underestimates rates of prior suicide attempts. In studies of older suicide completers, between 22% and 33% of the decedents were known to have made attempts (Robins et al. 1959; Dorpat and Ripley 1960; Barraclough et al. 1974). The Thompson study (1987) and our findings indicate females made twice the number of known prior attempts compared with males. Whereas this finding may simply reflect the preponderance of females who attempt suicide, it might also suggest that males are more likely to commit suicide without prior suicidal behavior, that is, end their lives in an impulsive act. Recent completers had higher rates of prior attempts; thus, attempts may be increasingly linked to later completions. It is worth noting that Pettifor and associates (1983) reported that suicidal ideation was the single variable that most discriminated between psychiatrically disturbed adolescents who did not eventually commit suicide.

Most of those studied in our report were rated as having experienced a precipitant that appeared to be related to their suicide. Ninety percent of Shaffer's (1974) and 64% of Poteet's (1987) samples had experienced precipitants before their deaths. Most of our subjects had experienced arguments; relationship breakups; problems at school, work, or with the police; or disappointing experiences. Similar rates were found in Thompson's study (1987) for breakups (26%), family disputes (22%), and legal problems (16%). Males appeared much more likely to have experienced a discrete precipitant before their suicides, suggesting that females may commit suicide as a function of the course of their psychiatric conditions. Females were more likely to commit suicide after an assault, which agrees with Robins's finding (cited in Holden 1986) that being assaulted is strongly predictive of suicidal behavior. In addition, the cohort differences in our study indicated that more recent suicide completers show a greater frequency of identifiable precipitants, particularly assaults.

Our findings suggest a heterogeneity of personality characteristics among youth who commit suicide. No single category defined more than 16% of the decedents. The most common categories employed were withdrawn, supersensitive, and angry. These results generally resemble those noted by Shaffer (1974) and Shafii and associates (1985). In the former study, the two most common personality descriptors suggest a supersensitive or withdrawn child, whereas in the latter study, 70% of the youth were rated as having "inhibited personalities" defined by withdrawal and supersensitivity.

Given the source of the data base involved in this study, namely medical examiners' records, several methodological issues need to be considered. First, no control or comparison groups are involved; thus, it is not clear if the characteristics of the young suicide victims are uniquely related to suicide or, for example, might be typical of any young person with a psychiatric disorder. More important perhaps, reliance on such records is likely to lead to an underrecognition of certain characteristics of young people who commit suicide. In particular, an archival study, like this one, is likely to underestimate the frequency and type of psychiatric diagnoses (especially, affective disorders, alcohol and substance abuse), previous suicide ideation and attempts, and specific precipitants. Nonetheless, despite the potential methodological issues, the results of this study are quite consistent with those of other studies of adolescent and young adult suicide. In integrating the findings of the available studies of young people who commit suicide, a number of conclusions appear to have a strong measure of support. In discussing these conclusions, it is important to emphasize that generalizations must be tempered with a sense that there is certainly heterogeneity in the characteristics of young suicide victims and that no single understanding of the nature of suicide will be appropriate.

Suicide is primarily an act of white males and its frequency increases with age. As with adult suicide, psychiatric conditions appear to be the most significant precondition to youth suicide; most, if not all young persons who commit suicide are experiencing a psychiatric episode or disorder. Generally speaking, these disorders seem to be of long duration or chronic in nature. Affective disorders and alcohol and substance abuse demonstrate a particular relationship to suicide in the young as they do in older suicide victims. The incidence of both of these types of disorders increases during the adolescent years. Each of these disorders is associated with a greater likelihood of suicidal ideation, which in turn predisposes for suicide attempts. At the same time, most depressed or substance-abusing young people neither attempt nor complete suicide; even most attempters do not proceed to take their lives. Moreover, the incidence of depression is twice as great for females as for males and yet males predominate in completed suicide. Thus, other characteristics must exist that differentiate those youth with psychiatric disorders who are at risk for suicide from those who are not. Shaffer (cited in Holden 1986) has argued that males may be at greater risk simply as a result of their comfort with and the relative availability of firearms. In addition, males may, as a group, be more prone to impulsivity and emotional explosiveness. It is noteworthy that in this and Shaffer's (1974) study, the youngest suicide victims were more likely to be angry and aggressive, antisocial youth.

The circumstances of suicides among youth also bear consideration. Precipitants do appear to precede most suicides; yet these stressors generally appear to be the same type of life events that occur for most adolescents (Hoberman et al. 1986). Stressors, in and of themselves, probably do not pose a risk for the average adolescent or young adult. Instead, it is their occurrence for particular individuals with preexisting psychiatric conditions that creates a climate of risk. Males appear to be more affected by relationship breakups, whereas suicides among females show an increasing association with assaults. Many of the stressors are a consequence of being depressed or abusing substances and may not be independently occurring traumatic events. The greater degree of distress experienced by males after relationship breakups was demonstrated in a study of dating couples by Hill et al. (1976).

The impulsive, crisis nature of the actual suicides was impressive. Few suicide victims revealed evidence of advance planning for the particular act, took precautions against being stopped or discovered, or left notes. Additionally, the extent and degree of intoxication suggests a mental state of impaired judgment; it raises questions about the capacity for these young people to make rational judgments about their current life circumstances, although it is possible that intoxication may, in some cases, indicate an attempt at disinhibition in order to commit suicide.

What are the implications of these findings for endeavors to reduce the rate of youth suicide? Several studies have demonstrated that suicide prevention programs have not made a significant impact on the rate of suicides (Bridge et al. 1977; Barraclough et al. 1978; Miller et al. 1979). Moreover, in recent years, a number of specific youth suicide prevention curricula have been developed. Garfinkel (1986) has noted that many of the curricula focus primarily on the circumstances surrounding suicides and tend to deemphasize the relationship between psychopathology and suicide.

It is apparent that a focus on precipitants, signs of premeditation, or planning is likely to be unproductive given the normative nature of the stresses experienced by young suicide victims and the largely impulsive nature of the actual suicidal act. The likelihood of preventing particular suicides at the time of the act seems low. Rather, we believe the emphasis in youth suicide prevention programs must be on the early identification and appropriate treatment of the episodes of psychopathology that underlie and precede most instances of suicide in young persons. Khuri and Akiskal (1983) have made a strong argument that energetic treatment and ongoing follow-up of patients with primary and secondary affective disorders will prove to be an effective method of preventing suicide.

Based on our findings, youth at risk for completed suicide are males who have either an affective disorder or alcohol or drug abuse and who have experienced an acute, proximal stressor that involves either a social loss or a blow to their self-esteem. These findings are consistent with other reports of youth suicide (Shaffer 1974; Shafii et al. 1985). Based on these data, it is strongly suggested that male adolescents identified as having a recent history of symptoms of an affective disorder and/or substance abuse undergo an evaluation to determine the type of intervention needed. It is also important to maintain close follow-up contact with such youngsters. This will enhance the possibility of offering intervention to prevent a suicidal act if the symptom severity increases and if stresses intensify. Finally, we appreciate the need for additional studies of youth who commit suicide and hope that the information obtained in this chapter will be helpful in developing a more accurate and comprehensive understanding of the factors involved in youth suicide. In turn, this information can provide the foundation of realistic and effective strategies to reduce the number of youths who tragically take their own lives in an impulsive desire to manage the distress of their psychiatric disorders.

───────────
    We thank Gary Peterson, M.D., J.D., and Michael McGree, M.D., Medical Examiners in Hennepin and Ramsey Counties, respectively. Their cooperation and support ensured the success of this endeavor.

REFERENCES

Andreasen NC, Endicott J, Spitzer RL, et al: The family history method using diagnostic criteria. Arch Gen Psychiatry 34:1229–1235, 1977

Barraclough BM, Bunch J, Nelson B, et al: A hundred cases of suicide: clinical aspects. Br J Psychiatry 125:355–373, 1974

Barraclough BM, Jennings C, Moss JR: Suicide prevention by the Samaritans: a controlled study of effectiveness. Lancet 2:868–870, 1978

Berman A, Cohen-Sandler R: Child and adolescent suicide research: a critique. Crisis 3:3–15, 1982

Bridge TP, Potkin SD, Sung WWA, et al: Suicide prevention centers. J Nerv Ment Dis 164:18–24, 1977

Centers for Disease Control: Youth Suicide in the United States, 1970–1980. Atlanta, GA, Centers for Disease Control, November, 1986

Dorpat TL, Ripley HS: A study of suicide in Seattle area. Compr Psychiatry 1:349–359, 1960

Garfinkel BD: School-based prevention programs. Unpublished paper presented at the National Conference on Prevention and Interventions in Youth Suicide, Oakland, CA, 1986

Garfinkel BD, Golombek H: Suicidal behavior in adolescents, in The Adolescent and Mood Disturbance. Edited by Garfinkel BD, Golombek H. New York, International University Press, 1983, pp 189–217

Garfinkel BD, Hoberman JM, Walker J, et al: Suicide attempts in a community of adolescents. Unpublished paper presented at the American Academy of Child Psychiatry, Los Angeles, CA, October 1986

Haim A: Adolescent Suicide. New York, International University Press, 1974

Hawton K: Suicide in adolescents, in Suicide. Edited by Roy A. Baltimore, MD, Williams & Wilkins, 1986, pp 135–150

Herjanic B, Weiner Z: Adolescent suicide. Advances in Behavioral Pediatrics 1:195–223, 1980

Hill C, Ruben Z, Peplau L: Breakups before marriage: the end of 103 affairs. Journal of Social Issues 33:147–168, 1976

Hoberman HM, Garfinkel BD, Parsons JH, et al: Epidemiology of depression in a community sample of high school students. Unpublished paper presented at the American Academy of Child Psychiatry, Los Angeles, CA, October 1986

Holden C: Youth suicide: new research focuses on a growing social problem. Science 233:839–841, 1986

Holinger PC: Adolescent suicide: an epidemiological study of recent trends. Am J Psychiatry 135:754–756, 1978

Jan-Tausch J: Suicide in Children 1960–63. Trenton, NJ, New Jersey Public Schools, Department of Education, 1964

Khuri R, Akiskal HS: Suicide prevention: the necessity of treating contributory psychiatric disorders. Psychiatr Clin North Am 6:193–207, 1983

Lefkowitz MM, Tesiny EP: Assessment of childhood depression. J Consult Clin Psychol 48:43–50, 1980

Leon GR, Kendal PC, Garber J: Depression in children: parent, teacher, and child perspectives. J Abnorm Child Psychol 8:221–235, 1980

Miller HI, Coombs DW, Mukherjee D, et al: Suicide prevention services in America. Ala J Med Sci 16:26–31, 1979

Murphy GE: Suicide and attempted suicide, in The Medical Basis of Psychiatry.

Edited by Winokur G, Clayton P. Philadelphia, PA, WB Saunders, 1986, pp 562–579

Pettifor J, Perry D, Plowman B, et al: Risk factors predicting childhood and adolescent suicides. Journal of Child Care 1983

Petzel SV, Cline D: Adolescent suicide: epidemiological and biological aspects. Adolesc Psychiatry 6:239–266, 1978

Petzel SV, Riddle M: Adolescent suicide: psychosocial and cognitive aspects. Adolesc Psychiatry 9:343–398, 1981

Poteet DJ: Adolescent suicide: a review of 87 cases of completed suicide in Shelby County, Tennessee. Am J Forensic Med Pathol 8:12–17, 1987

Rich CL, Young D, Fowler RC: San Diego suicide study, I: young vs. old subjects. Arch Gen Psychiatry 43:577–582, 1986

Robins E, Murphy GE, Wilkinson RH, et al: Some clinical considerations in the presentation of suicide based on a study of 134 successful suicides. Am J Public Health 49:888–899, 1959

Sacco W, Graves D: Correspondence between teacher ratings of childhood depression and child self-ratings. Journal of Clinical Child Psychology 4:353–355, 1985

Shaffer D: Suicide in childhood and early adolescence. J Child Psychol Psychiatry 15:275–291, 1974

Shaffer D: Completed suicide informant interview. Unpublished manuscript. New York State Psychiatric Institute, 1985

Shaffer D, Fisher P: The epidemiology of suicide in children and young adolescents. J Am Acad Child Psychiatry 20:545–565, 1981

Shafii M, Carrigan S, Whittinghill JR, et al: Psychological autopsy of completed suicide in children and adolescents. Am J Psychiatry 142:1061–1064, 1985

Thompson TR: Childhood and adolescent suicide in Manitoba: demographic study. Can J Psychiatry 32:264–269, 1987

Weissman M, Orvaschel H, Padian N: Children's symptoms and social functioning self-report scales: comparison of mother's and children's reports. J Nerv Ment Dis 168:736–740, 1980

3

Epidemiologic Issues in Youth Suicide

Paul C. Holinger, M.D., M.P.H.

Epidemiology is the study of the distribution and determinants of disease frequency in humans (MacMahon and Pugh 1970). The importance of epidemiology lies in its potential capacity to elucidate causal relationships, and, as a consequence, to generate intervention, prevention, and prediction models and strategies. Evaluating longitudinal trends in suicide rates also aids in protecting against the short-sighted sensationalism that often mars studies of self-destructiveness.

The purpose of this chapter is to present various forms of epidemiologic data on youth suicide, discuss prevention and intervention strategies from an epidemiologic viewpoint, and consider future research possibilities. The epidemiologic data to be evaluated include longitudinal, demographic, cross-cultural, and high-risk groups and relative risk.

DATA

Methodologic Considerations

There are several methodologic problems inherent in using national mortality data. These include under- and overreporting, data misclassification, and changes in data classification categories over time. These issues have been discussed in detail elsewhere (Holinger

Supported in part by the Center for Suicide Research and Prevention (Rush-Presbyterian-St. Luke's Medical Center) and the Harold W. Schloss Memorial Fund (Michael Reese Hospital and Medical Center). The author gratefully acknowledges the technical assistance of Daryl Michaels.

and Klemen 1982; Holinger 1987), but two aspects should be mentioned here. First, increases and decreases in suicide rates over time do not appear to be artifactual based on federal data classification over time, inasmuch as the comparability for suicide between revisions of the International Classification of Diseases is very high (Holinger and Klemen 1982). Second, the data used in this chapter are for the complete population, not samples; they include all suicides recorded among the indicated age groups in the United States. Mortality data before 1933 are not included because it was only after 1932 that all states were incorporated into the national mortality statistics (Alaska was added in 1959 and Hawaii in 1960).

Longitudinal Epidemiologic Data

This section will deal primarily with age and period effects in youth suicide. Age effects involve changes in specific rates of mortality or illness over the life span of the individual. Period effects refer to changes in rates of mortality or illness during a particular historical period (Holford 1983). National mortality data for youth are divided up, somewhat awkwardly, into 5-year age groups: 5–9, 10–14, 15–19, and 20–24 years. The psychological developmental tasks are overlapping: 5–9 years (childhood), 10–14 (preadolescence, early adolescence), 15–19 (middle to late adolescence), and 20–24 (late adolescence and early adulthood).

Suicides are not recorded in national mortality figures for the 0–4 years age group, and recorded suicides for 5- to 9-year-olds are very rare. Throughout this century, there have been usually from 0 to 10 suicides per year among 5- to 9-year-olds in the United States (Holinger 1987; Pfeffer 1986).

For 10- to 14-year-olds, the suicide rates are also very low relative to the older age groups. Every year there are about 100–200 suicides among 10- to 14-year-olds, for a rate of about 1 per 100,000. Rates for males are greater than those for females, and white males have the highest rates. Period effects are less discernible in this age group than in the older groups, with the exception of the rise in rates during the 1960s and 1970s.

For 15- to 19-year-olds, one finds rates 7–10 times higher than for 10- to 14-year-olds. In 1984, there were 1,692 suicides among 15- to 19-year-olds, with a rate of 9.0 per 100,000 (National Center for Health Statistics, Hyattsville, MD, unpublished data). Figure 1 shows rates for this age group over time by race and sex. Male rates are higher than female, and white males have the highest rates. Period effects demonstrate increases during the early 1930s (economic depression), de-

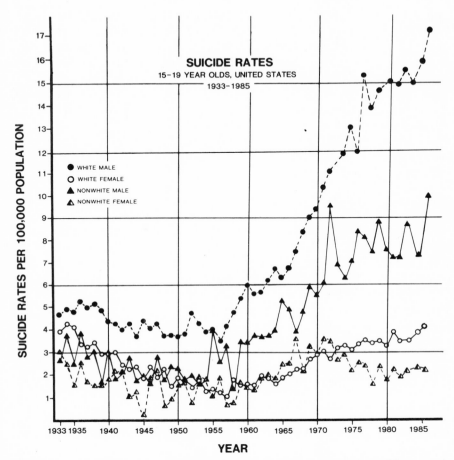

Figure 1. Suicide rates per 100,000 population for 15- to 19-year-olds, United States, 1933–1984. [Sources of data: Number of deaths: National Center for Health Statistics, unpublished data for 1933–1984. Population (for rate derivation): National Center for Health Statistics, unpublished data, 1933–1984.]

creases during the 1940s to the mid-1950s, and increases from the mid-1950s to the late 1970s. From the late 1970s to the present there has been a leveling off and decrease in suicide rates for nonwhite males, white females, and nonwhite females. In addition, the rate of rise for white males has decreased during this time (Holinger and Offer 1986).

As one moves to the next oldest age group, 20- to 24-year-olds, the suicide rates continue to increase: rates for 20- to 24-year-olds are approximately twice those of the 15- to 19-year-olds. There were 3,334 suicides among 20- to 24-year-olds in 1984, with a rate of 15.6 per

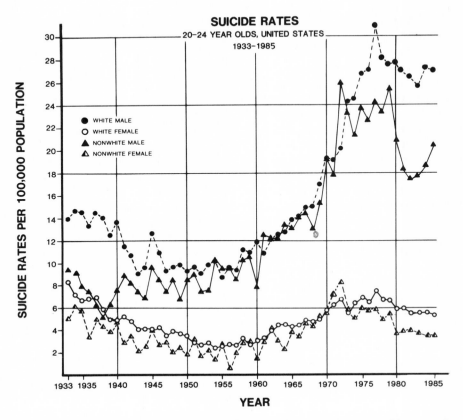

Figure 2. Suicide rates per 100,000 population for 20- to 24-year-olds, United States, 1933–1984. [Sources of data: Number of deaths: National Center for Health Statistics, unpublished data for 1933–1984. Population (for rate derivation): National Center for Health Statistics, unpublished data, 1933–1984.]

100,000 (National Center for Health Statistics, Hyattsville, MD, unpublished data). Figure 2 presents the suicide rates for 20- to 24-year-olds by race and sex in the United States, 1933–1984. Rates for males are higher than rates for females. Rates for whites have usually been higher than for nonwhites, but the difference between white and nonwhite rates are less for 20- to 24-year-olds than 15- to 19-year-olds. The period effects for 20- to 24-year-olds are quite clear, are similar for all race and sex groups, and resemble those for 15- to 19-year-olds. Period effects include the increases of the early 1930s, decreases during the 1940s until the mid-1950s, increases from the mid-1950s to the late 1970s, and recent leveling off and decreases. The rates in the late 1970s are the highest ever recorded in the United States for 20- to 24-year-olds.

As is well documented throughout the literature, suicide rates tend to increase with increasing age (Holinger 1987; Blazer et al. 1986). For young people, this trend is apparent over the last 50 years in the United States. The above data and Figures 1 and 2 show the increase in suicide rates as age increases from 5–9, to 10–14, to 15–19, and to 20–24 years. However, a more specific breakdown of age effects in suicide rates would enhance the understanding of youth suicide. In 1968, national mortality data became available by 1-year age intervals, and thus it became possible to explore the age effects in youthful suicide rates in a more definitive manner than simply utilizing the 5-year age groups (e.g., 5–9, 10–14 years). Figure 3 and Table 1 present the suicide rates for 0- to 30-year-olds by 1-year age intervals from 1968 to 1977, by race and sex. The rates were averaged over the decade 1968–1977 [complete methodology has been presented elsewhere (Holinger and Luke 1984)]. Suicides tend to begin at younger ages for males than females, and the rates for males are consistently higher than for females. The age patterns tend to be similar for all race and sex groups: suicide rates tend to increase from preadolescence into adolescence, leveling off in late adolescence and early adulthood. The significance of these findings with respect to the developmental tasks of childhood and adolescence has been explored elsewhere (Holinger and Luke 1984; Holinger et al. 1983–1985).

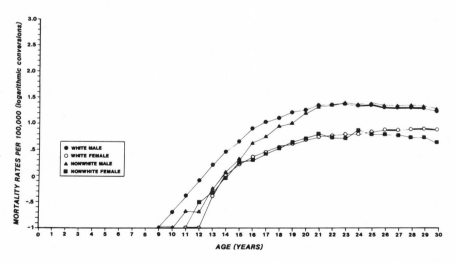

Figure 3. Suicide rates per 100,000 population, 0- to 30-year-olds by 1-year age intervals, United States, 1968–1977. [(Source of data: Holinger and Luke 1984.) Reproduced with permission from Suicide in the Young, Howard S. Sudak, Amasa B. Ford, and Norman B. Rushforth, editors, copyright 1984 by PSG Publishing Company, Inc., Littleton, Massachusetts.]

Table 1. Suicide Rates (per 100,000 population) by 1-Year Age Intervals, Race, and Sex, United States, 1968–1977

Age (years)	White male	White female	Nonwhite male	Nonwhite female
0 (0–11 mos)	0.0	0.0	0.0	0.0
1	0.0	0.0	0.0	0.0
2	0.0	0.0	0.0	0.0
3	0.0	0.0	0.0	0.0
4	0.0	0.0	0.0	0.0
5	0.0	0.0	0.0	0.0
6	0.0	0.0	0.0	0.0
7	0.0	0.0	0.0	0.0
8	0.0	0.0	0.0	0.0
9	0.0	0.0	0.1	0.0
10	0.2	0.0	0.1	0.0
11	0.4	0.1	0.2	0.0
12	0.8	0.1	0.2	0.3
13	1.7	0.4	0.6	0.5
14	3.0	1.0	1.2	1.1
15	4.7	1.7	2.1	1.9
16	8.3	2.4	4.2	2.2
17	11.2	2.9	6.1	2.8
18	14.9	3.7	9.8	3.5
19	17.7	4.4	14.0	3.7
20	19.7	5.1	16.4	5.2
21	23.2	6.0	21.5	6.4
22	23.5	6.2	21.8	5.8
23	24.9	6.7	24.0	5.7
24	23.4	6.9	22.7	7.7
25	23.5	7.4	23.9	6.6
26	22.1	8.2	22.6	6.9
27	21.9	8.0	22.2	6.4
28	22.1	8.4	24.0	6.0
29	21.9	8.7	22.8	5.8
30	20.3	8.4	20.1	4.9

Note. Reproduced with permission from Suicide in the Young, Howard S. Sudak, Amasa B. Ford, and Norman B. Rushforth, editors, copyright 1984 by PSG Publishing Company, Inc., Littleton, Massachusetts.

In conclusion, let us summarize the age and period effects in youth suicide. Suicide rates tend to increase with age over the 5-year intervals (5–9, 10–14, 15–19, 20–24 years of age). When examined in more detail by 1-year age intervals, suicide rates tend to increase gradually from early adolescence through late adolescence, with a leveling off in late adolescence to early adulthood. The period effects are apparent primarily in the 15–19 and 20–24 year age groups, and consist of increased rates during the 1930s, decreases into the 1940s and mid-1950s, increases from the mid-1950s to the late 1970s, and leveling off and decrease of rates from the late 1970s to the present. These period effects are consistent across virtually all age, race, and sex combinations.

Demographics

There is increasing evidence that demographic data may be of use in understanding suicide among the young (Easterlin 1980; Hendin 1982; Klerman et al. 1985; Murphy and Wetzel 1980; Solomon and Hellon 1980; Holinger and Offer 1987). This section will focus primarily on two types of studies that utilize population data: cohort analyses and population models.

Cohort analyses have provided many data to demonstrate the increase in suicide rates among the young (Klerman et al. 1985; Murphy and Wetzel 1980; Solomon and Hellon 1980; Hellon and Solomon 1980). Cohort effects involve differences in rates of mortality or illness among individuals defined by some shared temporal experience, for example, year or decade of birth (Holford 1983). Solomon and Hellon (1980), studying Alberta, Canada, during the years 1951–1977, identified 5-year age cohorts, and the suicide rates were followed as the cohorts aged. Suicide rates increased directly with age, regardless of sex. Once a cohort entered the 15- to 19-year-old age range with a high rate of suicide, the rate for that cohort remained consistently high as it aged. Murphy and Wetzel (1980) found the same phenomenon, in reduced magnitude, in birth cohorts of much greater size in the United States. Not only does each successive birth cohort start with the higher suicide rate, but it also has a higher rate at each successive 5-year interval than the preceding cohort had at that age. Klerman et al. (1985) noted a similar cohort effect in their study of depressed patients.

Whereas cohort studies follow a certain group of people (cohort) over time, the population model studies specific age groups (e.g., 15- to 24-year-olds) over time. Studying 15- to 19-year-olds and 65- to 69-year-olds, data suggested that as the proportion of 15- to 19-year-olds increased (and decreased) over time, the suicide rates for that age group increased (and decreased, respectively); the opposite trend was found for 65- to 69-year-olds (Holinger and Offer 1982). It should be noted that although one would expect the number of suicides to increase with an increased number of people in a specific age group, the rates should not necessarily increase. The model was subsequently expanded: from 1933 to 1982 suicide rates for 15- to 24-year-olds showed statistically significant increases and decreases with increases and decreases, respectively, in their proportion of the population, whereas virtually all adult groups (35–44, 45–54, 55–64 years of age) showed statistically significant decreases (and increases) in suicide rates with increases (and de-

Table 2. Suicide Rates for 15 to 24-Year-Olds in the United States

1977	13.6
1978	12.4
1979	12.4
1980	12.3
1981	12.3
1982	12.1
1983	11.9
1984	12.5
1985	12.9
1986	12.7

Note. Sources of data: Vital Statistics in the United States, Mortality, 1977–1982 (for 1977–1982) and National Center for Health Statistics, unpublished data (for 1983–1985); data for 1986 is provisional based on a 10% sample.

creases, respectively) of their proportion of the population (Holinger and Offer 1987). Possible explanations for this relationship between population changes and suicide rates have been discussed in detail elsewhere (Holinger and Offer 1986, 1987).

The importance of the demographic perspective lies in the capacity for prediction. Inasmuch as the numbers and proportions of various age groups can be determined years in advance based on the numbers in younger age groups, it may be possible to predict the suicide rates over time. If such epidemiologic predictions are substantiated over time, effective interventions can be established based on the relationships between population changes and suicide rates.

While at least decades are necessary to evaluate the epidemiologic propositions noted above, recent data appear to lend some support to the population model. The population model suggests that the suicide rates among young people would peak during the late 1970s (corresponding to the peak of the population of 15- to 24-year-olds), with a subsequent leveling off and decrease (corresponding to the projected leveling off and decrease in the proportion of 15- to 24-year-olds); the cohort studies implied that the suicide rates would continue to increase. In 1977, suicide rates for 15- to 24-year-olds were higher than ever recorded, and they have subsequently leveled off (Table 2). Figure 4 presents the actual and predicted suicide rates and the proportion of 15- to 24-year-olds in the United States, 1933–2000.

Cross-Cultural Data

Two types of cross-cultural data should be noted here as they relate to issues mentioned above, i.e., age effects and demographics.

In terms of age effects, Table 3 presents suicide rates in 1980 for

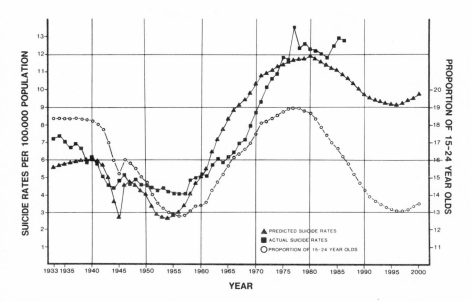

Figure 4. Suicide rates (actual and predicted) for 15- to 24-year-olds and population changes, 1933–2000. [Sources of suicide data: National Center for Health Statistics: Vital Statistics of the United States–Special Reports, vol. 43. Washington, DC, U.S. Government Printing Office, 1956 (for 1933–1953); Grove and Hetzel 1968 (for 1954–1960); National Center for Health Statistics: Vital Statistics of the United States—Mortality, 1961–1982. Washington, DC, U.S. Government Printing Office, 1963–1986 (for 1961–1982); and unpublished data from the National Center for Health Statistics (for 1983–1986). Sources of population data: Grove and Hetzel 1968 (for 1933–1960); National Center for Health Statistics: Vital Statistics of the United States—Mortality, 1961–1982, Washington, DC, U.S. Government Printing Office, 1963–1986 (for 1961–1982); and unpublished data from the National Center for Health Statistics (for 1983–1986). Reprinted with permission from Holinger PC, Offer D, Zola MA: A prediction model of suicide among youth. J Nerv Ment Dis 176: 275–279, 1988. Copyright 1988 by Williams & Wilkins.]

several countries by age. Two points are noteworthy in the present context. First, the suicide rates for the young in the United States can be seen to be approximately in the middle of the rates for the various countries listed. Second, for nearly all countries, the age effects are quite similar. That is, virtually regardless of culture, the suicide rates increase with age, with the youngest age groups having the lowest rates.

In terms of demographics, Offer et al. (in press) conducted an extensive psychological study of adolescents in 10 countries: Australia, Bangladesh, Hungary, Israel, Italy, Japan, Taiwan, Turkey, the United States, and West Germany. Using a cross-section approach, the investi-

Table 3. Suicide Rates (per 100,000 Population) by Age and Country for the Year 1980

	5–14	15–24	25–34	35–44	45–54	55–64	65–74	75+
Australia	0.2	11.2	15.0	16.8	15.9	15.8	14.1	17.3
Austria	2.3	18.0	23.9	29.2	39.5	36.5	46.0	50.7
Canada	0.6	15.3	18.8	17.0	22.2	19.9	17.5	18.3
Chile	0.2	6.9	7.0	7.3	6.9	8.7	5.4	9.5
England	0.0	4.7	8.7	11.8	13.2	14.7	15.4	14.4
Finland	0.5	23.6	33.2	33.5	38.2	32.9	38.0	25.3
France	0.4	10.7	18.7	23.3	27.2	28.6	37.5	49.7
Germany, Fed. Republic of	1.1	12.5	18.7	23.8	31.2	29.8	37.3	41.2
Greece	0.4	1.8	3.2	3.7	3.9	4.1	7.1	10.5
Hungary	2.3	20.0	37.6	56.2	69.9	67.0	79.8	130.9
Israel		6.1	7.2	6.1	8.9	10.4	14.9	29.4
Italy	0.2	3.9	5.8	6.6	10.3	12.4	17.4	20.2
Japan	0.3	12.5	18.2	20.7	24.1	24.2	37.8	65.4
Panama	0.4	2.9	4.6	2.3	3.9	2.4	16.7 [a]	
Portugal	0.5	4.6	6.6	8.6	10.6	13.8	16.6	26.5
Switzerland	1.1	23.4	25.7	30.0	33.6	41.0	40.7	43.5
Thailand	0.9	16.2	9.8	9.5	10.3	8.6	7.5 [a]	
United States	0.4	12.3	15.8	15.2	15.9	15.9	16.8	19.2
Yugoslavia	0.9	7.9	10.2	17.2	25.5	29.6	36.2	46.7

Note. Sources: World Health Statistics Annual. Geneva, World Health Organization, 1982, 1983, 1984, 1985.
[a] Rate for 65 years and older.

gators examined a total of more than 5,000 teenagers during the year 1983 in the 10 countries. A higher proportion of 14- to 18-year-olds in the total population of the countries was associated with more manifest psychopathology. A high proportion of adolescents was connected to adolescents reporting relatively poor mood, poor social relationships, and high psychopathology. These results tended to support the findings of Easterlin (1980), Hendin (1982), Klerman et al. (1985), and Holinger and Offer (1987, 1982).

High-Risk Groups and Relative Risk

Psychiatric patients and those who have previously attempted suicide represent a high-risk group for completing suicide, with rates far higher than those found in the general population. Those patients with diagnoses of affective disorders (major depression, manic-depressive illness) and schizophrenia are particularly at risk. These studies have been reviewed in detail elsewhere (Pokorny 1983; Sainsbury 1982; Diekstra 1982; Kreitman 1982). In addition, various groups of young people are at higher risk of suicide due to sociodemographic variables such as parental loss, divorce, and broken homes; recent loss and bereavement; unemployment; being white; being male; and belonging to younger age groups in the baby boom generation (for detailed reviews see Pfeffer 1986; Murphy and Wetzel 1980; Holinger and Offer 1981, 1982; Seiden 1969). The question arises, however, as to how use can be made of this knowledge about high-risk groups for the sake of prevention. The answer is far more complicated than it would first appear. Kreitman (1982), for example, has shown that if one screens even a large high-risk population for follow-up, one will catch relatively few suicides, and at high expense; and if one concentrates on smaller, higher-risk populations the yield is so low that the overall reduction in the total number of suicides is minimal. The technical derivations of these findings and the relative risk figures can be found in Kreitman (1982).

In addition to identifying various groups at high risk of youth suicide, one can also calculate the relative risk for a particular group exposed to a specific potentially influential variable. Relative risk refers to the ratio of the rate of the disease (usually incidence or mortality) among those exposed to the rate among those not exposed (MacMahon and Pugh 1970). Two sets of relative risks will be examined here: one dealing with age, race, and sex variables, and the other with demographics.

Table 4 presents the relative risk by age, race, and sex for 15- to 19-year-olds and 20- to 24-year-olds in 1984. The 20- to 24-year-olds can be seen to be approximately 1.5–2.5 more likely to die of suicide than the 15- to 19-year-olds, depending on race and sex. Table 5 gives relative risk figures for 1984 by utilizing race and sex differences, with nonwhite females as the comparison group. For example, for 15- to 19-year-olds, the white males are about 7 times (6.87) more likely to die of suicide than nonwhite females. Finally, Table 6 presents the relative risk for suicide rates in the years 1955 and 1977, i.e., when the proportion of adolescents in the United States was approximately at the lowest and highest, respectively. As shown in Table 5, adolescents were approximately 2–4 times at greater risk of dying by suicide in 1977 than in 1955. For instance, a white male 15–19 years old was nearly 4 times (3.83)

Table 4. Relative Risk for Suicide Rates by Age, Race, and Sex in the United States, 1984

	Suicide rates per 100,000		Relative risk
	15- to 19-year-olds	20- to 24-year-olds	
White males	15.8	27.5	1.74
White females	3.8	5.5	1.45
Nonwhite males	7.3	18.4	2.52
Nonwhite females	2.3	3.5	1.52

Table 5. Relative Risk for Suicide Rates by Age, Race, and Sex in the United States, 1984

	Suicide rates per 100,000 for 15- to 19-year-olds	Relative risk compared to nonwhite females	Suicide rates per 100,000 for 20- to 24-year-olds	Relative risk compared to nonwhite females
White males	15.8	6.87	27.5	7.86
White females	3.8	1.65	5.5	1.57
Nonwhite males	7.3	3.17	18.4	5.26
Nonwhite females	2.3		3.5	

Table 6. Relative Risk for Suicide Rates by Age, Race, and Sex in the United States, 1955 and 1977

	Suicide rates per 100,000 for 15- to 19-year-olds			Suicide rates per 100,000 for 20- to 24-year-olds		
	1955	1977	Relative risk	1955	1977	Relative risk
White males	4.0	15.3	3.83	8.7	30.8	3.54
White females	1.4	3.5	2.50	2.6	7.5	2.88
Nonwhite males	4.0	8.1	2.03	9.5	24.3	2.56
Nonwhite females	1.0	2.4	2.4	2.7	5.8	2.15

more likely to die of suicide in 1977 than in 1955. Of course, in addition to the possible influences of the demographic variable on the increased risk, other period effects, such as unemployment, could account for the differences.

INTERVENTION AND PREVENTION

Another issue of importance in exploring self-destructiveness among adolescents is that of intervention and prevention. There exists a massive literature on intervention and prevention in suicide (e.g., see Rosenberg et al. 1984; and Holinger and Offer 1986).

Two issues should be addressed before turning to the specifics of the effectiveness of various suicide interventions. First, detailed examination of the epidemiology of suicide rates from 1900 to 1980 in the United States reveals that the major shifts in rates are due to socioeconomic factors such as war, population shifts, and the economy (Brenner 1971, 1979; Easterlin 1980; Holinger 1987). The shifts in rates due to such socioeconomic factors occur virtually invariably throughout the century for all age, race, and sex groups. This pattern is so striking it has been termed *the societal factor*, and this pattern needs to be considered whenever one evaluates the epidemiology of suicide with the intention of intervening to alter the rates (Holinger 1987). Second, the impact of potential interventions is extremely difficult to estimate due to the remarkable paucity of solid data demonstrating effectiveness of interventions on suicide rates. Thus, while an attitude of pessimism is not necessarily warranted, one must be extremely cautious in estimating the effectiveness of interventions given the state of our knowledge at this particular time.

Of the many concepts that could be used to explore issues of intervention and recommendations regarding suicide, two somewhat overlapping methods have been chosen. The first involves epidemiologic concepts of prevention (primary, secondary, and tertiary), and the second includes groups at high risk.

Mental disorders and suicide in particular do not lend themselves well to investigation through classic epidemiologic concepts. Thus, the epidemiologic categories of suicide prevention used here will be similar to those developed specifically for suicide by Shneidman (1975); some modifications in Shneidman's categories will be made in order to best meet the task at hand. *Primary prevention*, then, will refer to prevention proper. *Secondary prevention* relates to intervention and is particularly concerned with suicide attempts. *Tertiary prevention* will refer to "postvention," consisting of such possible interventions as those in the family or school system following an actual death by suicide. Obviously there are overlaps between primary, secondary, and tertiary prevention; it appears, however, that these divisions allow for some greater conceptual focus on the different levels of abstraction involved.

With these concepts of prevention, two population groups will be examined: the general population; and populations at high risk, divided into two subgroups—1) psychiatric patients, such as patients who have had psychiatric treatment and have been diagnosed, and suicide attempters; and 2) a high-risk group defined by sociodemographic variables, such as the unemployed, single or divorced, those suffering recent losses, whites, males, older persons, and adolescents.

GENERAL POPULATION

Primary Prevention

Five issues will be considered with respect to primary prevention in the general population: developmental aspects (public education), training of professionals and paraprofessionals in suicidology, agents, suicide prevention centers, and population changes and cohort effects.

Developmental aspects (public education). Developmental issues in prevention have important potential. Of all the things children are taught in school and parents-to-be are taught about their children, there is little attention paid to affects. Why the emphasis on affects? Current infant research and the study of affects have productively challenged older theories and helped clarify much about what human beings feel, why they feel it, and how they communicate it. The research of such persons as Arnold (1968), Tomkins (1962, 1963), Stern (1985), Basch (1976), and Kohut (1971, 1977, 1984) should be noted. For example, research indicates that six to nine basic affects are identifiable as early as the first few days of life, e.g., joy, anger, interest, disgust, and fear. Kohut's studies (1971, 1977, 1984) on self-esteem disorders in adults have implications for how one understands and handles a child's pride, enthusiasm, and grandiosity. Recommendations would include studies specifically on the impact of the following: school classes that deal with this topic (helping the children to understand just what they are feeling, why they are feeling it, and how to communicate their feelings); the training of teachers; and parents obtaining this information via the schools, obstetricians, and other physicians (e.g., through brochures or classes). In terms of suicide prevention, decrease of self-destructive behaviors, and enhancement of mental health in general, it appears necessary to examine carefully the potential value of raising a generation of children who have a solid understanding of identifying and communicating affects and feelings.

Training of professionals and paraprofessionals in suicidology. The second aspect of primary prevention is that of training. The training referred to here is training in suicide assessment and prevention by physicians and paraprofessionals. The importance of training psychiatrists to adequately assess suicide potential is apparent. However, not so apparent, and perhaps even more important in terms of numbers of people, is the need to train other physicians (e.g., internists, family practitioners, obstetricians) and paraprofessionals in suicide assessment. As the Joint Commission on Mental Illness and Health (1961) demonstrated, far more people with problems first consult either paraprofessionals or physicians rather than psychiatrists. Sainsbury (1982) recently reviewed some of the relevant issues regarding suicide prevention and the competence of various groups to assess depression and suicidal intent. Perhaps the group with the most potential but least attention paid to it in terms of suicide prevention is the clergy. The joint commission found that more people seeking help for problems went to the clergy than to any other professional or paraprofessional group, and Kulka et al. (1979) reported similar findings 15 years later. Holinger (1985) has examined the treatment roles of the clergy and the potential public health impact the clergy have, given appropriate training.

Agents. Guns and medications are currently among the most common causes of successful, overt suicide (National Center for Health Statistics, Hyattsville, MD, unpublished data). The frequency of use of these agents in suicide and the potential for their regulation necessitates concentrating on them for purposes of suicide prevention. Other methods of suicide (e.g., hanging, jumping off buildings and bridges, jumping in front of trains and cars) are not only less frequent but have less regulatory and therefore less prevention potential. With respect to guns, there is a large literature relating to the use of guns in suicide and the potential for gun control to decrease the suicide rates. The issues become particularly problematic not only because gun control is controversial as a political concern but also the scientific data on the relationship between gun control and decreased suicide rates are not clear-cut. The importance of having solid data about agents of suicide was highlighted by the decrease in suicide rate in England following the conversion of domestic gas from a toxic to a nontoxic form. Miller et al. (1984) have reviewed the coal-gas findings, and their discussion demonstrates the critical need for data when attempting recommendations about the agents of suicide. Firearms have been shown to be not only the leading cause of suicide but also the one cause that has increased significantly with the recent increase in suicide rates (Boyd 1983). However, the issue of gun control as a method of suicide prevention is controversial, although the bulk of the evidence seems to suggest that it would be effective (Westermeyer 1984; Browning 1974; Markush and Bartolucci 1984; Boyd 1983; Hudgens 1983; Lester and Murrell 1980, 1982; Lester 1983). One might recommend gun control on a limited basis, e.g., prohibiting those with a history of previous suicide attempt (i.e., high-risk groups) from owning a gun, or differentiating between handguns and other guns in firearm regulations. The passage of gun control laws in specific communities (e.g., Morton Grove, IL) may make further epidemiologic research on this possible.

Another leading cause of suicide, poisoning by medications, may also lend itself to intervention with consequent decrease in rates. First, evidence suggests that restrictions of the number of tablets or capsules permitted for each prescription may decrease suicide rates (Oliver and Hetzel 1973; Goldney and Katsikitis 1983). Oliver and Hetzel (1973) argued persuasively that this kind of legislative restriction on the prescription of sedative and hypnotic drugs (especially barbiturates) was responsible for the decline in suicide rates in Australia during the late 1960s and early 1970s. Second, there exists the possibility that tricyclic antidepressants (and other medications frequently used in suicide attempts) could be manufactured with an emetic drug or antidote, so that if a person overdosed and the blood levels reached a certain level, the emetic or antidote would take effect. Third, many suicide victims get medication from a variety of physicians; with the use of computers, it would seem feasible for pharmacists filling prescriptions for certain dangerous drugs to have access to information regarding the patient's recent medication purchases in order to prevent some instances of stockpiling of drugs.

Suicide prevention centers.   This refers to groups such as the Samaritans, "hotlines," and mental health agencies, that attempt to respond specifically to those in crisis and especially to suicidal crisis. A detailed review of this literature has been recently presented by Miller et al. (1984). The success of such organizations and centers in decreasing suicide rates is controversial (Lester 1972). Much more sophisticated research examining communities before and after such interventions is needed. Miller et al. (1984) in a large study of this issue in which the investigators presented both a review of previous studies as well as new data, found that such centers consistently reduced the suicide rates of only one group, young white females, with decreases of approximately 1.75/100,000.

Population changes and cohort effects.   Another area of primary prevention involves the aforementioned population changes and prediction of suicide (Holinger and Offer 1982, 1984, 1987; Hendin 1982) and the cohort studies (Solomon and Hellon 1980; Hellon and Solomon 1980; Murphy and Wetzel 1980; Klerman et al. 1985). Holinger and Offer (1982, 1984, 1987) suggested that when the population of young people increases, the suicide *rates* (not just numbers of suicides, as one would expect) among the young also increase. They have outlined the implications of these findings for the prediction of suicide (prediction is possible inasmuch as the number of adolescents is known years ahead based on the number of children and preadolescents) and the intervention and prevention of suicide. Preventive interventions involve, especially, increasing the awareness of government, educational institutions, and private corporations to decrease the lag time between the increase of adolescents and young adults and society's response (i.e., increased high school and college enrollment and facilities, increased employment opportunities, increased health services).

Secondary Prevention

Secondary prevention refers to intervention and, in the current scheme, involves suicide attempters. This group will be addressed as a high-risk category. It is well documented that suicide attempters are at high risk of another attempted or successful suicide (e.g., Souris and Elefteriadis 1982; Schneider et al. 1976; Sainsbury 1982; Kreitman 1982). It seems critical, then, that treatment and follow-up plans be devised for both individual physicians as well as for medical centers. For example, this could take a form similar to a cancer registry. Unfortunately, as documented by Souris and Elefteriadis (1982), only a small percentage of attempters take advantage of voluntary programs. In addition, various regulations might be considered with respect to suicide attempters, especially in terms of firearms and medications.

Tertiary Prevention

Tertiary prevention, or postvention, refers to efforts directed toward those people and institutions who have been psychologically close to someone who committed suicide. Clinically, this involves family members and friends of someone who has suicided. These people become at risk of psychological problems, including suicide, and intervention may be necessary [e.g., see Cain (1972) regarding survivors of suicide]. Recommendations here would include public awareness (e.g., specific brochures describing reactions to suicide given to the survivors by physicians, hospitals, coroner's office) and treatment availability. On an epidemiologic level, tertiary prevention takes the form of preventing epidemics of suicide. High schools and small communities may be particularly vulnerable to such epidemics. Recommendations would include training of public health mental health workers to intervene quickly and effectively when such situations arise. Again, public awareness may be most effective (e.g., brochures, talking to the student body involved) with treatment being made available to those who need it.

HIGH-RISK POPULATIONS

Psychiatric Patients and Suicide Attempters

The three forms of prevention—primary, secondary, and tertiary—will be considered together in this high-risk group. Psychiatric patients and those who have previously attempted suicide represent a high-risk group for completing suicide, with rates far higher than those found in the general population (e.g., see Pokorny 1983; Sainsbury 1982; Diekstra 1982; Kreitman 1982). Those patients with diagnoses of affective disorders (major depression, manic-depressive illness) and schizophrenia are particularly at risk. As noted above, Kreitman (1982) has discussed the difficulties involved in preventive strategies in high-risk groups. However, some preventive possibilities might be considered. The first obvious one is training: focusing on psychiatrists, other physicians, and other mental health workers with a goal of demonstrating the high-risk nature of these groups in order to lead to increased awareness and follow-up in both the private and public sectors in medicine. Second, research is enhancing the efforts of suicide prediction on a clinical level. Prospective studies are particularly valuable, e.g., the current National Institute of Mental Health (NIMH) Collaborative Depression Study has massive amounts of data on patients with various forms of depression; several of those patients have subsequently suicided, and data analyses are being conducted and show patterns that may aid in clinical prediction. Also being studied is the use of specific biochemical tests to establish the suicidal potential of individual patients with psychiatric disorders, especially depression (Van Praag 1982). The third possibility involves the agents of suicide, especially guns and medication: a possible form of firearm regulation limited to certain patients or those with previous suicide attempts and stricter regulation of medication use for previous attempters. A fourth possibility would be various methods for follow-up, by either public or private facilities, of those persons combining various high-risk factors, e.g., young or old white males with an affective disorder or previous suicide attempt.

High-Risk Group Defined by Sociodemographic Variables

Referred to in this section are people at high risk of suicide due to sociodemographic variables such as loss and bereavement; single, divorced, widowed; unemployed; white; male; older age groups; and younger age groups in the baby boom generation (Murphy and Wetzel 1980; Holinger and Offer 1982). Recommendations for primary, secondary, and tertiary prevention are focused around training and health education of the wide variety of people involved with these high-risk groups, e.g., physicians, paraprofessionals, and clergy. More specifically, there is a need to have training in suicidology for judges and lawyers (especially those involved with divorce cases); those working with the unemployed and homeless; those in emergency rooms who deal with the survivors of death; persons working with geriatric patients; and high school and college counselors and advisors. In addition, literature should be available for dissemination by such workers to those who are at high risk.

In terms of these high-risk groups, it should be noted that a follow-up of those combining various high-risk factors (e.g., psychiatric disorder, older white male, unemployed, previous suicide attempt) would lead to increased accuracy in the prediction of suicide and would aid prevention; however, as Kreitman (1982) described, such a strategy, while being accurate, would leave out so many suicides as to make the overall impact on suicide rates minimal.

FUTURE RESEARCH

Various types of future research seem essential, in terms of both improving the epidemiologic data base as well as enhancing the effectiveness of intervention and prevention strategies. The first involves increasing the accuracy of national mortality data in order to better utilize longitudinal epidemiologic studies. Methodologic advances in separating age, period, and cohort effects are necessary (Holford 1983; Wasserman 1987), as are interfaces between clinical, biologic, and epidemiologic studies in order to discover the means by which clinical and biologic discoveries might have greater large-scale public health effects.

Second, with the increase in knowledge in the fields of developmental psychology and affect theory, it appears important to know whether or not such understanding of affects can be conveyed to children, with what short-term and long-term results, and how best to do it. Furthermore, methods of evaluating young children's affect states are required. Techniques need to be developed that embody systematic observational ratings of infant and young children's affect states and their consequences for behavior. Prospective research on changes in affects and their relation to self-destructive behaviors would enhance our efforts for primary suicide prevention. Such endeavors are complex and require the collaboration of professionals in the fields of developmental psychology, psychiatry, education, and medical practice.

Third, the data in suicide prevention suggest that intervention at the level of agents of suicide, especially with respect to handguns and medications, may be the most effective intervention in terms of beginning to save lives as soon as possible. However, further epidemiologic studies are needed to more thoroughly examine the relationship between firearm control and suicide rates; to study the effect of regulating the prescribing of medications as described above; and to evaluate the potential for decreasing the lethality of certain medications (e.g., by adding emetics or antidotes).

Fourth, further research should be conducted on suicide prevention centers; in light of the negative findings with respect to prevention, one needs to know if there are some centers effective in prevention and, if so, how they differ from ones less effective, or how the population they serve differs.

Fifth, biological markers of suicide potential need to be pursued: biochemical screening tests that would indicate high-risk patients would probably have enough potential on an epidemiologic level to make an impact on suicide rates (Van Praag 1982).

Sixth, further work is necessary on the interventions suggested by the population model and prediction of suicide rates described above. The population model may be a viable model for the prediction of suicide on an epidemiologic level, and the implied interventions for suicide prevention need exploring.

Seventh, prospective studies on a clinical level, e.g., the NIMH Collaborative Depression Study, are critical in further identifying high-risk patients on a clinical level. For example, there is preliminary evidence from the NIMH Collaborative Depression Study that suggests the possibility of prospective screening data so specific that widespread use on a clinical level could make an impact on suicide rates.

Finally, cross-cultural studies are necessary on biological, clinical, and epidemiologic levels. Such research could determine which aspects, if any, of suicide might be considered universal rather than culture-bound.

REFERENCES

Arnold MB: The Nature of Emotion. Baltimore, MD, Penguin Books, 1968

Basch MF: The concept of affect: a re-examination. J Am Psychoanal Assoc 24:759–777, 1976

Blazer DG, Bachar JR, Manton KG: Suicide in late life: review and commentary. J Am Geriatr Soc 34:519–525, 1986

Boyd JH: The increasing rate of suicide by firearms. N Engl J Med 308:872–874, 1983

Brenner MH: Times Series Analysis of Relationships Between Selected Economic and Social Indicators. Springfield, VA, National Technical Information Services, 1971

Brenner MH: Mortality and national economy. Lancet 2:568–573, 1979

Browning CH: Suicide, firearms, and public health. Am J Public Health 64:313–317, 1974

Cain AC (ed): Survivors of Suicide. Springfield, IL, Charles C. Thomas, 1972

Diekstra RFW: Epidemiology of attempted suicide in the EEC. Bibl Psychiatr 162:1–16, 1982

Easterlin RA: Birth and Fortune. New York, Basic Books, 1980

Goldney RD, Katsikitis M: Cohort analysis of suicide rates in Australia. Arch Gen Psychiatry 40:71–74, 1983

Grove RD, Hetzel AM: Vital statistic rates in the United States: 1940–1960. Washington, DC, U.S. Government Printing Office, 1968

Hellon CP, Solomon MI: Suicide and age in Alberta, Canada, 1951–1977. Arch Gen Psychiatry 37:505–510, 1980

Hendin H: Suicide in America. New York, WW Norton, 1982

Holford TR: The estimation of age, period, and cohort effects for vital rates. Biometrics 39:1311–1324, 1983

Holinger PC: Pastoral Care of Severe Emotional Disorders. New York, Irvington Publishers, 1985

Holinger PC: Violent Deaths in the United States: An Epidemiologic Study of Suicide, Homicide and Accidents. New York, Guilford Press, 1987

Holinger PC, Klemen EH: Violent deaths in the United States, 1900–1975. Soc Sci Med 16:1929–1938, 1982

Holinger PC, Luke K: The epidemiologic patterns of self-destructiveness in childhood, adolescence, and young adulthood, in Suicide in the Young. Edited by Sudak HS, Ford AB, Rushforth NB. Littleton, MA, PSG Publishing, 1984

Holinger PC, Offer D: Perspectives on suicide in adolescence, in Social and Community Mental Health, Vol 2. Edited by Simmons R. Greenwich, CT, JAI Press, 1981

Holinger PC, Offer D: Prediction of adolescent suicide: a population model. Am J Psychiatry 139:302–307, 1982

Holinger PC, Offer D: Toward the prediction of violent deaths among the young, in Suicide Among Children and Adolescents. Edited by Sudak HS, Ford AB, Rushforth NB. Littleton, MA, PSG Publishing, 1984

Holinger PC, Offer D: Suicide, homicide, and accidents among adolescents: trends and potential for prediction, in Advances in Adolescent Mental Health, Vol 1, Part B. Edited by Feldman R, Stiffman A. Greenwich, CT, JAI Press, 1986

Holinger PC, Offer D: Suicide and homicide in the United States: an epidemiologic study of violent death, population changes, and the potential for prediction. Am J Psychiatry 144:215–219, 1987

Holinger PC, Offer D: The epidemiology of youth suicide. Proceedings of the Department of Health and Human Services Secretary's Task Force on Youth Suicide, Work Group on Risk Factors, NIMH, May 8, 1986 (in press)

Holinger PC, Holinger DP, Sandlow J: Violent deaths among children in the United States, 1900–1980: an epidemiologic study of suicide, homicide, and accidental deaths among 5–14 year olds. Pediatrician 12:11–19, 1983–1985

Hudgens RW: Preventing suicide. N Engl J Med 308:897–898, 1983

Joint Commission on Mental Illness and Health: Action for Mental Health. New York, Basic Books, 1961

Klerman GL, Lavori PW, Rice J, et al: Birth-cohort trends in rates of major depressive disorder among relatives of patients with affective disorder. Arch Gen Psychiatry 42:689–693, 1985

Kohut H: The Analysis of the Self. New York, International Universities Press, 1971

Kohut H: The Restoration of the Self. New York, International Universities Press, 1977

Kohut H: How Does Analysis Cure? Chicago, University of Chicago Press, 1984

Kreitman N: How useful is the prediction of suicide following parasuicide? Bibl Psychiatr 162:77–84, 1982

Kulka RA, Veroff J, Douvan E: Social class and the use of professional help for personal problems: 1957–1976. J Health Soc Behav 20:2–17, 1979

Lester D: The myth of suicide prevention. Compr Psychiatry 13:555–560, 1972

Lester D: Preventive effect of strict handgun control laws on suicide rates. Am J Psychiatry 140:259, 1983

Lester D, Murrell ME: The influence of gun control laws on suicidal behavior. Am J Psychiatry 137:121–122, 1980

Lester D, Murrell M: The preventive effect of strict gun control laws on suicide and homicide. Suicide Life Threat Behav 12:131–140, 1982

MacMahon B, Pugh TF: Epidemiology: Principles and Methods. Boston, MA, Little, Brown, and Company, 1970

Markush RE, Bartolucci AA: Firearms and suicide in the United States. Am J Public Health 74:123–127, 1984

Miller HC, Coombs DW, Leeper JD, et al: An analysis of the effects of suicide prevention facilities on suicide rates in the United States. Am J Public Health 74:340–343, 1984

Murphy GE, Wetzel RD: Suicide risk by birth cohort in the United States, 1949–1974. Arch Gen Psychiatry 37:519–523, 1980

National Center for Health Statistics: Vital Statistics of the United States— Mortality, 1961–1982. Washington, DC, U.S. Government Printing Office, 1963–1986

National Center for Health Statistics: Vital Statistics of the United States— Special Reports, Vol 43. Washington DC, U.S. Government Printing Office, 1963–1986

Offer D, Ostrov E, Howard KI, Atkinson RR: The Teenage World: A Study of Adolescent Self-Image in Ten Countries. New York, Plenum Publishing (in press)

Oliver RG, Hetzel BS: An analysis of recent trends in suicide rates in Australia. Int J Epidemiol 2:91–101, 1973

Pfeffer CR: The Suicidal Child. New York, Guilford Press, 1986

Pokorny AD: Prediction of suicide in psychiatric patients. Arch Gen Psychiatry 40:249–257, 1983

Rosenberg ML, Gelles RJ, Holinger PC, et al: Violence: homicide, assault, suicide, in Carter Closing the Gap Health Project. Atlanta, GA, Centers for Disease Control, 1984

Sainsbury P: Depression and suicide prevention. Bibl Psychiatr 162:17–32, 1982

Schneider PB, Martini P, Meyland D: Contribution to l'etude du suicide: etudes d'un group de 372 sujets de 28 a 35 ans apres une tentative de suicide. Schweiz Arch Neurol Psychiatr 118:307–355, 1976

Seiden RH: Suicide among youth: a review of the literature, 1900–1967. Bulletin of Suicidology (Suppl), 1969

Shneidman ES: Suicide, in Comprehensive Textbook of Psychiatry, 2nd ed. Edited by Freedman AM, Kaplan HI, Sadock BJ. Baltimore, MD, Williams & Wilkins, 1975

Solomon MI, Hellon CP: Suicide and age in Alberta, Canada, 1951–1977. Arch Gen Psychiatry 37:511–513, 1980

Souris M, Elefteriadis C: The practitioner and suicide prevention: an inquiry. Bibl Psychiatr 162:33–41, 1982

Stern D: The Interpersonal World of the Infant. New York, Basic Books, 1985

Sudak HS, Ford AB, Rushforth NB (eds): Suicide in the Young. Littleton, MA, PSG Publishing Company, 1984

Tomkins SS: Affect, Imagery, Consciousness, Vols I and II. New York, Springer, 1962–1963

Van Praag HM: Biochemical and psychopathological predictors of suicidality. Bibl Psychiatr 162:42–60, 1982

Wasserman IM: Cohort, age, and period effects in the analysis of U.S. suicide patterns: 1933–1978. Suicide Life Threat Behav 17:179–193, 1987

Westermeyer J: Firearms, legislation, and suicide prevention. Am J Public Health 74:108, 1984

4

Suicide, Depression, and Related Problems Among the Baby Boom Cohort

Gerald L. Klerman, M.D.

This volume addresses a serious mental health and national social problem—the recent increase in suicide attempts and deaths among adolescents and young adults. This increase has been well documented (Hirschfeld and Cross 1984; Klerman 1986a; Murphy et al. 1986; Pfeffer 1986) and has become the subject of public attention, initiating hearings before Congress and the creation of a task force by the Secretary of the U.S. Department of Health and Human Services.

During the same period that this alarming increase in youth suicide was occurring, there has been a parallel rise in rates of depression, as well as an increase in rates of related disorders, notably alcoholism, among this birth cohort. An unprecedented rise in the use of drugs and their abuse has also occurred.

There is a complex relationship between depression and suicide. Many depressed patients are suicidal, and, conversely, most, but not all, suicidal individuals manifest depressive mood and symptoms, if not depressive illness. Also, important similar epidemiologic trends among the baby boom generation, the birth cohort born after World War II now in its late 20s to early 40s, indicate an earlier age of onset of depression.

The full understanding of these complex phenomena would have

Supported in part by grants U-01-MH-43077 and R-01-MH-43044 from the National Institute of Mental Health; Alcohol, Drug Abuse, and Mental Health Administration; Public Health Service; U.S. Department of Health and Human Services, Washington, DC.

important clinical, public health, and theoretical benefits. Clinically, demonstration of temporal trends would help in understanding the changes in the patients' psychopathology and the need for modification of diagnostic expectations and treatment decisions. From the public health point of view, changes in rates of a disease and in the characteristics of those afflicted influence the techniques used for monitoring the aggregate health of the population, the types of data and modes of statistical reporting, and plans for the deployment of existing resources to treat the increased numbers of depressed individuals. Theoretically, important issues would be raised about the role various risk factors play in the onset of depression and its most insidious outgrowth, suicide, noted particularly in that youthful segment of the population this chapter addresses.

TEMPORAL CHANGES IN EPIDEMIOLOGY

Investigating possible temporal trends of disorders and diseases is usually considered within the province of epidemiology—the medical science concerned with the distribution of disease in populations and the variations in those distributions by factors of time, place, and person. Variations in rates over time are usually referred to as temporal trends (or secular changes) (MacMahon and Pugh 1970; Susser et al. 1985).

Temporal trends are well established in the epidemiology of many medical disorders, such as Parkinson's disease, coronary artery disease, and some forms of cancer (Frost 1939; Case 1956; Day and Charnay 1982; Magnus 1982). Changes in the rates of mental illnesses may also have occurred (Häfner 1985). During the first half of the twentieth century, there was a decrease in the frequency of general paresis caused by central nervous system (CNS) syphilis. In the psychiatric complications of pellagra there were decreases due to effective treatments and to prevention of the infectious and nutritional causes of these disorders. In the past decade, the frequency of Acquired Immune Deficiency Syndrome (AIDS) has been increasing dramatically in North America and Africa, along with increases in frequency of one of its major complications, AIDS dementia syndrome.

Temporal trends are usually divided into three types: age, period, and cohort effects. Often two effects interact; for example, age and period effects (Holford 1983; Susser et al. 1985).

1. *Age effect* occurs if the frequency of a disorder varies with age. An example of an age effect would be Alzheimer's disease, which is rare below the age of 50, increases after the age of 60, and increases further after the age of 75. As changes occur in the age distribution of

the general population—which is the case in most industrialized nations—the prevalence of Alzheimer's disease may increase, but that does not necessarily mean there has been a change in the age-specific incidence.

2. *Period effect* refers to changes in rates of a disease during a particular time period, usually defined in terms of months or years, seldom more than a decade. The popular term *epidemic* refers to such a period effect. A classic example of a major epidemic was the bubonic plague, which decimated the population of Western Europe in the fourteenth century. Another example would be the large number of deaths due to radiation after the atomic bomb attacks on Hiroshima and Nagasaki in 1945. Psychiatric examples would include the increase in Parkinson's disease due to CNS viral infections after World War I and the impact of unemployment after the economic crash of 1929 on suicide rates (MacMahon et al. 1963; Cormier and Klerman 1985).

3. *Cohort effect* refers to effects among individuals defined by some temporal experience, effects which are usually sustained over the life of the cohort. The most common cohorts are those defined by year or decade of birth. An example would be the baby boom birth cohort showing increased rates of suicide as it entered adolescence and young adulthood (Offer et al. 1984).

4. *Age-period interactions* occur if the impact of the period effect varies with age-related vulnerability, as reflected in recent increases in substance abuse in adolescents (O'Malley et al. 1984).

There are complex statistical problems associated with making independent estimates of age, period, and cohort effects. Distinguishing birth cohort effects from age-period interactions can be conceptually and statistically difficult; however, a number of psychiatric investigators have approached this problem. Two techniques have been used, Feinberg and Mason's model (1983) and Holford's model (1983). In the Feinberg/Mason model, the simultaneous equations are partially solved by assuming a tentative solution based on nonmathematical, substantive knowledge of the field and then adjusting the mathematical calculations accordingly. Lavori and associates (1987) have extended the Feinberg/Mason mathematical model to data on depression. The Feinberg/Mason model has also been recently applied to data on anorexia nervosa, and these temporal effects have been incorporated into mathematical models of genetic transmission by using information from pedigrees (Rice et al. 1984; Reich et al., in press; Williams and King 1987). Holford's method involves the use of variation of multiple regression in the attempt to calculate nonlinear aspects of the multiple regression equations. Weissman and Wickramaratne have collaborated with Holford on analyses of temporal trends in data from the National Institute of Mental Health Epidemiologic Catchment Area Study (NIMH-ECA) (Wickramaratne et al., in press).

The Ideal Design: Successive Birth Cohorts Studied Prospectively

In order to test hypotheses about increases in depression, the ideal design would be to follow successive birth cohorts systematically and prospectively. Such a design would involve multiple samples of successive cohorts defined either at birth, after puberty, or in midadolescence (before the age at risk for depression), who would be assessed periodically by systematic assessments allowing for the detection of age of onset and of case criteria for selective disorders, particularly depression. Conditions with high degrees of comorbidity with depression, such as alcoholism, drug abuse, and anxiety disorders, should also be assessed.

The conduct of multiple prospective cohort studies would be expensive and time-consuming. However, the methodologies for sampling and survey techniques and for establishing psychiatric diagnosis by standardized interview have improved considerably so that it is not unreasonable to expect such undertakings in the near future. With such designs, it will be possible to generate estimates of cumulative probability of reaching criteria for a given disorder up to an established time point. Just as modern nations currently maintain ongoing data collection and report statistical trends for population data (births, deaths, fertility) and for economic indicators (unemployment, gross national product, inflation), in the not-too-distant future, ongoing collections of indices of mental health—including rates of specific disorders such as alcoholism, drug abuse, depression, and suicide—will become standard.

Approximations of the Ideal Design

Although the ideal design of multiple successive birth cohorts followed longitudinally through life is not feasible now, it is possible to approximate this design by use of appropriately analyzed data from available cross-sectional or longitudinal surveys, which have established lifetime prevalence and age of onset of community samples and/ or family study samples.

Approximate designs to test hypotheses regarding temporal trends should have the following characteristics:

1. Large samples (over 2,000 subjects), including subjects from different birth cohorts. These samples could be from three sources: clinically treated patients, families of patients, or community surveys.
2. A reliable and valid assessment system that generates categorical diagnoses, which are applied uniformly to all subjects in the sample.
3. Information as to the age of onset, essential for reconstructing cumulative probability curves, allowing for an approximation of a prospective incidence estimate. Reliable age of onset data are also required to test population models for detecting possible genetic modes of transmission.
4. The technical capacity to store, process, and manage large data sets. The availability of high-speed electronic computers makes this feasible.
5. Statistical techniques to analyze data with variable sample size. The use of life table statistical methods is a powerful tool in this effort.
6. Appropriate statistical methods to disentangle interactions among age, period, and cohort effects.

EVIDENCE FOR INCREASED RATES OF DEPRESSION AMONG THE BABY BOOM COHORT

In the 1970s, a number of psychiatrists in the United States speculated that the rates of depression might have greatly increased (Schwab 1974; Klerman 1976, 1979, 1980). This speculation was based on several observations:

1. Treatment settings, particularly outpatient clinics and psychiatric units in general hospitals, reported an increase in patients diagnosed as depressed.
2. Depressed patients were younger than the textbook description of depressed patients as being in middle-aged and involutional periods.
3. Childhood depressions became the focus of considerable clinical and research attention (Kovacs et al. 1984).
4. More coverage was given to depression in the lay press, particularly in women's magazines (Scarf 1980).

These observations occurred during a period of increased clinical and research attention to depression and affective disorders. New knowledge was being generated from investigations in genetics, psychopathology, and biological psychiatry, and from experience with new forms of psychotherapy and new psychopharmacologic agents specifically employed for the treatment of depression.

NIMH (Katz and Klerman 1979) and the World Health Organization (WHO) Division of Mental Health (Sartorius et al. 1983) initiated large multicenter studies to investigate the symptomatology, diagnosis, and classification of depression and to document its clinical course and natural history.

Changes in the official diagnostic systems were undertaken. In 1980, the American Psychiatric Association issued the third edition of its Diagnostic and Statistical Manual (DSM-III), which abandoned the long-standing major classification division between psychotic and neurotic conditions and created separate categories for affective disorders and for anxiety disorders. Similarly, the draft of the 10th edition of the WHO International Classification of Diseases (ICD-10) proposed a new category for mood disorders. The creation of separate categories for affective disorders (or mood disorders) does not represent a classification based on etiology, because it is likely that multiple etiologies are involved in these conditions, including genetic, developmental, and stress factors. Rather, the creation of categories based on dominant symptoms of affect and/or mood is parallel to the classification of medical disorders according to the organ involved (heart disease, kidney disease). In the case of psychiatric disorders, the mental faculty (emotion, cognition, memory, behavior) becomes the equivalent of the anatomical organ as the basis for classification.

These professional and scientific activities, while valid in their own right, probably also reflected changes in the frequency of depression, particularly among adolescents and young adults. The epidemic of suicide attempts and death by suicide among the baby boom birth cohort, however, was worldwide, documented in the United States (Murphy and Wetzel 1980), Canada (Solomon and Hellon 1980), the United Kingdom (Murphy et al. 1986), Australia (Goldney and Katsikitis 1983), New Zealand (P. Joyce, personal communication, 23 July 1987), and parts of Western Europe (Metropolitan Life Suicide-International Comparisons 1972).

Sources of Evidence

In the late 1970s and early 1980s, reports began appearing from a number of studies that met the requirements described above. These studies supply the empirical basis for confirming the hypothesis that there had been an increase in depression in youthful cohorts. These research programs used samples of two types: samples derived from community surveys and high-risk samples derived from families of probands with affective disorders.

The community surveys (see Table 1) include:

Table 1. Community Studies Relevant to Temporal Trends of Depression

Investigator	Country	Sample size	Diagnostic system
Canino et al. 1987	Puerto Rico	1,551	DSM-III
Hagnell 1982	Sweden	2,550	ICD
Hallstrom 1984	Sweden	453	ICD
Karno et al. 1987	United States (Mexican American)	1,243	DSM-III
Murphy et al. 1984	Canada	1,736	DSM-III
Robins et al. 1984	United States	18,000	DSM-III
Weissman and Myers 1978	United States	511	RDC

Note. DSM-III, Diagnostic and Statistical Manual, Third Edition, American Psychiatric Association; ICD, International Classification of Diseases, World Health Organization; RDC, Research Diagnostic Criteria.

1. The NIMH-ECA Study conducted in five sites—New Haven, CT; St. Louis, MO; Baltimore, MD; Piedmont County, NC; and Los Angeles, CA (Regier et al. 1984; Robins et al. 1984; Klerman 1986c). Over 20,000 interviews were conducted using the Diagnostic Interview Schedule (DIS), which generates DSM-III diagnoses. Data were reported for current and lifetime prevalence of major disorders, including depression.

2. The 25-year follow-up study from Lundby, Sweden (Hagnell 1982), begun by Essen-Muller more than 25 years ago. This community survey of a district in southern Sweden represents one of the few prospective and intensive studies of a community using consistent diagnostic methods. Hagnell reported findings of temporal trends in depression as well as in alcoholism.

3. An epidemiological study of mental disorder conducted in Göteborg, Sweden (Hallstrom 1984). Göteborg is Sweden's second largest city, and the Hallstrom study provides a valuable cross-sectional analysis of depression, particularly among females.

4. The Stirling County Study in Nova Scotia, Canada, analyzed by Murphy et al. (1984). Of particular note is the analysis that indicates shifts in the male/female ratio of depressive disorders.

5. The Puerto Rican Study of rural and urban Puerto Ricans done by Canino and associates (1987). Using methodology similar to the NIMH-ECA Study, this study of Puerto Rico also used the DIS as the main diagnostic instrument.

6. The Mexican-American study in California done by Karno and associates (1987). This study is an intensive study of a subsample of one of the five ECA sites in Los Angeles in which there was a heavy concentration of Mexican Americans.

7. The five United States communities study done by Weissman and associates (1988). The earlier New Haven community study undertaken by Weissman and Myers was reported in 1978.

The family studies (Table 2) include:

1. The clinical studies of the NIMH Collaborative Program on the Psychobiology of Depression (Klerman 1979).
2. The NIMH family study (Gershon et al. 1987).
3. The Yale family study (Weissman and Myers 1978).

A significant advance in understanding these phenomena occurred with the application of life table methodology to these data. In the life table method, also called survival analysis, the cumulative probability of obtaining a given end point (in this case, depression) is calculated for a given group (or cohort). A key element in this calculation is the requirement that the age of onset be reliable and validly estimated. This technique allows the reconstruction of longitudinal data from cross-sectional studies in which past episodes have been assessed and their dates of onset recorded. Life table methodology has mainly been used in vital statistics, but recently has been applied to clinical trials of outcomes of treatments for cancer, as well as for psychiatric illness, and also in naturalistic studies. The first application of this method to the problem of temporal effects of depression was to the family data in the NIMH Collaborative Program. The sample was divided into birth cohorts based on decade of birth, and the cumulative probability of the individual's having an episode that reached criteria for major depression up to a given time point was calculated. Separate calculations were done for males and females. The data indicated increasing rates of depression for cohorts born through the twentieth century (Klerman et al. 1985) (Figure 1).

Similar statistical methods were applied to community survey data from the New Haven site of the NIMH-ECA Study (Weissman et al. 1984). Again, there were successive increases and earlier age of onset in each birth cohort. Wickramaratne and associates (in press) subse-

Table 2. Family Studies

Investigator	Country	Sample size	Diagnostic system
Gershon et al. 1987	United States	823	RDC
Klerman et al. 1985	United States	2,500	RDC
Weissman et al. 1982	United States	300	RDC

Note. RDC, Research Diagnostic Criteria.

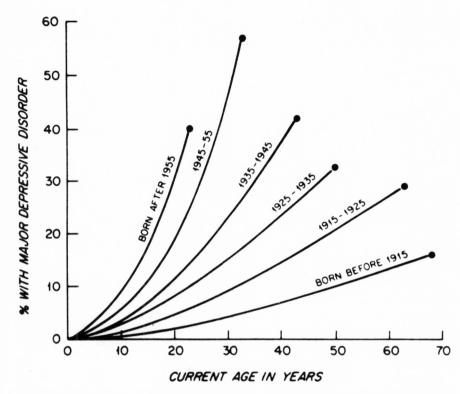

Figure 1. Cumulative probability of major depression for relatives and controls by birth cohort (life table method). [Reprinted with permission from Klerman GL: Evidence for increase in rates of depression in North America and Western Europe in recent decades, in New Results in Depression Research. Edited by Hippius H, Klerman GL, Matussek N. Berlin, Springer-Verlag, 1986. Copyright 1986, Springer-Verlag.]

quently applied these analyses to all five ECA sites (New Haven, CT; St. Louis, MO; Baltimore, MD; Los Angeles, CA; Piedmont County, NC). The temporal findings were similar in all five sites.

These methods were also applied to data from an NIMH study of bipolar and schizophrenic patients (Gershon et al. 1987). Again, a significantly higher cumulative risk of major depression in relatives born after 1940, as compared with relatives born in previous cohorts, was found. Similar trends were reported from a 25-year follow-up of a sample from a geographically defined area of Sweden (Hagnell 1982). Hagnell calculated age- and sex-standardized incidence rates for each 5-year period as well as cumulative probabilities of ever developing a depressive illness. A 10-fold increase in the risk of depression was found for the young adult group (ages 20–39) in the period 1957–1972 compared with the period 1947–1959. Also, Hallstrom (1984) reported temporal trends in a community survey of depression in Göteborg, Sweden.

Familial Aggregation

Similar temporal trends are evident in the general population samples surveyed and in the studies of families of probands with major depression and other affective disorders, but the rates are two to three times higher among samples of family members than in the general population samples (Weissman et al. 1982). Previous studies with case-control designs had established that the relative risk for depression was about three times higher in relatives of individuals with history of depression. In the family studies of temporal effects, rates for biologically related relatives of affectively ill probands were consistently higher than those of community samples across all birth cohorts.

Gender Differences

A replicated finding in previous epidemiologic and clinical studies from different geographic areas and time periods is the high female risk for depression (Weissman and Klerman 1977). In recent studies of temporal effects, females show higher lifetime prevalence of major depression than males across all birth cohorts. Females have predominated over males in a ratio of 2–3 to 1. However, there is some suggestion from recent studies that the magnitude of the male/female differences may have diminished in recent years (Hagnell 1982; Murphy et al. 1984).

Distinguishing Period from Cohort Effects

Having established an overall increase in depression and an earlier age of onset, investigators have attempted to separate period from cohort effects. Lavori and associates (1987) found a strong trend toward increased lifetime risk and an earlier age of onset for major depression in successive cohorts born since 1930. Age-period-cohort analysis suggested a powerful period effect occurred between 1965 and 1975 for both sexes. It was also suggested, however, that the period effect was decreasing after 1975.

Wickramaratne and associates (in press) independently analyzed the data from the ECA study using a modification of Holford's methods (Holford 1983) and reported both cohort and period effects (Figure 2). They found a sharp increase in the rate of major depression among both men and women in the cohorts born after 1935–1945, the cohorts that came to their maturity after World War II. This increase was most notable during the period 1950–1975.

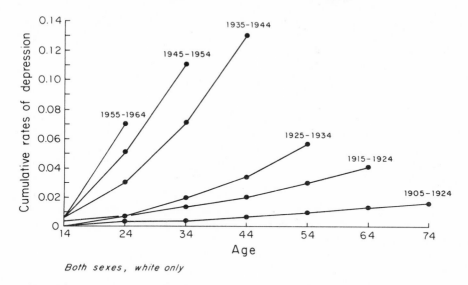

Both sexes, white only

Figure 2. Temporal trends (period-cohort effects). Lifetime prevalence of major depression shown in the National Institute of Mental Health–Epidemiologic Catchment Area Study's five sites. [Reprinted with permission from Journal of Chronic Diseases, Wickramaratne PJ, Weissman MM, Leaf PJ, et al., Age, period, cohort effects on the risk of major depression: results from 5 U.S. communities. In press, Pergamon Journals, Ltd.]

Possible Artifacts

A number of possible artifacts could account for these findings. These artifacts include the following:

1. There could be *differential mortality*, such that depressive-prone individuals die young, particularly by means of accidental death and suicide. In that case, they would not have survived to the 6th, 7th, and 8th decade and would be underrepresented in older age cohorts.
2. There could be *differential institutionalization*, particularly among the very elderly, who are more likely to be in nursing homes and chronic illness hospitals.
3. There have been *changing diagnostic criteria*, with the resultant shift of many patients from the schizophrenic category into the affective disorder categories due to the impact of DSM-III and DSM-III-R. Furthermore, the elimination of the previous concept of neurosis, and it replacement by major depression, also resulted in the greater increase in diagnostic assignment to depressive categories. However, this would not account for the changes noted in community and family surveys, which include nontreated as well as treated cases.

4. There have been *changes in the attitudes* of mental health professionals toward adolescents. Mental health professionals are less likely to explain the problems of adolescence in terms of exclusively developmental phenomena, such as "adolescent turmoil," and are now more willing to see psychopathologic conditions, such as depression, in children and adolescents.

5. Overall, there have been dramatic *changes in societal attitudes* about psychological mindedness, including depression and anxiety. Middle-class and better-educated groups are now more likely to interpret events in terms of psychological categories, rather than as "God's will" or destiny.

6. In general, there are *reporting biases*, such that some subjects respond "yes" to all questions or inquiries about symptoms. This could result in an inflated symptom account in structured interviews and checklists and requires attention to the wording of questions, so as to balance for "yea-saying" or "nay-saying."

7. The most serious potential artifact is *problems in recall and memory*. This, in particular, becomes a problem in the elderly. Because many of the studies using lifetime prevalence depend on retrospective recall of previous episodes and dating of age of onset, the opportunity for error in recall and memory is potentially of serious impact.

Space does not permit detailed examination of the evidence supporting the conclusion that these artifacts are not of sufficient magnitude to invalidate the findings. The artifacts of differential mortality, differential institutionalization, and problems with recall and memory might influence hypotheses about changes in rates of depression among the elderly, but the most significant increases have been among youthful cohorts, the age group under discussion in this chapter, called the baby boom cohort (Klerman 1988).

THE MENTAL HEALTH PROBLEMS OF THE BABY BOOM COHORT

Thus far, this chapter has focused on evidence for increased rates of depression in adolescents and young adults, the cohorts born after World War II. It is also important to examine possible trends for other disorders in the same cohorts.

If the evidence for increased rates of mental health problems among the more recent birth cohorts were exclusively for depression, it would allow for a focused search, albeit a complex one, concentrating on those social, biological, and environmental risk factors, sometimes collectively called "Agent Blue," which might be interacting with familial factors, or with changes related to year of birth and/or sex (Klerman 1988).

In this birth cohort, increased rates have been reported for suicide (Murphy and Wetzel 1980; Solomon and Hellon 1980; Holinger and Offer 1982; Goldney and Katsikitis 1983; Klerman 1986b), for homicide among black men (Klerman 1980), for automobile accidents and other forms of violent death (Holinger et al. 1987), and for substance abuse (O'Malley et al. 1984; Fowler et al. 1986; Murphy et al. 1986).

In parallel domains, temporal trends have been described for several important social and economic events possibly related to mental health problems, including the age of entrance into the labor force (Easterlin 1980), the age of marriage (Hogan 1981), fertility (Easterlin 1980), and the age of termination of maternal child-rearing function, referred to as the "empty nest" (Deykin et al. 1966; Goldman et al. 1984).

Demographers and economists have documented the consequences of large birth cohort size and, especially, the relationship between the relative size of birth cohort in the total population. Easterlin (1980, 1985, 1986) theorizes that the economic and demographic destinies of a cohort are shaped by its relative size. When a cohort is relatively large, it will have depressed earnings, a higher unemployment rate, and a lower upward job mobility. Accepting this theory, it follows that the baby boom generation, with the largest birth cohort ever recorded, has had a high rate of depression and suicide.

There are important differences by sex and race in these trends among adolescents and young adults. The greatest absolute number of suicide deaths occurs in young white males. Young black males have also had an increase in suicide rate, but the absolute rate is still not as high as among young white males. More significant is the dramatically increased homicide rate for young black males (Klerman 1980).

Temporal trends have also been reported for drug use and abuse. In a longitudinal study of drug use, over 1,000 New York adolescents were selected from high schools. Kandel and Davies (1986) found high rates of drug use and depression symptoms, with depression usually preceding the drug use.

Temporal changes in rates of bipolar disorder have been reported by Gershon and associates (1987). Relatives of those afflicted also showed increasing rates of bipolar disorder. Temporal changes have not been found for all psychiatric disorders.

Inasmuch as the changes in rates are not limited to depression, but also involve drug abuse and suicide attempts and deaths, a comprehensive explanation would have to account not only for the overall increased rates of mental health problems among young adults of the baby boom generation within the period 1960–1980, but also for the diagnostic differentiation to explain why some individuals, exposed to the pathogenic factors yet to be determined, manifest their vulnerability as depression, whereas others develop drug abuse or substance abuse.

To further complicate matters, there are high levels of comorbidity among many of these disorders, and a comprehensive explanation would have to take into effect the general increase in psychiatric morbidity for the younger cohorts during this period, as well as the differentiated rates of drug abuse, eating disorder, suicide, and affective disorders.

Gene/Environment Interactions

These trends cannot be explained by a simple-factor genetic theory of the etiology of affective disorders. The evidence for a genetic contribution to causation of depression is strong, particularly for bipolar illness. The strongest evidence is derived from twin studies and cross-rearing studies in addition to familial aggregation studies. In this respect it is noteworthy that Gershon and associates (1987) recently reported evidence for temporal effect among bipolar patients.

One must conclude that some complex form of gene/environment interaction is operating. Given a probable distribution of liability based on genetic determination, environmental factors must be operating to make that liability manifested in clinical illness. Whatever these environmental factors are, they have shifted, such that there are increases of depression, particularly at earlier years of onset.

Most observers have agreed it is unlikely that these changes can be explained in exclusively genetic terms, although Crow (1986) has attempted to reinterpret the evidence of temporal trends using, exclusively, genetic interpretations based on assortative mating and selective fertility.

Most models of genetic transmission presuppose constant age of onset. The demonstration of changing age of onset, both in familial samples and in population surveys, has required recalculation of the complex genetic models. These recalculations have recently been completed and reports have been offered by Reich et al. (in press). The presence of a cohort effect does not mitigate against the powerful role of familial aggregation. In fact, the cohort effect seems concentrated most intensely in families that have high rates of intrafamilial affective disorder.

Although some forms of major depression are familial and may be genetically determined, current evidence does not conclusively support a specific mode of genetic transmission, whether the mode of transmission is a single major locus or is polygenic. Genetic factors are more conclusively implicated in bipolar disorder. The demonstration of temporal trends, however, does not rule out genetic contribution to the vulnerability to depression. Environmental factors often are required to make manifest a genetic vulnerability, as demonstrated for diabetes, phenylketonuria, and other genetic disorders.

Acknowledging some genetic influence in the development of clinical depression, one must concede there is also an environmental contribution causing the overall increase in rates and shifts in age of onset. The environmental risk factors could be biological, including changes in nutrition, the possible role of viruses, or the effects of an unknown depressogenic chemical agent in the air or water. Other risk factors could be nonbiological, such as historical, cultural, or economic. They would include urbanization, demographic fluctuation, changes in family structure, an increased role of women in the work force, and anomie (Easterlin 1980; Hagnell 1982; Murphy et al. 1984).

PROSPECTS FOR THE FUTURE
OF THE BABY BOOM COHORT

The baby boom generation experienced high rates of suicide, drug abuse, and depression during the period 1960–1980. There are important sex and ethnic differences in these rates: females are more prone to depression, whereas males are more prone to suicide, drug abuse, and alcohol abuse; black males are more prone to homicide, particularly with firearms. Mental health problems have reached epidemic proportion in young people since 1960, with important age-period effects (Klerman 1980).

The baby boom cohort is now approaching its maturity. Members of the first wave of this cohort are now in their early 40s. It is instructive to anticipate what the future trends might be. There are many possibilities, one being that the current high rates of depression, suicide, and drug abuse will continue, in which case the cumulative probabilities of mental illness will rise. At this point it is important to distinguish between a specific incidence and prevalence. The prevalence of depression in this cohort may continue to increase because of chronicity and recurrences, even though the peak of onsets may have already occurred.

On the other hand, it is possible that if only a circumscribed period effect were operative, the peak of the exposure to "Agent Blue" having passed, there will be a decline in age-specific incidence. This seems to be the case for suicide, because the rates among young adults and adolescents peaked in 1978–1980 and have been declining slowly since then.

In addition to tracking suicide rates, incidence of new depressive episodes, recurrence, and lifetime prevalence in the baby boom cohort, it would be desirable to document comparable mental health trends among the "post baby boom" cohort, those individuals born after 1970. These individuals are now entering adolescence and, if the period effect hypothesis is true, the rates of suicide attempts, suicide deaths, and depression should be lower in adolescents and young adults over the next decade. These possibilities make all the more cogent the need to maintain ongoing sampling of multiple cohorts for detection of future trends.

CONCLUSIONS

A number of trends have been discussed:

1. An overall increase in prevalence of depression, particularly since World War II.
2. A marked increase in depression among individuals in the cohorts born after World War II, adults now in their 30s and 40s. Whereas previously depression had its onset predominantly in the middle aged and the elderly, it is now the young adults who are at greatest risk.
3. An earlier age of onset of depression.
4. An effect for family aggregation resulting in increased risk of depression in the first-degree relatives of ill patients, suggestive of, but not conclusively establishing, genetic transmission for certain forms of depression.
5. An increase in risk for females in rates of depression across all cohorts.

Based on these considerations, it is reasonable to conclude that the baby boom cohort has experienced serious mental health problems manifested by depression, drug abuse, alcoholism, and suicide. The high comorbidity among these conditions indicates response to some common features, most likely in the environment. However, the interplay of genetic and environmental factors remains to be investigated.

REFERENCES

Canino GJ, Bird HR, Shrout PE, et al: The prevalence of specific psychiatric disorders in Puerto Rico. Arch Gen Psychiatry 44:727–735, 1987

Case RAM: Cohort analysis of mortality rates as an historical or narrative technique. British Journal of Preventive Medicine 10:159–171, 1956

Cormier HJ, Klerman GL: Unemployment and male/female labor force participation as determinants of changing suicide rates of males and females in Quebec. Soc Psychiatry 20:109–114, 1985

Crow TJ: Secular changes in affective disorder and variations in the psychosis gene (letter). Arch Gen Psychiatry 43:1013–1014, 1986

Day NE, Charney B: Time trends, cohort effects, and aging as influence on cancer incidence, in Trends in Cancer Incidence. Edited by Magnus K. New York, Hemisphere, 1982

Deykin EY, Jacobson S, Klerman GL, et al: The empty nest: psychosocial aspects of conflict between depressed women and their grown children. Am J Psychiatry 122:1422–1426, 1966

Easterlin RA: Birth and Fortune. New York, Basic Books, 1980

Easterlin RA: The struggle for economic status. Unpublished paper presented at the Conference on Non-Replacement Fertility, Hoover Institution, Stanford University, CA, November 1985

Easterlin RA: Easterlin hypothesis, in New Palgrave. London, Macmillan Press, 1986

Feinberg SE, Mason WM: Discrete archival data: age, period, cohort effects for vital rates. Biometrics 39:311–324, 1983

Fowler RC, Rich CL, Young D: San Diego Suicide Study, II: substance abuse in young cases. Arch Gen Psychiatry 43:962–968, 1986

Frost WH: The age selection of mortality from tuberculosis in successive decades. American Journal of Hygiene 30:91–96, 1939

Gershon ES, Hamovit JH, Guroff JJ, et al: Birth cohort changes in manic and depressive disorders in relatives of bipolar and schizoaffective patients. Arch Gen Psychiatry 44:314–319, 1987

Goldman N, Westoff CF, Hammerslough C: Demography of the marriage market in the US. Population Index 50:5–25, 1984

Goldney RD, Katsikitis M: Cohort analysis of suicide rates in Australia. Arch Gen Psychiatry 40:71–74, 1983

Häfner H: Are mental disorders increasing over time? Psychobiology 18:66–81, 1985

Hagnell O: The 25-year follow-up of the Lundby Study: incidence and risk of alcoholism, depression and disorders of the senium, in Mental Disorders in the Community. Edited by Barrett J, Rose RM. New York, Guilford Press, 1982

Hallstrom T: Point prevalence of major depressive disorder in a Swedish urban female population. Acta Psychiatr Scand 69:52–59, 1984

Hirschfeld RMA, Cross CK: Psychosocial aspects of depression: personality. Unpublished paper presented at Workshop on the Measurement of Depression, The Queen's Medical Center, Hawaii, March 21–23, 1984

Hogan DP: Transition and Social Change: The Early Lives of American Men. New York, Academic Press, 1981

Holford TR: The estimation of age, period, and cohort effects for vital rates. Biometrics 39:311–324, 1983

Holinger PC, Offer D: Prediction of adolescent suicide: a population model. Am J Psychiatry 139:302–306, 1982

Holinger PC, Offer D, Ostrove E: Suicide and homicide in the United States: an epidemiologic study of violent deaths, population changes and the potential for prediction. Am J Psychiatry 144:215–219, 1987

Kandel DB, Davies M: Adult sequelae of adolescent depressive symptoms. Arch Gen Psychiatry 43:255–264, 1986

Karno M, Hough RL, Burnam MA, et al: Lifetime prevalence of specific psychiatric disorders among Mexican-Americans and non-Hispanic whites in Los Angeles. Arch Gen Psychiatry 44:695–701, 1987

Katz MM, Klerman GL: Introduction: overview of the clinical studies program of the NIMH Clinical Research Branch Collaborative Study on the Psychobiology of Depression. Am J Psychiatry 136:49–51, 1979

Klerman GL: Age and clinical depression: today's youth in the 21st century. J Gerontol 31:318–323, 1976

Klerman GL: The age of melancholy. Psychology Today 12:36–42, 88, 1979

Klerman GL: Homicide among black males: concluding remarks. Public Health Rep 95:549–550, 1980

Klerman GL: Evidence for increase in rates of depression in North America and Western Europe in recent decades, in New Results in Depression Research. Edited by Hippius H, Klerman GL, Matussek N. Berlin, Springer-Verlag, 1986a

Klerman GL (ed): Suicide and Depression Among Adolescents and Young Adults. Washington, DC, American Psychiatric Press, 1986b

Klerman GL: The National Institute of Mental Health–Environmental Catchment Area Program (NIMH-ECA). Soc Psychiatry 21:159–166, 1986c

Klerman GL: The current age of youthful melancholia. Br J Psychiatry 152:4–14, 1988

Klerman GL, Lavori PW, Rice J, et al: Birth cohort trends in rates of major depressive disorder among relatives of patients with affective disorder. Arch Gen Psychiatry 42:689–695, 1985

Kovacs M, Feinberg TL, Krouse-Novak MA, et al: Depressive disorders in childhood. Arch Gen Psychiatry 41:229–237, 1984

Lavori PW, Klerman GL, Keller MB, et al: Age, period, cohort analysis of secular trends in onset of major depression: findings in siblings of patients with major affective disorders. J Psychiatr Res 21:23–25, 1987

MacMahon B, Pugh TF: Epidemiology: Principles and Methods. Boston, Little Brown, 1970

MacMahon B, Johnson S, Pugh TF: Relationship of suicide rates to social conditions. Public Health Rep 78:285–293, 1963

Magnus K (ed): Trends in Cancer Incidence. New York, Hemisphere, 1982

Metropolitan Life: Suicide—international comparisons. Statistical Bulletin 58:2–5, 1972

Murphy E, Lindsay J, Grundy E: 60 years of suicide in England and Wales. Arch Gen Psychiatry 43:969–977, 1986

Murphy GE, Wetzel RD: Suicide risk by birth cohort in the United States. Arch Gen Psychiatry 37:519–523, 1980

Murphy JM, Sobol AM, Neff RK, et al: Stability of prevalence. Arch Gen Psychiatry 41:990–997, 1984

Offer D, Ostrov E, Howard KI: Epidemiology of mental health illness among adolescents, in Significant Advances in Child Psychiatry. Edited by Call J. New York, Basic Books, 1984

O'Malley PM, Bachman JG, Johnston LD: Period, age, and cohort effects on substance use among American youth, 1976–1982. Am J Public Health 74:682–688, 1984

Pfeffer CR: The Suicidal Child. New York, Guilford Press, 1986

Regier DA, Myers JK, Kramer M, et al: The NIMH–Epidemiologic Catchment Area Program. Arch Gen Psychiatry 41:934–941, 1984

Reich T, Van Eerdewegh P, Rice J, et al: The familial transmission of primary major depressive disorder. Journal of Psychiatric Review (in press)

Rice J, Reich T, Andreasen NC: Sex-related differences in depression: familial evidence. J Affective Disord 7:199–210, 1984

Robins LN, Helzer JE, Weissman MM, et al: Lifetime prevalence of specific psychiatric disorders in three sites. Arch Gen Psychiatry 41:949–958, 1984

Sartorius N, Davidian H, Ernberg G, et al: Depressive Disorders in Different Cultures: Report on the WHO Collaborative Study on Standardized Assessment of Depressive Disorders. Geneva, World Health Organization, 1983

Scarf M: Unfinished Business. New York, Basic Books, 1980

Schwab JJ: Perception of social change and depressive symptomatology, in Social Psychiatry, Vol I. Edited by Masserman JH, Schwab JJ. New York, Grune & Stratton, 1974

Solomon MI, Hellon CP: Suicide and age in Alberta, Canada, 1951–1977. Arch Gen Psychiatry 37:511–513, 1980

Susser M, Watson W, Hopper K: Sociology in Medicine, 3rd ed. New York/Oxford, Oxford University Press, 1985

Weissman MM, Klerman GL: Sex differences and the epidemiology of depression. Arch Gen Psychiatry 34:98–111, 1977

Weissman MM, Myers JK: Affective disorders in U.S. urban community: the use of Research Diagnostic Criteria in an epidemiologic survey. Arch Gen Psychiatry 35:1304–1311, 1978

Weissman MM, Kidd KK, Prusoff BA: Variability in rates of affective disorder in relatives of depressed and normal probands. Arch Gen Psychiatry 39:1397–1403, 1982

Weissman MM, Leaf P, Holzer C, et al: The epidemiology of depression: an update on sex differences in rates. J Affective Disord 7:179–188, 1984

Weissman MM, Leaf PJ, Tischler GL, et al: Affective disorders in 5 U.S. communities. Psychol Med 18:141–154, 1988

Wickramaratne PJ, Weissman MM, Leaf PJ, et al: Age, period, cohort effects on the risk of major depression: results from 5 U.S. communities. J Chronic Dis (in press)

Williams P, King M: The epidemic of anorexia-nervosa: another medical myth? Lancet 1:205–207, 1987

5

Suicide Clusters
and Youth

Lucy E. Davidson, M.D., Ed.S.

Epidemic suicides ... can under favorable circumstances spread as rapidly as epidemics of physically contagious diseases. Once these epidemics are recognized as such ... is it beyond the possibilities of art and science to prevent their occurrence?" (Rovinsky 1988, p. 239). The rise in adolescent and young adult suicide in the last two decades has made a major impact on the need to understand this self-destructive epidemic among youth. Furthermore, the fact that some youth suicides cluster within similar time periods and communities emphasizes the complex nature of the epidemic of youth suicide that has occurred in the 1960s through the 1980s. Records of epidemic suicides, in fact, have stretched back through ancient history. Part of the public concern in recent times has been the fear that some contagious element about suicide might incite others to kill themselves. This chapter will review reports of suicide epidemics or clusters to identify their characteristics and identify risk factors that may increase the likelihood of killing oneself during a cluster of suicides. Evidence for suicide contagion will be assessed, and several recent clusters will be examined. This chapter will also outline community prevention approaches to forestall the spread of youth suicide clusters.

DEFINITION OF SUICIDE CLUSTER

Efforts to document the existence of suicide clusters statistically are hampered by our lack of a standard definition for clusters. Time and geographic boundaries of suicide clusters vary. When direct social linkages are documented among decedents, longer time frames seem plausible. For example, teens from the same circle of friends might pattern their suicides after each other and kill themselves over a 6-month span. Geographic limits are stretched by mass communication techniques, which may provide details of a celebrity suicide to millions of young people across the country. The validity of some suicides being clustered in time and space seems self-evident, as in the report of three suicides on one hospital ward in 6 months where none had occurred in that hospital for the preceding 10 years (Anonymous 1977). Again, the numbers speak for themselves in a cluster of suicides among physicians on probation in Oregon. Eight of the 40 physicians committed suicide in 13 months, with 2 others attempting. By extrapolation, this is a suicide rate of 20,000 per 100,000! (Crawshaw et al. 1980).

Niemi (1978) has applied statistical techniques that addressed detecting clusters of diseases such as cancer to detecting clusters of suicide. He used Mantel's procedure, in which time and space measurements between all possible pairs of the suicide cases are made. Their distribution is compared statistically with the normal distribution with regression methods (Mantel 1967). Niemi showed that the numbers of suicides in jail occurring within 24 or 48 hours of a preceding suicide were significantly greater than expected (Niemi 1978). Attempts to demonstrate simultaneous time and space clustering are more problematic. Recently, Davis and Hardy (1986) have developed a mathematical model of suicide epidemics based on time-space clustering. Using a system of differential equations, their model predicts an asymptotic cumulative number of suicides in cluster. The parameters they estimated for immunity and susceptibility to suicide may help generate more refined specifications for time-space clustering of suicides.

In this chapter, suicide is considered as a self-inflicted, intentional death. The term *cluster* refers to three or more suicides that occur within a defined space and time. It is hoped that information derived from these accounts of suicide clusters may contribute to further precision in definitions and hypotheses regarding the mode of spread of suicide.

HISTORICAL REPORTS

Young women of Miletus in ancient Greece committed suicide in an epidemic wave. Other suicide epidemics among women occurred in Rouen in 1806, Stuttgart in 1811, and at the Valoris in 1813 (Mathews 1891). In 665, during a siege of the plague in England, men and women jumped to their deaths from seaside cliffs. They chose a certain and speedy death over potential agony from the plague (Bakwin 1957). Centuries later in England (1772) a lottery mania was followed by a suicide epidemic (Mathews 1891). Epidemic suicides have also been reported among young people, with 70 children in one Moscow school district killing themselves between May 1908 and October 1910 (Popow 1911).

Suicide epidemics have been patterned after the suicide of someone famous or of an immensely appealing fictional character. Castlereagh committed suicide with his penknife in 1822, touching off a spate of suicides by the same method among Englishmen (Mathews 1891). Goethe published *The Sorrows of Young Werther* in 1774 and unwittingly instigated an epidemic of imitative suicides. Young men adopted the same dress as Werther and, in this most renowned example of imitative suicide from literature, also shot themselves (Weigand 1962).

Instead of enacting his own suicidal impulses, Goethe wrote the novel to transform them into an artistic creation. His novel, however, had a reverse effect on readers:

> I had saved myself from a tempestuous element with this composition . . . but just as I felt relieved and lighthearted because I had succeeded in transforming reality into poetry, my friends were confusing themselves by believing that they had to turn poetry into reality, enact the novel and shoot themselves! What actually took place now among a few, happened later en masse, and this little book that had done me so much good acquired the reputation of being extremely harmful! (Goethe 1962, p. 147)

CONTEMPORARY ACCOUNTS

More detailed accounts of epidemic or cluster suicides occur in contemporary scientific literature. Most are descriptive studies that lack a comparison group or statistical analysis. Thus, characteristics of the suicide-cluster victims may not necessarily differentiate them from other persons who commit suicide or from the general population. Because there is no systematic surveillance or reporting system for suicide clusters, the published accounts may have selection biases that affect their representativeness. Most accounts of suicide clusters in the scientific literature are studies of adults, whereas the popular press has highlighted recent suicide clusters among youth.

Similarity of Methods

Many authors have commented on choice of similar method in suicide clusters. When the method is unusual for the geographic area or bizarre, choice of method may allow a small cluster of imitative suicides to be identified. A recent group of suicides by jumping from expressway overpasses in Seattle was apparent because the method was novel in Seattle; the number of suicides alone would not have been an obvious marker in a city that size.

Walton's account of a series of suicides by antifreeze poisoning illustrates the contagious effect that news of an unusual method of death may have (Walton 1978). A group of seven garage employees consumed fluid they had found in a cherry brandy bottle in a car. The car owner, however, had stored antifreeze (ethylene glycol) in the brandy bottle. One of the employees died and a second required hemodialysis, events which became headline news and the subject of local radio reports for several days. In the next few months, five suicides and six suicide attempts from antifreeze poisoning occurred in the community. One of the victims was found with the antifreeze newspaper story beside his bed and two other victims told their spouses that they had drunk antifreeze like they had read about in the newspaper. In this series a readily available, relatively pleasant tasting, lethal fluid was given extensive publicity as a means of death, and potentially suicidal persons were influenced to kill themselves by this method.

Hospital suicides of two middle-aged, depressed men 2 weeks apart, using the same suicide methods, prompted Crawford and Willis (1966) to review their hospital records for inpatient suicides. In the 100 years since the hospital opened, they found 24 suicides, 10 of which seemed to occur in pairs. Victims in three pairs used identical methods. Additionally, an unpaired suicide victim leaped into a chalk pit where a patient from another hospital had committed suicide a few days earlier. Because the hospital suicide records counted those patients who died while on pass, the choice of available methods in this series was unlimited. The authors reason that knowledge of a patient's suicide by a given method may lead another patient to enact suicidal impulses by the same, presumably effective method.

Sacks and Eth (1981) explore pathological identification with a suicide victim "as the result of a history of similar past experiences." The psychological identifications Sacks and Eth describe may, however, lead a subsequent potential victim to enact the same method as the index suicide. Conversely, the article raises the possibility that a history of attempt by similar method may serve as a nidus for identification. In their report, a psychiatric inpatient committed suicide while on a pass by jumping from a rooftop. Two days later, another patient jumped from his apartment window hours after hospital discharge. A third patient became preoccupied with suicidal ideation. After discharge, she visited the second patient in the intensive care unit. Several years earlier the third patient had attempted suicide by jumping from the roof of a seven-story building.

Seiden (1967) has described a series of suicides by jumping from buildings on the Berkeley campus. Five men, none of whom were students, killed themselves within a month. He reports,

> Each successive case was given front-page news coverage to the point where the University community was gripped in a state approaching hysteria. . . . Almost everyone was afraid that, whatever the underlying cause, the immediate trigger to the outbreak was an imitative influence contributed by preceding cases, or in more formal terms, the concept of behavioral contagion. (p. 364)

Seiden concludes that a contagious influence was negligible because none of the victims knew each other personally; the second and third victims jumped within minutes of each other, making the third victim probably unaware of the second's suicide; the suicides stopped abruptly; and all of the decedents had histories of severe mental disorder.

An alternative view of these five cases is that behavioral contagion in suicide does not require direct observation of the victim or require social acquaintance. Indirect exposure, for example, through the media, is sufficient (Bandura 1977). The second and third victims may have each been influenced by the index suicide. Measures were taken to halt the epidemic by preventing access to the top floors of campus buildings, which may have contributed significantly to ending the series. Finally, those persons with serious mental illness may be more susceptible to the influence of another's suicide and may express that identification by a similar choice of method.

Certain methods or locations for committing suicide acquire a significance that attracts the victim (Kurtz et al. 1987). The location or method acquires a symbolic value, and the suicide victim's death acquires a larger meaning and significance. Those who traverse the Bay Bridge en route to the Golden Gate Bridge to jump illustrate the powerful significance that the Golden Gate Bridge holds for suicide. Nalin (1973) describes epidemic suicide by malathion poisoning among the Guyanese. This insecticide is freely available and has become such a prevalent method of suicide that in rural areas the equivalent of "Go jump in a lake" is "Go take malathion." Malathion suicides in cases of unrequited love received widespread publicity, enhancing malathion's symbolic value in lovers' suicides.

Emulating the suicide of a celebrity or cult figure makes a statement about the victim's feelings without speaking directly or leaving a note. In April 1986 a teenage Japanese singing idol, Yukiko Okada, committed suicide by jumping. Extensive news coverage broadcast her despondence over a broken love affair (Snyder 1986). The following wave of imitative suicides among Japanese teenagers tapped into all that was publicized about Ms. Okada's sense of loss and hopelessness.

These reports of suicide epidemics or clusters by similar methods offer several approaches to understanding the relationship between choice of method and the potential suicide victim's decision to die. Public knowledge of an available and seemingly effective or painless method of suicide may overwhelm the more life-affirming side of the potential victim's ambivalence about killing himself or herself (Ashton and Donnan 1981). If the method is a novel one, victims may be attracted to it in expectation that it will circumvent noxious qualities of other methods they may have considered. Choice of an identical method may be an outward expression of identification that potential victims make with the feelings and life circumstances they assume were the decedent's. In some cases, method itself may be the point around which an identification grows if the potential victim has had a similar, nonfatal experience. Additionally, a particular method may acquire a publicly known symbolic value in the community and thereby assure that the victim's suicide makes a public statement. In such cases, the suicidal act may then express sentiments otherwise culturally prohibited. Methods such as self-immolation or jumping are generally public and witnessed. The victim may imagine that the attendant publicity would speak powerfully to those left behind.

Milieu Effects on Suicide Clustering

Suicide epidemics in closed environments, such as mental hospitals, have been used to illustrate the impact of the social environment or milieu on suicide. Among these already high-risk populations, "fragmented leadership, faulty supervision and staff demoralization and anomie" may overpower intrapsychic prohibitions against suicide and foster clusters of suicide (Anonymous 1977, p. 331). Kobler and Stotland (1964) emphasize the social expectations created within the hospital milieu more than the intrapsychic impetus to suicide. The four suicides they reported were certainly patients with intrinsic risk factors for suicide. However, the authors felt that the ensuing suicide cluster was a response to hopelessness and helplessness among the staff, conveyed as an expectation that these patients would kill themselves.

As the numbers of suicides in a community increase, Rubinstein (1983) believes that familiarity with the idea of suicide has an additive effect with contagion. This familiarity fosters acceptance of the idea of suicide and begins to trivialize its lethality. Youth in conflict may come to regard suicide as an ordinary option and feel no particular aversion to this seemingly commonplace way out of their problems.

Elements of Identification and Modeling

Rubinstein (1983) describes clusters of suicides among adolescents in the Marshall Islands following the suicide of a prominent young man who was torn between two women. His hanging served as a model of a lover's dilemma suicide. Over the next 12 years, others followed the same method when they were addressing a similar dilemma. Suicide victims and youth who attempted suicide reported having a vision of the previous victim circling the island in a boat and beckoning potential victims to join him. Rubinstein (1983) believes that these suicides illustrate "how a single case appears to have become a dramatic model for successive suicides [and how] the suicide *act* acquires a specific local meaning as a culturally-patterned solution to certain kinds of dilemmas" (p. 663).

Eight young Canadian Indians from a community of 37 families committed suicide within a 12-month period (Ward and Fox 1977). Interviews with families and neighbors of the decedents contributed to a picture of the victims as vulnerable, stressed, and overdependent on their troubled families. Ward and Fox view the intrapsychic and interpersonal problems of the victims as a "tinder-dry forest" to which the spark of one suicide sets off a spreading fire. They surmised that potential victims identified with the seemingly intolerable life situation of the person who committed suicide and that suicide became a model for escaping their similar life situation.

During a cluster of suicides, potential victims may identify more strongly with the decedents if their own past has been affected by people who attempted suicide, committed suicide, or died violently. The first case in a hospital cluster had a younger sister who had made several suicide attempts. He committed suicide 10 days after his sister killed herself. The second victim had begun to feel suicidal after he assumed the job of a man who had committed suicide. As a child, this patient had witnessed his alcoholic father's inadvertent and fatal self-immolation (Anonymous 1977). These earlier kinds of identifications with persons who committed suicide or died violently can induce a feeling of inevitability about one's own suicide that may be irresistible during a cluster (Sacks and Eth 1981).

The model exerting some contagious influence need not have been a fatality. The cluster of suicides reported by Kobler and Stotland (1964) was heralded by a nonfatal suicide attempt on the hospital ward. The five antifreeze suicides reported by Walton (1978) were instigated by reports of a fatal, unintentional poisoning.

Role of Mental Illness

Mental illness is widely recognized as a risk factor for suicide. Some reports indicate that psychiatric illness may be more prevalent among those who commit suicide in a cluster. Some of the literature on suicide clusters comes from patient populations, because psychiatric hospitals represent a small community of high-risk persons in which multiple suicides are readily noted and are cause for corporate concern. Nonetheless, victims of suicide clusters occurring outside the hospital environment demonstrate a high incidence of psychiatric pathology. Five of the six antifreeze victims had long-standing mental illness (Walton 1978). Eighty-one percent of train suicides in Lindekilde and Wang's (1985) study were psychiatric patients. Ninety percent of the self-immolation victims reported by Ashton and Donnan (1981) had psychiatric problems, and 46% had been hospitalized for mental illness at some time. All of the victims in the Berkeley cluster of suicides had histories of chronic mental illness (Seiden 1967), as did all of the physicians on probation in Oregon whose suicides clustered (Crawshaw et al. 1980).

A special predilection of mentally disturbed persons toward epidemic suicide has long been suspected. In 1895, Winslow attributed an outbreak of suicide to "the force of imitation being so great and acting prejudicially on weak minded persons or on those predisposed to mental disorders" (Winslow 1895, p. 337). Another early observer of epidemic suicides noted that "it is difficult to determine how much was due to the psychopathic tendencies of the actors . . . and how much to the external circumstances which probably served only as the spark applied to the inflammable material" (Rovinsky 1898, p. 239). Poor emotional health, then, may increase one's susceptibility to suicide in a cluster. Those with seriously disordered thinking may also have a pathological capacity to identify with tangential elements of another's suicide and be more easily influenced by it. Efforts to establish psychiatric diagnoses in studies of nonepidemic suicides may be quite exhaustive (Robins 1981); while some of the suicide-cluster reports count only treated cases. These sorts of differences make it difficult to determine whether the proportion of noncluster suicides with psychiatric illness actually differs from proportions reported in case series of cluster suicides.

Age Susceptibility to Cluster Suicides

Phelps (1911) in an early diatribe against "morbid and sensational" literature as factors inciting suicide pointed out the special sensitivity of youth to such influence:

There is a moral or psychic contagium in certain books that is as
definite and disastrous as that of the plague. . . . The pubescent reader
is in the greatest danger from unhealthful reading. He or she is in a
condition of unstable equilibrium—adjustment to environment is
not yet perfect; the emotions are keyed to the highest pitch; the
centers of ideation are plastic. (p. 273)

The relative susceptibility of youth to imitative suicide has been examined for cases reported in the media.

Several studies have looked at the association between newspaper
reporting of suicide and subsequent changes in suicide rates. These
studies show greater susceptibility among younger victims. Barraclough et al. (1977) found a statistically significant association between
published reports of coroners' inquests in suicide cases and subsequent
suicide of men under 45 years old. Motto (1970) compared suicide rates
before, during, and after a newspaper blackout in Detroit. Those 15–34
years old showed the greatest drop in suicide rates during the blackout.
A replication of this study in New York City during a partial newspaper
strike found significant reductions in the suicide rate only among younger women under age 35 (Blumenthal and Bergner 1973).

None of these studies separated out youth suicides (less than 24
years old) from the changes among suicides reported for younger ages.
Recently, Phillips and Carstensen (1986) correlated fluctuations in the
daily number of suicides among 10- to 19-year-olds with television news
stories about suicide broadcast during 1973–1979. They found that the
observed number of suicides 0–7 days after broadcast was greater than
expected and that the increase was age-specific for teens.

The statistical procedures used in all these studies, however, may
be inadequate to control for daily, weekly, seasonal, and yearly trends in
suicide among youth. Also, these studies look at aggregate data and
attribute the results to an imitative or contagious factor. This etiologic
hypothesis cannot be demonstrated by any similar aggregate study.
Without analysis on the individual level, we can never demonstrate that
those who committed suicide were actually exposed to the newspaper,
broadcast, or other presumed influence. Over 75 years ago, Hemenway
(1911) outlined a study to link individual suicide victims and exposure
to suicide. Coroners would collect the following information:

1) Dates of prominent publication of details of suicides, with the
method selected by the unfortunates. 2) Dates of subsequent suicides
with special references to the grouping of cases according to
methods. 3) Direct evidence by asking at inquests for information as
to the possible relationship of the suicide being investigated to
previous cases either read about or known of. (p. 254)

Published studies have not yet taken a similar approach and analyzed suicide imitation among youth at the individual level.

Without some surveillance system for suicide clusters, one cannot conclude that the proportion of known clusters involving youth reflects the actual age distribution of persons who commit suicide in clusters. Youth suicide clusters may be preferentially reported because they are perceived as more newsworthy. Neither are data available to compare the proportion of all youth suicides that appear clustered with those for adults. Youth have psychological characteristics consistent with greater susceptibility to imitative suicide, but we lack data to document their representation among suicide clusters.

Influence of Suicide Aftereffects

Suicide contagion shows many parallels with the process of imitative learning. Among those factors influencing imitative learning are the consequences or rewards associated with the behavior (Bandura 1977). Hankoff (1961) reported a cluster of suicide attempts among Marines stationed in a desolate area. In the beginning, those who attempted suicide were transferred back to installations in more populous and desirable areas. Only when this secondary gain was thwarted by a no-transfer policy that quickly returned the young men to their duty assignments was the epidemic of attempts stopped.

The aftereffects of a young person's suicide can reinforce the image of suicide as more desirable than anything else a potential youth victim might achieve. Hochkirchen and Jilek (1985) emphasize the ways community reaction to a youth suicide can trigger further attempts and suicides in a cluster:

> The latest suicide victim may be talked of as a martyred hero. Posthumously he gets attention as never during his lifetime. His entire life is glorified and his "good old days" are emphasized rather than his more recent, possibly antisocial behaviour. Suicide is seen as the crowning event of his life. His funeral is a big social occasion and the time between death and funeral is filled with memorial services and commemorative gatherings. The attention of the whole community is focused on this particular suicide and on suicide in general, thus making suicidal acts interesting and attractive for predisposed young people. (p. 27)

These examples suggest that the process of imitative suicidal behavior is complex and probably involves factors associated with vulnerability for an individual's narcissism and self-esteem regulation. Certainly the interactions between cognitive processes and behavior are also important.

Instituting adverse sequelae to suicide has been tried as a deterrent to cluster suicides. Authorities in Lyons and Miletus squelched epidemic suicide among the women by ordering that the bodies of all suicide victims be publicly exposed in the marketplace (Winslow 1895). Helping the potential victims to more realistically perceive the probable effects of their actions may be a deterrent. Ashton and Donnan (1981) felt that the public impression of self-immolation during an epidemic was that burning resulted in instantaneous death. Had the potential victims known what a lingering, painful death many of the suicide victims endured, they might have been less easily influenced to follow suit.

Negating the positive aura in identification has also been proposed. Kaminer (1986) recommended labeling suicidal behavior among adolescents as something likely to be imitated. The potential adolescent victim would then be less likely to imitate the suicide, because adolescents are rebellious and do not wish to appear as unthinking followers. This approach would aim at deterring the potential victims by devaluing the imitative aspect of the behavior they are considering.

The converse approach has also been reported. Stack (1983) showed no change in suicide rates attributable to the mass suicides at Jonestown. He felt that the absence of a discernible imitative effect may have resulted from the type of news coverage surrounding the events. The victims were portrayed as easily intimidated cult members and horrifying photographs of decaying bodies were shown. Thus, the news coverage devalued the suicides as acts worthy of imitation. Shepherd and Barraclough (1978) described patterns in newspaper reporting of suicide inquests, which accord more numerous and larger stories to youth suicides and/or violent suicides. They concluded that newspaper reporting of suicide distorts the facts for entertainment value. Thus, the tone and slant of media coverage in portraying the suicide and its aftereffects may either act as a deterrent or enhance the likelihood of imitative suicide among youth.

Illustrative Clusters

A cluster of suicides in 1985 among enrolled members of the Arapahoe and Shoshone tribes, cohabitants of the Wind River Reservation, is illustrative. These data were obtained by the Centers for Disease Control with the cooperation of the county coroner, the Bureau of Indian Affairs, and state vital registrars. Thirteen suicides (12 Arapahoe and 1 Shoshone) occurred between January 2, 1985, and October 18, 1985. No suicides had occurred among tribal members in 1983, and 1 Shoshone committed suicide in 1984. There were 12 males and 1 female decedent, all of whom killed themselves by hanging. Decedents were between 14 and 25 years old.

Tribal enrollment records were used to calculate suicide rates (per 100,000 population) for males 15–24. By comparison, the United States suicide rate for males 15–24 was 19.8, that of the Wind River tribes was 1592.9, and the rate for the Arapahoe was 2492.2—over 125 times the United States rate. During the time course of this cluster, suicide was the only cause of death for Arapahoes under 35 years old. Since tribe-specific suicide rates could be calculated, this cluster could be verified by a significant increase in suicide rates. A discrete cluster, however, occurring within a large metropolitan county might not increase suicide rates beyond background variability.

All of these decedents hanged themselves, and their selection of method may have been culturally influenced as well as affected by the immediate cluster. Not all suicides occurred on the reservation. Six were off site with two in the local jail and one at boarding school. However, all bodies were returned to the small reservation community for burial. Thus, it is unlikely that any of these suicides were unknown to the population at risk; although news coverage focused on the deaths between August and October, and direct social connections were not universal. The extraordinarily high prevalence of suicide among young tribal members may have fostered identification with the decedents. Bleak employment prospects, alcoholism, poverty, and disparities between tribal perspectives and government programs contribute to a pervasive sense of hopelessness. In such a situation, making a statement by one's suicide may appear to be a liberating and courageous act to potential victims.

Two teen suicide clusters in Texas were investigated by the Centers for Disease Control. Each cluster included victims who were close personal friends and victims who only knew of the other decedents through the media or by word of mouth. The first decedent in one cluster of eight teens was powerfully affected by the death of a close friend who had been fatally injured as a bystander in a mock drag race. Although he had not directly caused the friend's death, he felt distressed and guilty over it. A mutual friend of the pedestrian victim and the first suicide victim also killed himself. His bulletin board displayed newspaper clippings of the pedestrian fatality. He was known to be upset by both deaths. A third decedent was also a good friend of the first suicide victim. A boyfriend-girlfriend pair in this series committed double suicide. All the suicide victims in this cluster attended school in the same section of town. The other cluster of six suicides involved three victims who were personal friends.

Among the decedents, then, exposure to suicide was indirect as well as direct. In both series, the second and subsequent suicide victims were aware of the preceding teen suicides. Many of the victims' parents felt that their children's suicides were patterned after another suicide or suicide attempt.

RECOMMENDATIONS FOR COMMUNITIES

Recommendations to prevent suicide contagion emphasize preparedness. As with infectious diseases, the most effective means to prevent contagion is to prevent the first case. However, this chapter focuses on the situation a community finds itself in after a suicide or suicide attempt has occurred. The school system will be used as the example of the unit experiencing the suicide because the school system is a near-universal framework for youth, not because schools are pathogenic. Analogous recommendations could be made for hospitals, neighborhoods, military installations, and so on.

Having a response plan serves many goals. Ideally, school system personnel, mental health professionals, community leaders, parents, and student representatives should collaborate in forming this plan. Their involvement in working out the plan itself models the type of coordinated effort that is necessary after a suicide. Familiarity with the response plan helps avert panic. When people in the school system know their roles and how anticipated situations will be handled, their attention is less likely to be diverted from children in need to their own anxieties. Their composure and organization maintains a more secure environment for youth troubled by the suicide; whereas a milieu of panic and confusion may increase the potential victim's sense of hopelessness, urgency, and alienation.

A key element of the plan is establishing a referral network. Fears of one's own inability to manage a suicidal child may lessen one's receptiveness to communications of suicidal intent. Simple and explicit procedures for referring youth during the crisis should be widely known. Self-referral should also be easily available to students. Local mental health resources for youth may be woefully inadequate. An alliance of public and private caregivers may need to be arranged with provisions for contingent state health department resources.

School system personnel should be aware of the types of students who are likely to be at high risk for suicide in a cluster. These include youth in the same social network as the decedent, those with previous suicidal behavior, and those with poor baseline mental health. Students whose life circumstances or past history parallel the victim's may have stronger identifications. Having family members or acquaintances who have died by suicide, accident, or homicide may strengthen the identification. Also, youth who have a history of impulsive or violent behavior that is directed either toward self or others are at increased risk.

In responding to the suicide, the school system strives to avoid glorifying the suicide. Stopping classes for a funeral conveys that suicide can make the youth's world stop and take notice. Mass assemblies focusing on the individual decedent can intensify the prestige that potential victims view suicide as providing. In smaller counseling sessions or homeroom discussions, school system personnel can help students understand many important concepts:

1. Death is permanent, and the decedent will not gain satisfaction from any of the postmortem events.
2. Suicide can be portrayed as a permanent solution to temporary problems for which help is available.
3. Many people have suicidal thoughts when a suicide has occurred in the community. Students should understand that having thoughts of suicide does not mean that they are "crazy." Persistent and intrusive suicidal thoughts are a signal that something important is troubling the person and he or she should seek help. Teachers can provide information about available mental health resources.
4. The student who committed suicide can be portrayed as seriously disturbed and as someone who, sadly, had not found an avenue to effectively work on his or her problems. Students can be helped to disidentify with the decedent without abusing the victim's character.

Providing reasonable access to information, controlling rumors, and protecting students from intrusive news reporters are important concerns. The school system should have an identified spokesperson to whom all information requests should be directed. Other school system personnel and students should be protected from media requests. Regrettably, some of the media have an insatiable appetite for stories of death and violence. Schools may need to station employees to monitor access to the campus and buildings to prevent a circus of camera crews and interviewers from pursuing students.

Rumors may proliferate rampantly during a suicide crisis. Such rumors may predict further suicides in an incendiary way that would lend notoriety to subsequent suicides. Rumors of suicide pacts can be especially troublesome. Occasionally such rumors can be traced to one or two emotionally disturbed students who can then be engaged in treatment. The official spokesperson and other school personnel, in their contact with students, will need to help dispel such rumors.

Provisions for the needs of teachers and other caregivers during the crisis should be planned. Those committed to meeting students' needs during a suicide crisis are under tremendous pressure. They also need opportunities to ventilate feelings, seek reassurance, get outside assistance, and exchange information. Teaching often isolates the educator from peers, and increased contact with coprofessionals during the crisis is valuable.

CONCLUSION

This review of suicide clusters has been based on case series in the literature and data from several clusters studied by the author. Although much empirical research remains to be done, the following conclusions can be made:

1. Time-space clusters of suicides occur among youth and adults and are not a new phenomenon.
2. Direct or indirect exposure to other suicides may induce imitative behavior among vulnerable people. Depression, narcissistic loss, poor self-esteem, chronic feelings of emptiness, and psychosis are examples of concurrent psychological states inducing vulnerability to suicide. Imitation alone does not produce suicide.
3. Younger people and people with mental illness may be more susceptible to epidemic suicide.
4. Sociocultural meanings attached to suicide may facilitate suicide clusters.
5. Identification with a suicide victim fosters imitative behavior.
6. Identification with a suicide victim is more likely among persons with similar life experiences, especially previous exposures to suicide and violence.
7. Imitative suicide is more likely when the model is highly regarded and the potential victim views the outcome of the model's behavior as rewarding.

REFERENCES

Anonymous: A suicide epidemic in a psychiatric hospital. Diseases of the Nervous System 38:327–331, 1977

Ashton VR, Donnan S: Suicide by burning as an epidemic phenomenon: an analysis of 82 deaths and inquests in England and Wales in 1978–79. Psychol Med 11:735–739, 1981

Bakwin H: Suicide in children and adolescents. J Pediatr 50:749–769, 1957

Bandura A: Social Learning Theory. Englewood Cliffs, NJ, Prentice Hall, 1977

Barraclough B, Shepherd D, Jennings C: Do newspaper reports of coroners' inquests incite people to commit suicide? Br J Psychiatry 131:529–532, 1977

Blumenthal S, Bergner L: Suicide and newspapers: a replicated study. Am J Psychiatry 130:468–471, 1973

Crawford JP, Willis JH: Double suicide in psychiatric hospital patients. Br J Psychiatry 112:1231–1235, 1966

Crawshaw R, Bruce JA, Eraker PL, et al: An epidemic of suicide among physicians on probation. JAMA 243:1915–1917, 1980

Davis BR, Hardy RJ: A suicide epidemic model. Soc Biol 33:291–300, 1986

Goethe JW: Reflections on Werther. New York, New American Library, 1962

Hankoff LD: An epidemic of attempted suicide. Compr Psychiatry 2:294–298, 1961

Hemenway HB: To what extent are suicide and other crimes against the person due to suggestion from the press? Bulletin of the American Academy of Medicine 12:253–263, 1911

Hochkirchen B, Jilek W: Psychosocial dimensions of suicide and parasuicide in Amerindians of the Pacific Northwest. Journal of Operational Psychiatry 16:24–28, 1985

Kaminer Y: Suicidal behavior and contagion among hospitalized adolescents (letter). N Engl J Med 315:1030, 1986

Kobler AL, Stotland E: The end of hope: a social-clinical study of suicide. The Free Press (London) 1964

Kurtz RJ, Pizzi WF, Richman H, et al: Jumping from the Brooklyn Bridge. Surg Gynecol Obstet 165:60–62, 1987

Lindekilde K, Wang AG: Train suicide in the county of Fyn 1979–82. Acta Psychiatr Scand 72:150–154, 1985

Mantel N: The detection of disease clustering and a generalized regression approach. Cancer Res 27:209–220, 1967

Mathews W: Civilization and suicide. The North American Review 1891, pp 470–484

Motto JA: Newspaper influence on suicide. Arch Gen Psychiatry 23:143–148, 1970

Nalin DR: Epidemic of suicide by malathion poisoning in Guyana. Trop Geogr Med 25:8–14, 1973

Niemi T: The time-space distances of suicides committed in the lock-up in Finland in 1963–1967. Israel Annals of Psychiatry and Related Disciplines 16:39–45, 1978

Phelps EB: Neurotic books and newspapers as factors in the mortality of suicide and crime. Bulletin of the American Academy of Medicine 12:264–306, 1911

Phillips DP, Carstensen MS: Clustering of teenage suicides after television news stories about suicide. N Engl J Med 315:685–689, 1986

Popow NM: The present epidemic of school suicides in Russia. Nevol Nestnik (Kazan) 18:312–355, 592–646; 1911

Robins E: The Final Months. New York, Oxford University Press, 1981

Rovinsky A: Epidemic suicides. Boston Medical and Surgical Journal 138:238–239, 1898

Rubinstein DH: Epidemic suicide among Micronesian adolescents. Soc Sci Med 17:657–665, 1983

Sacks M, Eth S: Pathological identification as a cause of suicide on an inpatient unit. Hosp Community Psychiatry 32:36–40, 1981

Seiden RH: Suicidal behavior contagion on a college campus, in Proceedings of Fourth International Conference for Suicide Prevention. Edited by Farberow NL. 1967, pp 360–365

Shepherd D, Barraclough BM: Suicide reporting: information or entertainment? Br J Psychiatry 132:283–287, 1978

Snyder J: Wave of suicides rocks Japan. United Press International, April 22, 1986

Stack S: The effect of Jonestown on the suicide rate. J Soc Psychol 119:145–146, 1983

Walton EW: An epidemic of antifreeze poisoning. Med Sci Law 18:231–237, 1978

Ward JA, Fox J: A suicide epidemic on an Indian reserve. Canadian Psychiatric Association Journal 22:423–426, 1977

Weigand HJ: Foreword to The Sorrows of Young Werther, by J.W. Goethe. New York, New American Library, 1962

Winslow F: Suicide considered as a mental epidemic. Bulletin of the Medico-Legal Congress. New York, 1895, pp 334–351

6

Effects of Mass Media News Stories on Suicide, with New Evidence on the Role of Story Content

David P. Phillips, Ph.D.
Lundie L. Carstensen, M.S.
Daniel J. Paight, B.A.

For many years, parents, teachers, and network television censors have acted on the assumption that people—especially young, "impressionable" ones—are prone to imitate the actions of others. This insight has prompted some people to avoid setting a bad example for children, students, and the mass media audience. The same insight suggested to Goethe's contemporaries that his novel *The Sorrows of Young Werther*, in which the lovesick hero commits suicide, was responsible for a rash of suicides following the publication of the book. Because of these fears, the book was banned in many European cities.

Until recently, however, many researchers have failed to examine the hypothesis that part of the fluctuation in suicides results from the influence of suicidal models. Perhaps this was because early research on the topic produced findings that were inconclusive (Motto 1967; Blumenthal and Bergner 1973), contradictory (Crawford and Willis 1966; Seiden 1968), or readily explainable by other causes (Weiss 1958;

We thank the following for providing data on suicide: the California Department of Health Services, the Central University Library and Associate Librarian James Jacobs, and the Vanderbilt Television News Archives.

Kreitman et al. 1969). Recently, interest in imitative suicide has revived, and there is now an increasing number of studies that have suggested that publicized models do indeed affect the suicide rate, particularly among teens.

In the first part of this chapter, we review recent research on the impact of mass media stories about suicide. In the second part of the chapter, by analyzing new data, we consider whether the manner in which these stories are presented affects the degree to which they are imitated.

The first convincing, quantitative evidence in support of the "Werther effect" came in 1974 with Phillips's study of the relation between the incidence of suicide and news stories about suicides in the United States (Phillips 1974). Phillips systematically generated a list of 35 publicized suicide stories that appeared in *Facts on File* and the front page of the *New York Times* between 1946 and 1968. A few of these stories occurred at nearly the same time; to avoid problems of statistical dependence, these overlapping stories were treated as one, leaving 33 stories for analysis. Phillips consulted official United States statistics from 1946–1968 for the number of recorded suicides in the months before, during, and after publicized suicide stories. He compared the number of suicides in the month of a story with 1) the number of suicides 12 months after the story and 2) the number of suicides 12 months before the story. By averaging the values for these two control periods, he was able to estimate the number of suicides that should occur in the month of the suicide story (the experimental period) if suicide stories have no effect on suicides. Because the two control periods straddled the experimental period and occurred in the same month as the experimental period, this procedure also corrected for the influence of seasons and of linear trends.

Having followed this procedure for each of 33 stories, Phillips found that suicides in the United States increased significantly ($p = .00066$) after nearly all of the publicized suicide stories (binomial test, $p = .5$, $n = 33$, $r \geq 26$). He named this increase *the Werther effect* in honor of Goethe's suicidal hero. Phillips suggested that this effect occurred because the publication of news stories about suicides tended to trigger some additional, imitative suicides.

Two additional findings help to support this interpretation of the data: 1) The most heavily publicized suicide stories are associated with largest increases in suicides. Using the number of days a story ran in the *New York Daily News* as an indicator of the level of publicity a story received, Phillips found that suicides in the United States increased (on average) by 28.54 in the month after "1-day" stories in the *Daily News*, by 35.25 after "2-day" stories, by 82.63 after "3-day" stories, and by

197.5 after "4-day" stories ($p = .0083$). 2) Phillips also found that the Werther effect is strongest in the geographic area in which the stories are run. If a story runs primarily in the New York City area, then the rise in suicides is larger in New York City than in the rest of the country; similarly, Phillips found that a story that was publicized primarily in the United States (and very little in Britain) was followed by a larger rise in America than in Britain. Several alternative explanations for these findings appeared to be initially plausible. Phillips assessed, but finally rejected, four of these.

First, it is possible that the publicized suicide affects coroners, rather than suicidal persons. That is, suicide stories may not prompt a real increase in the suicide rate, but rather an increase in the *recording* of suicides. After suicide stories, coroners may be more likely than usual to record deaths occurring under dubious circumstances as suicides, rather than as accidents, murders, or "undetermined whether purposefully or accidentally inflicted." If coroners do indeed act in this way, then it should be possible to detect a decrease in the frequencies of these latter categories, a decrease that corresponds to the increase in recorded suicides. But the data do not exhibit this compensatory decrease. The affected-coroner hypothesis is, therefore, empirically untenable.

Second, publicized suicides may do nothing more than prompt persons to commit suicide a little sooner than they would otherwise have done. (Durkheim believed in this "precipitation hypothesis.") If this were the case, however, then the poststory rise in suicides should be followed by a compensatory drop in suicides below normal, caused by some persons "moving up" their death dates as a result of the story. However, no such compensatory decrease has been found and this undermines the precipitation hypothesis.

A third alternative explanation for these findings is that the observed increases in suicides following suicide stories result from grief generated by the stories, rather than from imitative behavior. Phillips argued that this explanation was unlikely for two reasons. On one hand, many of the stories were about individuals whose deaths would be unlikely to produce an outpouring of grief (e.g., obscure persons, Nazi officials, Ku Klux Klansmen, underworld leaders). On the other hand, Phillips found that the deaths of United States Presidents (events which should produce more grief than the average suicide story) were not followed by a statistically significant increase in suicides.

A fourth alternative explanation is that both the publicized suicides and the suicides following them are caused by some prior factor (such as a dramatic change in economic conditions). If this prior-factor hypothesis were correct, a publicized suicide should occur somewhere in the middle of the wave of suicides that is associated with it. Instead, however, one finds that publicized suicides always *precede* the wave of extra suicides. Figure 1 shows that, in the month just before a suicide story, suicides were generally less frequent than expected; in contrast,

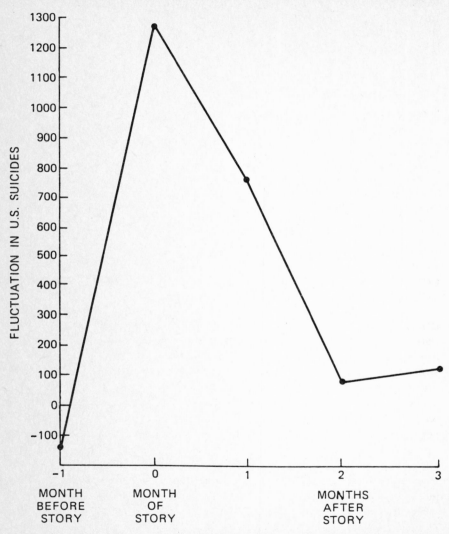

Figure 1. Fluctuation in the number of suicides in the United States before, during, and after the month of the suicide story. (Reprinted with permission from Phillips DP: The influence of suggestion on suicide: substantive and theoretical implications of the Werther effect. American Sociological Review 39:340–354, 1974. Copyright 1974, The American Sociological Association.)

suicides were far more frequent than expected (by an average of 58.1 per story) in the month of the story and in the month just afterward.

These findings are suggestive but not conclusive, because Figure 1 leaves open the possibility that some of the surge in suicides in the month of the suicide story begins *before* the appearance of the story. In the absence of daily data, this possibility cannot be checked directly, but it can be checked indirectly:

> If suicides rise only after a story appears, then stories appearing late in the month should elicit a relatively small rise in suicides in the month of the story, and a relatively larger rise in suicides in the month after the story. Conversely, stories appearing early in the month should elicit a relatively large rise in suicides in the month of the story, and a relatively smaller rise in the month after the story. These predictions are consistent with the available data: Stories appearing on or before the 15th of the month are associated with a total rise of 636 suicides in the month of the story and in the month thereafter; 98% of this rise (624/636) occurs in the month of the story. In contrast, for stories appearing after the 15th of the month, only 47% of the rise (651/1398) occurs in the month of the story. (Phillips 1986a, pp. 215–216)

In sum, the findings suggest that the publicized suicide story always precedes the wave of ordinary suicides, and this undermines the prior factor hypothesis under assessment.

These findings have since been replicated repeatedly in studies using different types of data (daily, weekly, and monthly), different statistical techniques (the quasi-experimental methods described above and time-series regression techniques), and different types of suicide stories (those appearing on television and in the newspapers) (Bollen and Phillips 1982; Phillips and Bollen 1985; Stack 1986, 1987; Phillips and Carstensen 1986; Wasserman 1984). The results of all these studies were fully consistent, with the exception of Wasserman's study, which replicated only part of the original findings. Extending the data set to cover 1948–1977, and using Phillips's original quasi-experimental design, Wasserman found a significant increase in suicides after all suicide stories. However, upon subjecting the data to regression analysis, and adding corrections for the effects of economic conditions and the celebrity status of the person in the story, he found a significant increase in suicides only after celebrity suicides. Stack (1987), however, discovered that Wasserman had inadvertently omitted a relatively large number of suicide stories from his analysis; after including these stories, Stack found that regression analysis revealed suicide peaks after news stories about both celebrated and uncelebrated persons.

The most recent replication (Phillips and Carstensen 1986)—a regression analysis that corrected for the effects of seasons, day of the week, holidays, and linear trends—focused on the daily fluctuations in suicides among teenagers in the United States (1973–1979) and found a total increase of 110.58 suicides in the 0- to 7-day periods following 38 network television news stories about suicide ($p = .008$, two-tailed Wilcoxon test). The size of the increase following each story was significantly correlated with the amount of coverage the story received. The more programs carrying a story, the larger the increase, and stories covered by only one television program (which typically receive very brief coverage) were not followed by an increase at all. The authors found a much larger increase for teenagers than for adults; within the teenage group, the poststory increase was larger for teenage girls (13.46%) than for teenage boys (5.18%). The authors assessed alternative explanations for their findings, including those discussed above, and concluded that the best available explanation for the data is that suicide stories elicit some additional suicides, apparently because of imitation.

Perhaps the most striking findings in this research area concern the association between publicized suicides and the incidence of motor vehicle fatalities (MVFs) (Phillips 1977, 1979; Bollen and Phillips 1981). Researchers have long suspected that some MVFs are not really accidents at all, but disguised suicides. If this is true, then MVFs should increase after suicide stories in the same way that recorded suicides do.

Phillips (1979) detected such an increase. After correcting for the impact of day of the week, holidays, seasons, and trends, and using much the same quasi-experimental method as that described above, he found that California MVFs increased by an average of 9.12% in the week following suicide stories that appeared on the front pages of the *Los Angeles Times* and *San Francisco Chronicle*, with the bulk of the increase occurring on the 3rd day ($p = .011$, one-tailed t test). The source of this 3-day lag—which has shown up in a replication of the present study (Bollen and Phillips 1981) and in similar studies (see Phillips 1986a, 1986b)—is unknown, but part of it can probably be attributed to the lag between crashing and expiring (Figure 2).

Paralleling the earlier study on suicide, Phillips also found a significant, positive correlation between the amount of publicity given stories and the size of the increase in MVFs following them ($r = .59; p < .005$). He also found that the increases in MVFs were concentrated in areas where the suicides were publicized. Phillips argued that if these "extra" MVFs were disguised suicides, then the data should support several other predictions as well. One would expect to find, for example, that single-vehicle accidents make up an unusually large proportion of the increase in MVFs after suicide stories and that the drivers in these

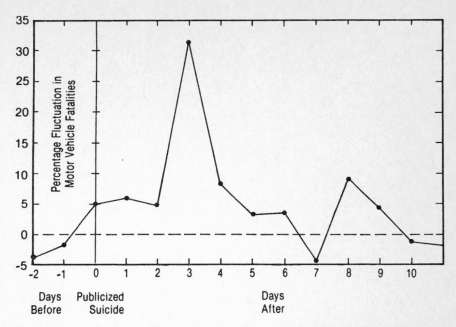

Figure 2. Daily fluctuation in motor vehicle accident fatalities for a 2-week period before, during, and after publicized suicides, California, 1966–1973. (Reprinted with permission from Phillips DP: Suicide, motor vehicle fatalities, and the mass media: evidence toward a theory of suggestion. American Journal of Sociology 84:1150–1174, 1979. Copyright 1979, the University of Chicago Press.)

accidents are unusually similar to the person in the story. Conversely, one would not expect the publicized suicide to be unusually similar to 1) *passengers* dying just after suicide stories or 2) drivers in *multiple*-vehicle MVFs or 3) drivers who crash just *before* the suicide story. The data are consistent with all these expectations.

Focusing on the 3rd day after suicide stories (where the increase is the most heavily concentrated), Phillips found that 88% of these MVFs died in single-vehicle accidents; the comparable figure was just 43% for matched control periods ($p = .0213$, hypergeometric, one tail). The drivers in these single-vehicle accidents—but *not* the passengers, *not* the multiple-car fatalities, and *not* the control-period fatalities—were unusually close in age to the publicized suicide victim ($r = .46$, $p = .023$). (Because almost all the publicized suicides were white males, Phillips was unable to test for similarities in race and sex.) It is difficult to find an alternative explanation for findings that have been reviewed above. At present, the only explanation that seems to fit all the data we

have discussed is that publicized suicides elicit some additional suicides, some of which are disguised as automobile accidents.

METHODS OF STUDYING IMITATIVE EFFECTS

For the purposes of a methodological discussion, it is useful to distinguish between two kinds of processes leading to suicide: chronic and
acute. Chronic processes are those that work themselves out over the
course of years or decades; acute processes unfold over the course of
days or weeks. Most people probably commit suicide under the influence of both types of processes, and it is neither necessary nor desirable
to think of chronic and acute processes as mutually exclusive. They are,
rather, supplementary to each other. It may be useful to think of chronic
processes as those that push suicidal persons "to the edge" and to think
of acute processes as those that push them over.

Despite their many differences, the studies reviewed here all have at
least one thing in common: they all trace an acute causal process—the
imitation of models in the mass media. There is a reason for this focus
on acute processes: they are much more easily susceptible than chronic
processes to rigorous, causal analyses.

Where chronic processes are concerned, an analysis of statistical
data can yield suggestive but not conclusive findings and can therefore
help direct, but not replace, a more clinical approach. The reasons for
this are several. First, by definition, chronic processes operate over
many years, and during this long period a host of extraneous variables
can easily mask any causal link between independent and dependent
variables. Second, the suicide-related factors most often implicated in
chronic processes (e.g., divorce, unemployment, alcoholism) can logi-
cally be understood to either cause, or result from, thoughts of self-
destruction. It is often difficult to determine empirically which came
first: a change in the independent variable (like unemployment) or a
change in the dependent variable (like suicidal ideation). Finally, the
independent variables implicated in these chronic processes usually
change subtly—and often irregularly—over time; they do not, for example, increase and then decrease suddenly. This lack of pronounced,
sudden change in the independent variable makes it more difficult to
measure the causal effect it might have.

These methodological problems are alleviated, however, in the
analysis of acute causal processes. By definition, these processes operate over the very short term. This facilitates accurate measurement of
the variables (which, to make things even easier, are often of the on-off
variety, as in the case of the appearance or nonappearance of suicide
stories). In addition, the short time period reduces the likelihood that

extraneous variables will have a chance to mask the statistical "signal," and makes it relatively easy to determine the time order of changes in the independent and dependent variables. These features of acute processes facilitate the rigorous testing of causal hypotheses.

Aside from their focus on acute processes, studies of imitation share two other methodological features: 1) the use of *found experiments* (Phillips 1986b) and 2) the use of precollected official data. These features further facilitate the careful analysis of causal hypotheses. The found experiment differs from its laboratory cousin in that the population under study, rather than the researcher, collects the research data (e.g., by operating a National Center for Health Statistics) and establishes the experimental conditions (e.g., by publishing suicide stories). The examination of monthly suicides in the United States around the time of Marilyn Monroe's death is one example of a found experiment using precollected data. The month of Monroe's death (August 1962) can be thought of as a natural experimental period, whereas August 1961 and August 1963 can be thought of as natural control periods.

The use of precollected, machine-readable data to conduct a found experiment offers the researcher several advantages over the laboratory experiment. First, some topics are not amenable to laboratory experimentation, e.g., the study of suicide. Second, the subjects in a found experiment are studied in a natural setting, in contrast to the subjects of a laboratory experiment, who are typically examined in an artificial context. Third, subjects in a found experiment are unaware that they are being studied, in contrast to laboratory subjects, who sometimes modify their behavior by trying to please or impress the experimenter. Finally, the use of precollected, machine-readable official data in the found experiment often allows the researcher to study whole populations (rather than small, nonrandom samples) and facilitates the cheap, rapid testing of hypotheses.

But the found experiment is not without its disadvantages, the most obvious of which is that researchers are unable to test many hypotheses with this method simply because they lack reliable data on many topics that interest them. For example, it would be extremely valuable to know whether publicized suicides trigger an increase in *attempted* suicides, but large-scale high-quality data on this topic do not seem to be available. A related problem is that precollected data often do not provide very much detail on topics that interest the experimenter. To revert to our example of Marilyn Monroe's suicide in August 1962—it would be very important to learn how persons who committed suicide in this month learned of Monroe's suicide: by television, radio, newspaper, word of mouth, or by a combination of media. Did these people have a history of identifying with the film star? Were they already depressed and suicidal before learning of her death? Had they made previous attempts? Were they similar to the film star in some crucial psychological features? Answers to these questions would greatly facilitate our understanding of the imitative process, but these answers are not available from the precollected death-certificate data that have been studied.

In short, studies that use precollected, machine-readable data to conduct found experiments on acute causal processes are very well suited for some research topics and not at all for others. This approach can best serve as a complement, rather than as a substitute, for more traditional methods of studying suicide.

THE INFLUENCE OF STORY CONTENT ON IMITATION

It is evident from the findings reviewed above that suicides in the United States (particularly teen suicides) tend to increase after publicized suicide stories. In view of these findings, it is important to discover whether certain types of suicide stories or particular methods of presenting a story are more or less likely to trigger imitative behavior. Are some stories safe to broadcast while others are particularly dangerous? A definitive answer to this question could provide guidelines that would help to minimize the harmful impact of suicide stories.

This research question has been left largely unexamined, with the exception of studies on the impact of publicity (Phillips 1974, 1977, 1979; Bollen and Phillips 1981, 1982; Phillips and Carstensen 1986) and on the celebrity status of the publicized suicide (Stack 1987). Many other story characteristics have yet to be explored. Is a story particularly likely to trigger imitation if it provides information about the method of suicide or if it facilitates identification with the suicide victim by providing a photograph of her or him? Is it easier to identify with an American's suicide rather than that of a foreigner? Does the reporting of the suicide victim's motive encourage imitation? If the suicide is described as "apparent" rather than as definite, is it less likely to be imitated? These and similar questions are investigated in the second part of this chapter.

To address this issue of story content and style of presentation, we analyzed videotapes of the same network news broadcasts that made up the data set in the Phillips and Carstensen (1986) study of teenage suicide reviewed above. We were able to obtain videotapes for 32 stories from the Vanderbilt TV News Archives. Tapes were not available for stories that appeared on morning or afternoon news programs or for those that were special broadcasts. There were 6 such stories in Phillips and Carstensen's original list of 38, and these had to be omitted from the present analysis. The 32 videotaped stories were classified along 12 different lines:

1. Whether the suicide was reported as apparent or definite;
2. Whether the story displayed a photograph of the victim as he or she appeared in life;
3. Whether the story displayed a photograph of the victim's body or coffin;
4. Whether the method of suicide was reported;
5. Whether the family or friends of the victim were interviewed or mentioned in the story;
6. Whether the motive for suicide was specified;
7. Whether the suicide was central to the story or peripheral (e.g., news about Salvador Allende's reported suicide was peripheral to coverage of the political upheaval in Chile);
8. Whether the suicide occurred in the United States;
9. Whether the victim was identified as a foreigner;
10. Whether the victim was a celebrity (as defined by Stack 1987);
11. Whether the victim was reported to be a relative of a celebrity;
12. Whether the victim was male or female.

Information on the first 7 variables was obtained directly from the videotapes and was available for 29 stories about individual suicides (the other 3 were feature stories about suicide). Information on variables 8–12 could also be gleaned from sources other than the videotapes, and in these cases we could include three additional stories for which videotapes were not available. Once the stories were classified according to the characteristics listed above, we calculated the mean fluctuations in suicides following stories with, and stories without, each characteristic. In order to determine whether the content of a story influences its effect, one must first correct for the influence of day of the week, seasons, holidays, secular trends, and publicity. Phillips and Carstensen (1986) calculated a set of story effects that was corrected for the influence of all but the last of these variables. In this analysis, we have corrected for the influence of publicity by regressing the story effects calculated by Phillips and Carstensen against the amount of publicity accorded to each story. The residuals from this regression equation provided an estimate of the impact of each story, controlling for day of the week, seasons, holidays, trends, and publicity. We then compared these story effects to determine whether one type of story produced a significantly larger effect than another. For example, the mean decrease after stories reporting a definite suicide was compared with the mean increase after stories reporting an apparent suicide.

Table 1. The Relationship Between Story Characteristics and the Fluctuation of Teen Suicides Thereafter, Correcting for the Amount of Publicity Accorded Each Story

Story characteristic	n^a	Mean[b]	Confidence interval for difference between means		t	p
Definite suicide	9	−1.98	−5.348	1.378	−1.21	.24
Apparent suicide	20	0.00				
No photo of person	13	−1.94	−6.226	1.427	−1.29	.21
Photo of person	16	0.46				
No photo of suicide	25	−0.45	−3.533	5.909	0.62	.56
Photo of suicide	4	−1.64				
Method not reported	7	−1.99	−6.615	2.987	−0.84	.42
Method reported	22	−0.17				
No mention of family/friends	25	−1.44	−19.51	7.575	−1.40	.26
Mention of family/friends	4	4.53				
Suicide central story issue	21	−0.48	−4.125	5.063	0.22	.83
Suicide peripheral to story	8	−0.95				
Suicide committed in U.S.	27	−0.34	−10.19	8.153	−0.31	.77
Suicide committed overseas	5	0.67				
American	24	0.07	−5.291	6.686	0.27	.80
Foreigner	7	−0.63				
Victim a celebrity	6	−1.83	−1.813	5.865	1.15	.27
Victim not a celebrity	26	0.20				
Victim related to a celebrity	4	0.63	−5.990	4.118	−0.48	.65
Not related to celebrity	28	−0.30				
No motive stated	13	0.87	−1.244	6.608	1.41	.17
Motive stated	14	−1.61				
Male	20	−0.35	−4.512	3.630	−0.22	.82
Female	11	0.09				

[a] When 2 stories overlapped they were treated as 1 story. When the characteristics of those stories differed, they were excluded from the analysis.

[b] The weighted sum of these means does not necessarily add to 0, because some of the story residuals had to be omitted from the analysis. (See text for further details.)

Table 1 displays the average fluctuation in teen suicides after each type of story. Column 1 identifies the characteristics under examination. Column 2 indicates the number of stories displaying a particular characteristic (e.g., there are 9 stories reporting definite suicides). Column 3 shows the mean fluctuation of teen suicides after stories displaying the characteristic. Columns 4–6 compare the mean fluctuation in teen suicides after stories with a given characteristic with the mean fluctuation after stories without that characteristic, or with an opposing one (e.g., stories reporting a definite suicide are compared with those reporting an apparent suicide, and stories about a female are compared with those about a male).

Table 1 provides no evidence that certain types of story are more likely to cause imitation than others; no single characteristic is significantly associated with a particularly large increase or decrease in teen suicides. Thus, the *style* in which stories about suicide are told in the news media does not appear to make any difference to those (mostly teens) who imitate publicized suicides; instead, as evidenced in a series of replicated findings, what seems to matter is the *amount of publicity* devoted to the suicide story.

CONCLUSION

The practical lesson to be learned from all this is evident. Although suicide stories are not the only—and certainly not the most significant—cause of suicide, a series of replicated findings vindicate the judgment of Goethe's contemporaries: suicide stories do seem to elicit suicide. And the content analysis presented here suggests the tentative conclusion that—short of reducing the publicity accorded to these stories—there does not appear to be anything we can do to minimize their impact.

This last conclusion should be regarded as tentative for several reasons. The present analysis examined the effect of only 12 story characteristics, and it is possible that other characteristics may yet be found to enhance or diminish the effect of a story. This study was restricted to obvious characteristics, like the nationality of the publicized suicide. It is possible that subtle factors, like the intonation of a newscaster's voice, may have a demonstrable effect on the impact of a story. In this connection it is worth noting that laboratory research on imitative behavior suggests that a violent action is more likely to be imitated if it is presented as real, exciting, rewarded, and justified (Berkowitz and Rawlings 1963; Berkowitz and Geen 1966, 1967; Comstock 1977). The reporter's apparent attitude toward the suicide could influence its effect. An examination of this topic would be extremely valuable but difficult to conduct.

The present analysis examined the effect of one story characteristic at a time, rather than considering the impact of combinations of characteristics. It is possible that stories having some combination of characteristics might be unusually likely to trigger imitative action by teens, but this possibility could not be assessed in this study, because of the small sample of stories available.

At present, the statistical evidence identifies only one characteristic that distinguishes between influential and noninfluential suicide stories—the amount of publicity accorded to a suicide story. Future research should test this tentative conclusion, employ a larger sample of news stories, and cover a longer period of time. Such studies should shed more light on the differential effects of certain kinds of suicide stories.

In this chapter, we have noted several important gaps in the literature on imitative suicide. It may be valuable to list some other lacunae as well. Our review of the literature has focused entirely on the impact of nonfictional suicide stories presented through the mass media. This is because nearly all of the research on imitative suicide has concentrated on this type of suicidal model. Future research should also examine the influence of fictional stories, and indeed some work on the topic has already begun (Gould and Shaffer 1986; Schmidtke and Häfner 1986; Platt 1987; Phillips and Paight 1987). Using a sample of 31 deaths, Gould and Shaffer found an increase in New York City teen suicides after three television movies about suicide. Phillips and Paight examined a much larger sample ($n = 167$) in California and Pennsylvania, and found a slight drop in suicides after the same three television movies. This drop persisted even after Gould and Shaffer's New York City data were merged with the California and Pennsylvania data. Platt found a significant increase in attempted suicides in England after a soap opera character took an overdose of aspirin, but felt that his findings could be attributed most plausibly to factors other than imitation. Schmidtke and Häfner found a significant increase in suicides in Germany after a televised movie about suicide. In short, findings in this area are inconclusive, with some studies (Gould and Shaffer 1986; Schmidtke and Häfner 1986) uncovering evidence for an imitative effect and others (Platt 1987; Phillips and Paight 1987) failing to do so.

At present, almost all research has focused on the influence of models in the mass media. Future research should also examine the influence of suicidal models who are personally known to those at risk of suicide. Such personal models might include relatives, friends, and co-workers. After studies of these sorts have been completed, it may be possible to answer some important questions: which type of suicidal model has the greatest effect—one who is personally known or one who is known only through the mass media? One whose behavior is presented sympathetically or unsympathetically? Do fictional models have a smaller effect than nonfictional ones? Is a model most likely to affect persons who are exactly like her or him? Do prestigious models have a larger effect than ordinary ones? We are just at the beginning of understanding the imitation of suicidal behavior.

Although a great deal remains to be discovered, it is possible even now to draw some clinical implications from the available evidence. Many people, particularly teens, experience an increased risk of suicide just after mass media attention to this behavior. It may be possible for clinicians to reduce the risk by developing an increased sensitivity to the impact of suicidal role models. The impact seems to persist for at least a week after the death of the model. During this time, health professionals should be particularly alert for signs of suicide.

REFERENCES

Berkowitz L, Geen R: Film violence and the cue properties of available targets. J Pers Soc Psychol 3:525–530, 1966

Berkowitz L, Geen R: Stimulus qualities of the target of aggression: a further study. J Pers Soc Psychol 5:364–368, 1967

Berkowitz L, Rawlings E: Effects of film violence on inhibitions against subsequent aggression. Journal of Abnormal and Social Psychology 66:405–412, 1963

Blumenthal S, Bergner L: Suicide and newspapers: a replicated study. Am J Psychiatry 130:468–471, 1973

Bollen KA, Phillips DP: Suicidal motor vehicle fatalities in Detroit: a replication. American Journal of Sociology 87:404–412, 1981

Bollen KA, Phillips DP: Imitative suicides: a national study of the effects of television news stories. American Sociological Review 47:802–809, 1982

Comstock G: Types of portrayal and aggressive behavior. Journal of Communication 27:189–198, 1977

Crawford JP, Willis JH: Double suicide in psychiatric hospital patients. Br J Psychiatry 112:1231–1235, 1966

Gould MS, Shaffer D: The impact of suicide in television movies: evidence for imitation. N Engl J Med 315:690–694, 1986

Kreitman N, Smith P, Tan E: Attempted suicide in social networks. British Journal of Preventive and Social Medicine 23:116–123, 1969

Motto JA: Suicide and suggestibility. Am J Psychiatry 124:252–256, 1967

Phillips DP: The influence of suggestion on suicide: substantive and theoretical implications of the Werther effect. American Sociological Review 39:340–354, 1974

Phillips DP: Motor vehicle fatalities increase just after publicized suicide stories. Science 196:1464–1465, 1977

Phillips DP: Suicide, motor vehicle fatalities, and the mass media: evidence toward a theory of suggestion. American Journal of Sociology 84: 1150–1174, 1979

Phillips DP: Natural experiments on the effects of mass media violence on fatal aggression: strengths and weaknesses of a new approach. Advances in Experimental Social Psychology 19:207–250, 1986a

Phillips DP: The found experiment: a new technique for assessing the impact of mass media violence on real-world aggressive behavior. Public Communication and Behavior 1:259–307, 1986b

Phillips DP, Bollen KA: Same time, next year: selective data dredging for negative findings. American Sociological Review 50:364–371, 1985

Phillips DP, Carstensen LL: Clustering of teenage suicides after television news stories about suicide. N Engl J Med 315:685–689, 1986

Phillips DP, Paight DJ: The impact of televised movies about suicide: a replicative study. N Engl J Med 317:809–811, 1987

Platt S: The aftermath of Angie's overdose: is soap (opera) dangerous to your health? Br Med J 294:954–957, 1987

Schmidtke A, Häfner H: Die Vermittlung von Selbstmordmotivation und Selbstmordhandlung durch fiktive Modelle. Nervenarzt 57:502–510, 1986

Seiden RH: Suicide behavior contagion on a college campus, in Proceedings of the Fourth International Conference on Suicide Prevention. Edited by Farberow NL. Los Angeles, Delmaro, 1968

Stack S: Suggestion and suicide: aspects of differential identification in television news stories, 1969–1979. Unpublished paper presented at the annual meetings of the American Sociological Association, San Antonio, Texas, August 27–31, 1986

Stack S: Celebrities and suicides: a taxonomy and analysis. American Sociological Review 52:401–412, 1987

Wasserman I: Imitation and suicide: a reexamination of the Werther effect. American Sociological Review 49:427–436, 1984

Weiss E: The clinical significance of the anniversary reaction. General Practicioner 17:117–119, 1958

7

Do Televised Fictional Suicide Models Produce Suicides?

Heinz Häfner, M.D., Ph.D
Armin Schmidtke, M.D.

In the 1970s we began conducting epidemiological studies among suicide attempters to look for signs pointing to environmental factors that increase the risk of suicide. We were astonished to find that the frequency of attempted suicide varied markedly in both directions over short periods of time. This can be illustrated by the data taken from two studies carried out at the Central Institute of Mental Health in Mannheim, for the period 1966–1975 (Welz 1979) and for the period 1976–1985 (Schmidtke et al., in press). Both studies covered the whole city of Mannheim (in 1985 approximately 302,000 inhabitants) and registered all suicide attempts committed by Mannheim inhabitants who were receiving inpatient or outpatient care at a psychiatric hospital or the general hospital in Mannheim. Figure 1 shows a marked increase with a peak of 139/100,000 for males and 180/100,000 for females in 1976–1977 and a decrease thereafter.

The sizes of the increases depend on the periods compared. Because attempted suicides peaked in the various age groups in somewhat different years, it would have been misleading to compare the same periods for different age groups. For the 11-year period 1966–1977, a global increase of over 200% was calculated. The increase was the steepest for adolescents: for males 15–19 years of age it was approximately 340%, and for females of the same age group it was approximately 300%. In older age groups the increase was smaller. The rates for both sexes 65 years and older remained stable. By 1985, attempted suicides fell by 79% to 107/100,000 for males (15 years and older) and by 63% to 119/100,000 for females, compared with the maximum rates for 1976–1977. Similar trends in the frequency of attempted suicides, showing a maximum around the mid-1970s, have been reported by Wexler et al. (1978) for the United States, by Kreitman and Schreiber (1979) for Edinburgh, and by Schmidtke et al. (in press) for two other German cities.

Changes of considerable magnitude in the frequency of a deviant behavior occurring within particularly short periods of time provide indications of effects emanating from changes in environmental factors over time, which constitute a classic period effect. If both trends, increases and decreases, become continuously smaller in older age groups, the period effect is modified by an age-group effect. Thus, we set

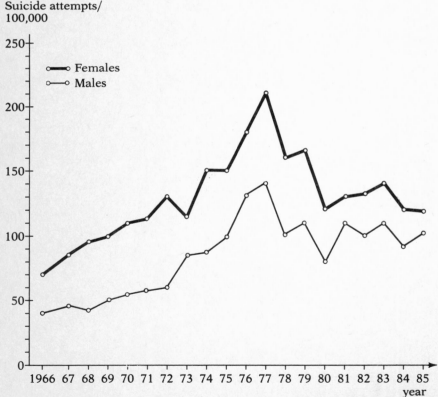

Figure 1.   Trends in suicide attempts in Mannheim (1966–1985) for males and females. (Sources of data: Welz 1979; Schmidtke et al., in press.)

out to look for relevant events that precede suicidal behavior and to which a large number of individuals at risk are exposed in an approximately equal way.

One of the longest discussed but never conclusively proven hypotheses suggests that suicidal behavior might be acquired by learning from models. It has been frequently suggested that real suicides or descriptions of suicides might have a suggestive effect on persons at risk. Early references are to be found in stories of suicide epidemics in antiquity, such as the mass suicide of Milesian virgins and the besieged defenders of Masada. There are other early references to the imitation hypothesis in the scientific literature. William Farr, who is famous for his contributions to the ecology of cholera (Farr 1852), wrote in 1841: "No fact is better established in science than that suicide (and murder perhaps may be added) is often committed from imitation" (Phelps 1911). If this were the case, the enormous expansion in the availability of suicide and violence models owing to the modern mass media should lead to unwanted side effects in the form of increasing suicide rates. Indeed, the growing expansion of daily newspapers and their sensational reporting on crime, violence, and suicide at the beginning of this century gave cause for concern, at least among experts. In 1910, the "Wiener Psychoanalytisher Verein" (the Viennese Psychoanalytical Society) organized a symposium on suicide among schoolchildren and stressed the suggestive power of suicide models in newspaper reports (Unus Multorum 1910). In 1911, a Commission of the American Academy of Medicine and the American Medical Association dealt with the suggestive effect of newspaper reports on suicide (Hemenway 1911; Phelps 1911; Rost 1912). This period, however, did not bring forth any empirical studies of sufficient methodological rigor, although some kind of agreement with journalists was reached not to report intensively on suicidal acts in newspapers.

Thereafter the topic seems largely to have fallen into oblivion. It was not until the tremendous expansion of television that the topic became of interest anew (Ringel et al. 1955; Cermak 1972; Blumenthal and Bergner 1973). Several authors have proposed that suicides committed with parathion and the increase in spectacular self-burning in the 1960s were induced by reports on such cases in the mass media (Dahm and Händel 1970; Henseler 1975; Grosby et al. 1977; Ashton and Donnan 1981). Suicide epidemics reported from certain units of the armed forces (Hankoff 1961), classes of schoolchildren (Popow 1911; Ringel et al. 1955; Harbauer 1978), groups of adolescents (Robbins and Conroy 1983; Doan 1984; Rubinstein 1983; Fox et al. 1984; Taylor 1984), and from institutions, such as hospitals (Offer and Barglow 1960; Crawford and Willis 1966; Kayton and Freed 1967; Matthews 1968; Olin

1980; Rada and James 1982; Walsh and Rosen 1985), reservations (Ward and Fox 1985), or ethnic groups (Rubinstein 1983) have been classified as analogous phenomena of learning by modeling. The imitation hypothesis has also been used to explain suicides committed on anniversary days in the manner of the suicides of reference persons. Seiden and Spence (1982) employed the imitation hypothesis even in explaining the higher frequency of suicides on the Golden Gate Bridge compared with other similar bridges in the San Francisco area.

Since the 1960s, increasing efforts have been made to prove the imitation hypothesis in empirical studies. The approaches that can be used in such studies are of two types: 1) a retrodirected design, which proceeds from individuals who have committed or attempted suicide and looks for suicide models whom these individuals have been exposed to in the recent past; and 2) a prodirected design, not necessarily a prospective assessment, which proceeds from models of suicidal behavior and tries to assess their effects on individuals at risk or on the frequency of suicide or attempted suicide in the population exposed to the observation of the model. Both designs have so far been applied in observation studies, especially because an experimental approach is not possible and quasi-experimental conditions have not been available (Figure 1).

RETRODIRECTED STUDIES

Several authors have reported an increased frequency of suicidal behavior in the social network of persons with suicidal behavior. Individuals who had committed or attempted suicide in short periods of time preceding the index cases were defined as models (e.g., Murphy et al. 1969; Dahm and Händel 1970; Flinn and Leonhard 1972; Lindsay and Nathan 1974; Holinger 1977; Heer and Städeli 1979; Henderson and Lance 1979; Murphy and Wetzel 1982; Pettifor et al. 1983; Roy 1983a, 1983b). These models seem to possess some predictive validity irrespective of the diagnosis of the suicide population (Pfeffer et al. 1983; Roy 1983b). Robbins and Conroy (1983) and other authors assume that models of suicidal behavior have a suggestive effect mainly on relatives, close friends, and probably also on fellow inmates of institutions (Beichl 1965; Stutte and Stutte 1967; von Schlieffen 1969; Diekstra 1974; Wellhöfer 1975; Harbauer 1978; Schier 1980; Pöldinger 1984). Diekstra (1974), conducting a study among 109 suicide attempters from a total of 580 psychiatric inpatients, attempted to assess the role social learning plays in the risk of suicide. He found that suicidal behavior of an important reference person in the close environment was one of four predicting behavioral indices and stressed that suicidal behavior "is a response learned directly (by practice) or vicariously (by observation) to certain stimuli or situations" (Diekstra 1974, p. 63).

Only a few controlled studies of the familial and social environment of persons who committed suicide or attempted suicide have so far been carried out. They have demonstrated that suicide models are more frequent among the suicide attempters than in the general population. One of the most sophisticated studies is that of Kreitman et al. (1969, 1970). The authors examined closer relatives and friends of 135 suicide attempters in Edinburgh. The frequency of suicidal behavior in this group ($n = 578$) was four times higher (17) than expected (4.23). Murphy and Wetzel (1982) found equally high frequencies of suicide models in the families of suicide attempters (38%). In our attempts to test the imitation hypothesis, we too carried out a controlled retrospective study starting from a representative sample of 103 suicide attempters in Mannheim (Welz and Häfner 1984). Evaluating the data of a pilot study, we found more persons who had committed a suicidal act in the previous 2 weeks in the overall social networks of persons with less serious suicidal acts compared to individuals with serious attempts and normal controls (Häfner and Welz 1980). This finding seemed to support our hypothesis. In the main study, however, the difference disappeared when allowance was made for the network size.

As Table 1 shows, in the final evaluation, the percentage of network members with a lifetime suicidal act was equal for both suicide attempters and controls, matched on age, sex, and residential area. The high proportion, that is, two-thirds, of individuals who know at least one person with suicidal behavior in their social environment in both groups shows that we are dealing with a common phenomenon. This does not make the proof of imitation effects easier. We also examined the assumption that suicide attempters might have contacts with network members who have committed suicidal acts more recently or in closer spatial contexts compared with controls. Both comparisons shown in Tables 2 and 3 did not reveal any significant differences in favor of the hypothesis. An unexpected difference emerged when the numbers of persons with suicidal acts in the closer and wider social

Table 1. Percentage of Persons with Any Reported Suicidal Acts Within the Social Network of Suicide Attempters

Number of network members with any reported suicidal acts	Suicide attempters ($n = 103$)	Controls ($n = 103$)
0	34%	33%
1 or more	66%	67%

Note. Source: Welz and Häfner 1984, pp. 63–76.

Table 2. Proximity in Time of the Index Suicidal Act and the Next Reported Suicidal Act of Any Person in the Social Network of Suicide Attempters

Period of time between the latest suicidal act within the social network and the index attempt	Suicide attempters (n = 103)	Controls (n = 103)	
Up to 1 year	11.7%	18.7%	NS
1–5 years	29.4%	28.7%	NS
More than 5 years	58.9%	52.5%	NS

Note. Reprinted with permission from Welz R, Häfner H: Imitation und Kontagiosität bei Selbstmordhandlungen, in Bestandsaufnahme der Suizidforschung. Edited by Welz R, Möller HJ. Regensburg, Roderer, 1984, pp. 63–76.

Table 3. Proximity in Distance of the Suicide Attempter and the Nearest Person with Any Reported Suicidal Acts Within the Social Network

Proximity in distance	Suicide attempters	Controls	
Neighborhood	49.3%	36.8%	NS
More distant than neighborhood	50.7%	63.2%	NS

Note. Reprinted with permission from Welz R, Häfner H: Imitation und Kontagiosität bei Selbstmordhandlungen, in Bestandsaufnahme der Suizidforschung. Edited by Welz R, Möller HJ. Regensburg, Roderer, 1984, pp. 63–76.

Table 4. Percentage of Persons with Any Reported Suicidal Acts in the Kin and Non-Kin Networks of Suicide Attempters

Number of network members with any reported suicidal acts	Kin (family)		Non-kin network	
	Suicide attempters	Controls	Suicide attempters	Controls
0	52%	72%	57%	43%
1 or more	48%	28%	43%	57%
	$p<.01$		$p<.01$	
	(Mann-Whitney U test)			

Note. Reprinted with permission from Welz R, Häfner H: Imitation und Kontagiosität bei Selbstmordhandlungen, in Bestandsaufnahme der Suizidforschung. Edited by Welz R, Möller HJ. Regensburg, Roderer, 1984, pp 63–76.

networks were compared. As shown in Table 4, contrary to our hypothesis and the findings of other authors, we observed a smaller number of individuals with suicidal behavior (43%) in the wider social network of the experimental group compared with the matched control group (57%). This unexpected finding could again be attributed to the larger number of persons in the wider social network of the control group (Welz and Häfner 1984). In line with the hypothesis, the proportion of persons who had ever attempted suicide was significantly higher in the closer social network of the experimental group than in the kinship of the control group (48% versus 28%), as shown by other controlled studies. But this does not yet prove the hypothesis conclusively.

A higher frequency of suicidal behavior among family members of suicide attempters may also be attributed to a genetic transmission of diseases carrying an increased risk (e.g., affective disorders) or to other predisposing or precipitating factors that are in familial covariation with the risk of suicide. For example, suicides of close family members have been discussed as leading to psychological distress and thus contributing to reactive depressions or precipitating suicidal behavior in other family members. The whole family or the wider social group under study may also be subject to the same risk factors or stressors, such as alcohol problems or unemployment.

All retrodirected similar studies so far conducted have failed to evaluate the relevant alternative explanations of the imitation hypothesis, such as genetic transmission, common exposure to certain risk factors, or the existence of a particular subcultural or familial coping style in the social networks of the individuals under study. All these factors may partly or wholly explain the elevated risk of suicide, as Kreitman et al. (1970) and Phillips and Carstensen (1986) point out. Alternative hypotheses also provide for more plausible explanations of the historical mass suicides committed to escape slavery, rape, or torture, which were described by Singer (1980a, 1980b) and Stepien (1980), than does the imitation hypothesis. Indeed, it is not possible to exclude all the relevant alternative explanations in a retrodirected design of the type described.

PRODIRECTED STUDIES

A direct examination of the imitation hypothesis is possible only in studies proceeding from the model event. In this context a distinction must be made between reports on real suicidal behavior and fictional suicide models presented in the mass media. For quantitative reasons and probably also because of the attractiveness of suicide models shown on television, the majority of which are fictional, these probably are of a far greater importance than directly observed suicidal behavior.

Effects of Reporting on Suicidal Behavior

As to studies on the effects of reporting on suicidal behavior, two studies conducted by Motto (1967, 1970) and that of Blumenthal and Bergner (1973) on changes in suicide frequencies after newspaper strikes can be mentioned. Most of the research on this topic has been conducted by Phillips and his group, who have investigated the effects of front-page newspaper stories and televised suicide reports in the United States and Great Britain. The increases were larger for those events receiving more publicity. The results, consistently showing increases in suicide rates and in some cases also in fatal automobile accidents in the first days after the reporting in the areas concerned, have been criticized by several authors (Wasserman 1984; Altheide 1981; Kessler and Stipp 1984; Baron and Reiss 1985b). Some of Phillips's findings proved untenable, but the positive relationship between the amount of publicity of the suicide reports and the size of the effect persisted. The latest study by Phillips and Carstensen (1986) on the effects of television reports or feature stories about suicide on adolescents in the United States between 1973 and 1979 takes into account part of the criticism. The study revealed significant increases in the nationwide suicide rates within 7 days after the reporting. The increases were approximately 7.5% (1,555 expected and 1,666 observed). This effect was independent of period effects. The increase was higher if more television networks reported on a suicide.

Effects of Fictional Suicidal Behavior

For more than 200 years the imitation of fictional suicide models has been known as the *Werther effect* (Phillips 1974, 1985). In 1774, Johann Wolfgang von Goethe, the leading German poet and writer of the eighteenth and nineteenth centuries, published his novel *The Sorrows of Young Werther*, whose hero shot himself after a sentimental, unhopeful love affair. In Goethe's own words the novel made "a great, well an immense impact." The imitation hypothesis was supported at another level in an impressive way: Werther's clothing (blue tailcoat with brass buttons, yellow vest, yellow breeches, brown turndown boots, felt hat, and loose, unpowdered hair), which Goethe had described so vividly, became the gentlemen's fashion of the last quarter of the eighteenth century and was known as the "Werther dress."

The term *Werther effect*, however, is not derived from gentlemen's fashions, but from the widespread impression that Goethe's novel led to an increase in suicides of the same type, that is, shooting with a pistol. This impression was so strong that authorities in Copenhagen, Saxony (Leipzig), and Milan banned the book. The question of whether the model of Werther had actually caused suicides to increase remained unanswered. Emil Durkheim (1897) believed that the fictional model in Goethe's novel had only precipitated suicides already planned and not increased their absolute numbers.

Television as a mass medium has again made the Werther effect of topical interest. In this medium, attractive models of suicidal behavior, portrayed in a realistic manner by sometimes avoiding the deterring impressions of suffering and dying, are presented to a great number of individuals, who may be susceptible to suicide, in the privacy of their own homes.

Only a few studies have yet investigated the effects of fictional suicides. Ostroff et al. (1985) reported increased hospital admissions of adolescent suicide attempters, compared with a similar time period of the preceding year, in 2 weeks after the broadcast of a television film showing the effect the suicide of a young couple had on their parents. In London, Ellis and Walsh (1986) observed the effects of the soap opera *East Enders*, in which the character Angie took an overdose. In the week after the broadcast, 22 patients with an overdose were admitted to the local emergency department. The average for the 10 preceding weeks had been 6.9, and for the 10 preceding years the average had been 6.7 per week. A similar effect was observed in two other English cities by Sandler et al. (1986) and Fowler (1986), and no effect was observed in another city (Daniels 1986). Recently, Platt (1987a, 1987b) extended the Ellis and Walsh study of attempted suicides committed in the wake of the two broadcasts of *East Enders* to 63 English hospitals. He could not confirm the significant increase observed by Ellis and Walsh.

Phillips (1982) investigated the impact on white Americans of 13 white suicide models in soap operas that were broadcast by United States television networks in 1977. In the second half of the following week, significantly more suicides occurred than were expected on the basis of the preceding period and the time trend. The number of car accidents with people who were severely injured (this could be controlled for California only) or killed also rose.

Gould and Shaffer (1986) studied the suicide rates for New York and the number of attempted suicides admitted to six hospitals in the New York area 2 weeks before and after the broadcast of four television movies showing suicide models between October 1984 and February 1985. The mean number of attempts in the 2-week period after the broadcasts for teenagers, aged 19 or younger, was significantly greater than the mean number before (22 versus 14, $p < .5$). Completed suicides also showed a significant excess after three of the movies compared with the number expected (13 versus 7.44, $p < .05$). To sum up, most of the studies referred to have revealed significant increases in suicidal acts shortly after the showing of a fictional suicide model. This finding, however, is not fully consistent. All the studies so far conducted show at least some methodological shortcomings.

METHODOLOGICAL PREREQUISITES FOR TESTING THE IMITATION HYPOTHESIS

The proof of a causal relationship between suicide models and increased suicidal behavior in exposed individuals is faced with several difficulties. This is illustrated by the problems posed by the operationalization of the outcome variable "suicide frequency." Studies on this topic are usually based on 1) public statistics on causes of death, 2) hospital admissions for attempted suicide, and 3) statistics on accidents. Public statistics usually comprise only completed suicides according to a few categories of method and these are often aggregated over time periods. In addition, it is presumed that between the suicidal act, which alone is of interest in this context, and the time of death (as far as it is at all precisely recorded), there can be unknown time lags of several days, so for example in the case of intoxications and injuries. Such time lags can level down a short-term increase. For the testing of the imitation hypothesis, however, data on attempted suicides are equally important and, with respect to certain methods like overdosing of medications, even decisive. In the case of hospital admissions, which provide fairly exact data on time and method, it is difficult to guarantee the representativeness of the suicide attempters under study for large populations. Therefore, it is also difficult to obtain sufficiently reliable data for comparisons over several time periods before and after exposure.

In the following, and also illustrated in Figure 2, we have tried to sum up briefly the main requirements for valid testing of the imitation hypothesis:

I. Assessment
   A. Independent variable (model): The method used, time of exposure of the suicidal act, and the main characteristics of the model must be determined exactly (which is an easy task in the case of television movies, but hardly possible in the case of books).
   B. Outcome variable (observer)
      1. The population exposed to the observation of the model must be large enough and clearly defined. Also the proportion of individuals exposed in the total population by age and sex should be known in order to be able to compare age- and sex-specific effects of more than one event and over time periods.
      2. The method, time of suicidal act, and the main characteristics of individuals who commit suicidal acts must be determined clearly for sufficiently long periods of time before and after.

ASSESSMENT OF DESIGN VARIABLES:

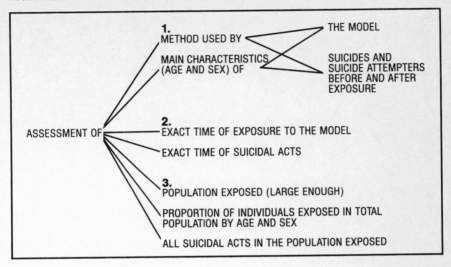

DESIGN:

| 1. PRODIRECTED DESIGN | STARTING FROM THE MODEL EVENT WITH A SUFFICIENT NUMBER OF CONTROL PERIODS BEFORE AND AFTER EXPOSURE |
| 2. QUASI-EXPERIMENTAL DESIGN | TO STUDY THE EFFECT AT REPEATED EXPOSURE UNDER DIFFERENT CIRCUMSTANCES |

THEORETICAL BASIS:

1. MAIN HYPOTHESES BASED ON BASIC-RESEARCH FINDINGS ON LEARNING BY MODELING

2. TESTING OF RELEVANT ALTERNATIVE HYPOTHESES

Figure 2. Some requirements for studies on the imitation of suicide models.

II. Design
   A. Prodirectional design starting from the model event and including a sufficient number of control periods before and after exposure.
   B. Quasi-experimental design with an opportunity of testing the effect after repeated exposure to the same model under changed conditions to rule out chance effects.

III. Theoretical basis
    A. The hypotheses tested should be based on the results of basic research on learning by modeling.
    B. Alternative hypotheses must be included in the design (trends over time; covariation with other relevant variables; increased referral to hospital; increased sensitivity to the type of suicidal behavior or risk groups mediated by the model; mediation of a suicide method or precipitation of suicidal acts that would be committed anyway, while long-term suicide figures remain unchanged).

THE CONCEPTUAL FRAMEWORK: LEARNING BY MODELING

Learning by modeling refers to the acquisition of new patterns of behavior by observation without a necessary reinforcement (Bandura 1976). The original paradigm of learning by modeling has been extended to comprise differing ways of perceiving the model, of which the degree of reality may vary, too (Bandura 1977). In experiments, the effect of modeling depends on the number of models; the characteristics of the model, such as age, sex, and social status; the degree to which the behavior of the model is reinforced; and the characteristics of the observer. Similarity between certain characteristics of the model and those of the observer increases the effects of learning from symbolic models (Bandura 1977). In psychotherapy it also seems to be important whether a coping or a mastery model is available to the patient (Meichenbaum 1971).

Learning by modeling is thus to be regarded as a function of the variable of both the model and the learner. It is also influenced by complex variables like self-esteem, which may moderate the probability of performance, that is, of using the learned behavior. Under specific circumstances, as in motivational states, a behavioral pattern learned from a model, but meanwhile latent, may be reactivated after some time (Michaelis 1976; Zumkley 1980). Stimulating events or motivating factors determine then whether the responses acquired by observation are actually performed at a later time (Bandura 1976, 1977; Groffman 1982). Applied to the imitation of fictional models, this means that the size of the effect upon the degree of similarity between the characteristics of the model and those of the observers must be examined. It is usually impossible to obtain information on predisposing personality or situational variables for the large numbers required for the testing of a hypothesis. But such information is necessary for the assessment of individual risks and the identification of risk groups. Also the assumption of a time lag, that is, the possibility that the effect of a suicide model might be reactivated by secondary factors, is worth examining.

THE STUDY

A six-episode television movie, broadcast twice by one of the two nation-wide television networks in Germany (ZDF) in 1981 and 1982, gave us a unique opportunity to fulfill all the above-mentioned methodological requirements more or less adequately and to apply a quasi-experimental design (Schmidtke and Häfner 1986, in press; Häfner and Schmidtke 1987). At the beginning of each episode, it was shown how a train slows down, the dead body of a student is found, and police investigations begin. Episodes two through six began by showing the 18- or 19-year-old student on his way to the rails in a mood of resignation, determined to let himself be run over by a train. After this initial scene, each episode showed, partly mirrored by the police investigations, one particular aspect of the student's life leading up to the suicide, as seen by the student himself, his parents, fellow students, teachers, and girlfriend. The movie has received several awards because of its outstanding aesthetic quality.

The movie was rebroadcast 1.5 years later, in 1982. By using this natural experiment, we were able to test repeated imitation effects in suicidal behavior, especially in relation to the size and the characteristics of both audiences.

Materials and Methods

Design. The movie was first broadcast in January and February 1981 on six successive Sunday evenings (January 18 and 25; February 1, 8, 15, and 22; each time at 8:15 P.M.). The second broadcast took place in October and November 1982 (October 24 and 31; November 7, 14, 17, and 21; Sundays at 4 P.M.). For obtaining a natural "ABABA-design" (A = baseline phase; B = intervening phase) we selected time periods before and after the transmission for a total period from January 1, 1976, to December 31, 1984, with an A-phase of about 1.5 years between the two broadcasts. This is shown in Figure 3. In addition, control time periods were included. We used various age and sex groups differing in their proximity to the age and sex of the model. In order not to overlook effects persisting over a longer time period, we chose time periods of differing lengths following the broadcasts, including the 5 weeks between the first and the last episode. The results presented here are based on a time period that began 2 hours after the broadcasting of the first episode and ended 70 days later (including March 29, 1981). Thus, the

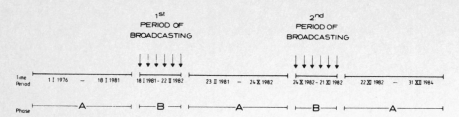

Figure 3. Study design: natural "ABABA" (A = baseline phase; B = intervening phase).

period studied after the last of the six episodes was 6 weeks or 35 days for both broadcasts. At the second broadcast (1982) the time span between the first and the last episode, but not the period afterwards, was shorter, as one of the episodes was broadcast on public holiday (Wednesday). The total period for which data on suicides were collected and compared thus had a length of 68 days. To control for long-term trends and seasonal and other covariations, we used analogous time periods in the years 1976–1984. We also used the periods immediately before the first episode at both broadcasts.

Model variables. The model variables were the method of suicide (be run over by a train), age (18 or 19 years), and sex (male). We were not able to assess socioeconomic status because of the strict data protection regulations in the Federal Republic of Germany. We collected information on all suicides and attempted suicides that had occurred on the entire German railway network (the Deutsche Bundesbahn) over the period January 1, 1976, to December 31, 1984. Suicides committed over the entire period under study were recorded exactly by the date and the hour. Problems of assessing attempted suicides and dating suicidal acts precisely did not arise, because all events on the railways were recorded precisely, and 92% of all the suicide attempts in the 9-year period under study ended lethally.

Methodology. To test differences in the suicide figures for each time period, parametric and nonparametric tests of significance were performed. To control for the effects of trends over time, Box-Jenkins univariate time-series analyses were performed. To test for the stationarity of the time series, the variances were used as a benchmark. The degree of differencing that was chosen was one that yielded the lowest variance of the time series (with a corresponding decrease, in order to avoid over-differencing). The test for serial dependencies of the time series on the values of the different groups were then performed with the original values or the residuals, depending on the degree of differencing.

Results

The evaluation of time-related data collected for various age groups and periods studied revealed an increase in the frequency of suicides for the age and sex groups similar to the model in the relevant time periods. This is shown in Figure 4.

In order to use an age grouping comparable with that used for the audience, 15- to 19-year-old males were used for the first age group. During the observation period of 70 days after the first broadcast, there were 62 suicides. The mean value for the remaining years studied was 33.25 ± 6.50, which amounted to an increase of some 29 suicides (86%). An increase of the same magnitude was obtained when the 62 suicides were compared with the mean of the year before and the year

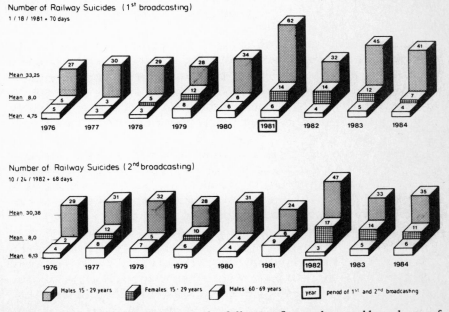

Figure 4. Number of railway suicides following first and second broadcasts of television movie. (Reprinted with permission from Schmidtke A, Häfner H: Die Vermittlung von Selbstmordmotivation und Selbstmordhandlung durch fiktive Modelle. Nervenarzt 57:502–510, 1986. Copyright 1986, Springer-Verlag.)

after the broadcast. For females of the same age, 14 suicides were found, amounting to a considerably lower increase of 6 suicides (75%) compared with the mean of the remaining years (8 ± 4.07) and of 4 compared with the same time period in the preceding and the following year. For males and females aged 15–29 years, the total increase in railway suicides was 33–35, depending on the method of calculation, in the time period of 70 days during and after the first broadcast of the movie.

When further differentiations were made, the effect was observed to be the strongest among males 15–19 years of age. This was the group most similar to the model in age and sex. Compared with the mean (7.63) of the same time periods in the remaining years, 21 ± 2.92 suicides occurred in the 70 days during and after the first broadcast of the suicide model, corresponding to an increase of 175%. Compared with the corresponding time periods in the preceding and the following year, the increase was 147%. For girls 15–19 years of age, the effect was slightly weaker: 6 suicides occurred, amounting to an increase of 167%, when compared with the figure expected, that is, 2.25 ± 1.98, the mean of all the corresponding control periods.

In age groups less similar to the model, the effect leveled off. Among males aged 30–39 years, suicides increased by 6 only, when compared with the mean of the remaining years, and by 10, when compared with the preceding and the following year. Among 40- to 49-year-old males, the small increase of suicides did not reach the standard deviation of the expected figure. For females, no increase could be observed in the age group of 30–39 years (7 suicides observed; 7.5 expected). In higher age groups of both sexes, especially in the age group of 60- to 69-year-olds, we did not observe any effect of the suicide movie.

The effects of the second broadcast were weaker than those of the first, but they still led to significantly higher suicide figures than expected. The number of suicides for males 15–29 years of age showed an increase of 54% (47 suicides observed; 30.38 expected). Compared with the time periods immediately before and after the broadcast, the increase was 61%. Females of the same age group showed a similar trend (an increase of 113%). As at the first broadcast, the effect was strongest in young males 15–19 years of age, the group most similar to the model: 18 suicides observed, compared with 8.4 expected, equaling an increase of 115%. Neither for other male age groups nor for females were such clear-cut effects found.

A striking finding was that suicides continued to increase for a longer period of time after the broadcast of the model than indicated in Phillips's studies, and longest in the group most similar to the model. As shown in Figure 5, suicides per week after the first broadcast of the movie are compared between the group most similar to the model and the group next similar to the model. Suicides in the group of 15- to 19-year-old males start to rise immediately after the first episode and persist with slight fluctuations above the figures expected for 16 weeks. In

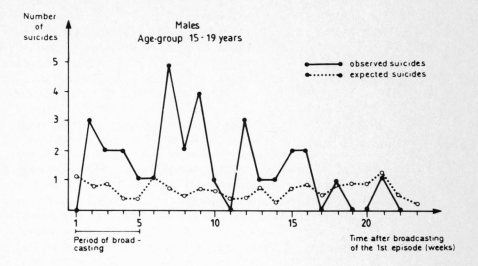

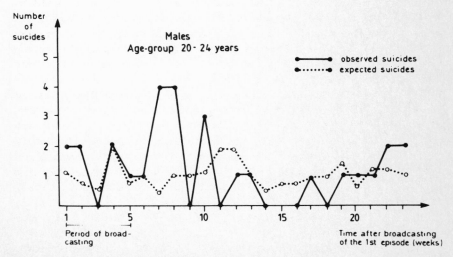

Figure 5. Suicides per week after broadcast of the first episode. (Source: Schmidtke and Häfner 1987.)

the group of 20- to 24-year-old males, which was less similar to the model, suicides ceased to increase after the 10th week. After the second broadcast, the increased suicide rate of the 15- to 29-year-old males kept declining slowly over the entire following year.

When the increases in the suicides of males 15–29 years of age in the period of the first and the second broadcast were compared with the audience figures, the ratio of the increases approximately corresponded to the ratio of the sizes of audience accounted for by the comparable age group of 14–29 years in the two periods of broadcast (on an average, 19% versus 8.85% of this age group). This is shown in Figure 6.

To control for time trends and seasonal and other covariations, we used time-series analysis. The various time periods were regarded as successive time-related measurements, standardized by the day on account of the differing lengths of the time periods studied. When the two experimental periods and the two immediately preceding and following control periods were considered, a total of 36 data were obtained for the whole period. Although the number of points of measurement used was lower than the number usually required, the procedure allowed us to make at least a rough estimate. However, neither did the autocorrelations, nor did the partial autocorrelations of the original values (no differencing) indicate a special ARIMA model (0,0,0-model). The differences, too, yielded higher variances after the first differencing (for example, for males aged 15–29, 1.69 to 3.63). Therefore, both serial dependencies of the data and trends over time could be ruled out for the relevant age groups. According to the procedure applied, the best estimate of a suicide figure in a specific time period would be equal to the average value of all time periods. The effect the movie had on the age group of 15- to 29-year-old males, that is, the group most similar to the model, is shown most clearly in Figure 7 when all of the time periods are considered simultaneously.

Of all the time periods studied (and this could still be demonstrated when further control periods were included), the "experimental" period during and after the first broadcast occupied rank 1, and the "experimental" period of the second broadcast occupied rank 2. The third rank was occupied by the first control period, starting at the end of the second experimental period.

Discussion

Durkheim's assumption (1897) that imitation only precipitates suicides that have already been planned, can be refuted as an alternative explanation, as already demonstrated by Phillips (1974), Phillips and Carstensen (1986), and our data. The decrease in suicides that should occur after a certain period of time following the suicides "brought forward" did not take place; rather a slowly decreasing trend of increase could be observed.

To forestall the objection that the model had only mediated the method for those individuals who were already determined to commit suicide by some other method, we examined the frequencies of suicides by other "hard" methods (hanging or jumping from a high place) in the relevant age groups during the observation period. The results did not

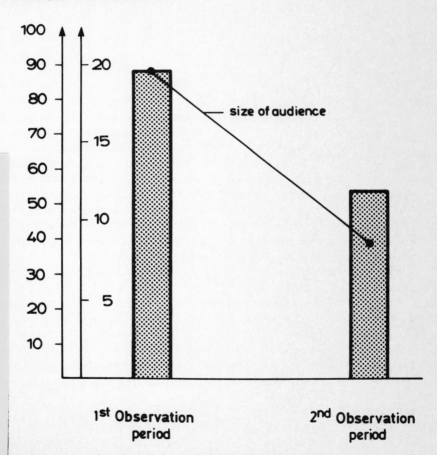

ure 6. Ratios of the increases in railway suicides among 15- to 29-year-olds
he observation periods at the first and the second broadcasts and ratios of the
s of audience (14- to 29-year-olds).

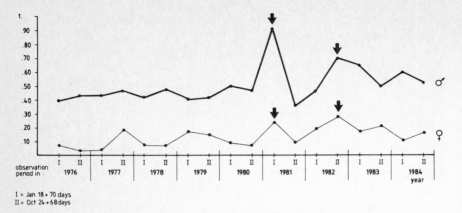

Figure 7. Daily average of suicides for males and females 15 to 29 years of age in time periods corresponding to the observation periods at the first and second broadcasts, 1976–1984.

support the alternative hypothesis. Suicides by the other two hard methods did not decrease while railway suicides increased in the two periods of broadcast; in contrast, they increased slightly, but nonsignificantly in the relevant age groups. Had the model in fact only mediated the method to persons who otherwise would have chosen a soft method, which is very unlikely, the overall frequency of suicidal behavior would have remained unchanged. The increased use of a highly lethal method, however, would have caused the number of deaths from suicide to rise, even if the number of attempted suicides had remained unchanged (Schmidtke and Häfner 1986, 1987, in press).

The repeated broadcast of a clearly defined suicide model with a well identifiable model variable and the collection of complete and precise nationwide data on the modeling effect over a period of sufficient length enabled us to assess the imitation effect with some experimental rigor. The findings show that the maximum of a significant increase in suicides occurred in the age and sex group of the model. The increase was lower if there was a greater difference from the model in terms of age and sex. The results support the results of laboratory research showing that imitation effects depend on the similarity of the variables of the model to those of the imitator.

Compared with the findings of the studies so far published (Phillips 1978, 1980, 1982; Gould and Shaffer 1986; Phillips and Carstensen 1986), our findings seem to suggest that the imitation effect probably persists much longer than a number of days after the perception of a model. After the second broadcast the increase fell particularly slowly, so that the mean figures for the age group at maximum risk remained slightly elevated well into the following year.

In view of the methodology and design used in the study, the objection that the observed increase in the suicide figures could result from artifacts, for example an increased classification of ambiguous cases of death as suicides (Phillips 1974) or a referral bias (Gould and Shaffer 1986), is irrelevant. Also, the point raised by Baron and Reiss (1985a) that differing suicide frequencies on different days of the week, months, and seasons of the year might lead to model effects, could be ruled out by choosing analogous control periods and by performing time-series analyses yielding an increasing long-term trend neither for the total group nor for special age or sex groups.

This study suggesting the role that fictional models can play in the precipitation of suicide has identified an important risk factor. In view of the predominantly unsuccessful attempts to prevent suicide in the past, it should be seriously considered whether this aspect could provide an opportunity of effective prevention.

Of course, some important questions still remain unanswered. For example, what makes suicide models so attractive to persons at risk that they overcome the instinct of self-preservation and are led to suicide, or what characteristics, besides age and sex, make individuals susceptible to the provocation of suicidal acts by suicide models?

Also, a more comprehensive question of some practical importance arises. Could the increase in suicide rates in the younger age groups, which has been observed for some decades now in several industrial countries such as for the United States (Murphy and Wetzel 1980), Canada (Solomon and Hellon 1980), Australia (Goldney and Katsikitis 1983), the Federal Republic of Germany (Häfner and Schmidtke 1985), and Switzerland (Häfner and Schmidtke 1985) from about 1950–1960 onwards, have something to do with the expansion of the mass media and their increasing tolerance of attractive models of destructive and autodestructive behavior in the same period of time?

REFERENCES

Altheide DL: Airplane accidents, murder, and the mass media: comment on Phillips. Social Forces 60:593–596, 1981

Ashton JR, Donnan S: Suicide by burning as an epidemic phenomenon: an analysis of 82 deaths and inquests in England and Wales in 1978–1979. Psychol Med 11:735–739, 1981

Bandura A: Lernen am Modell. Stuttgart, Klett, 1976

Bandura A: Self-efficacy: towards a unifying theory of behavioral change. Psychol Rev 84:191–215, 1977

Baron JN, Reiss PC: Same time, next year: aggregate analyses of the mass media and violent behavior. American Sociological Review 50:347–363, 1985a

Baron JN, Reiss PC: Reply to Phillips and Bollen. American Sociological Review 50:372–376, 1985b

Beichl L: Uber Selbstmordhäufung in einer Familie. Wien Klin Wochenschr 77:727–728, 1965

Blumenthal S, Bergner L: Suicide and newspapers: a replicated study. Am J Psychiatry 130:468–471, 1973

Cermak I: Suizid und Suizidversuch. Praxis der Psychotherapie 17:66–71, 1972

Crawford JP, Willis JH: Double suicide in psychiatric hospital patients. Br J Psychiatry 112:1231–1235, 1966

Dahm K, Händel K: Untersuchungen uber Selbstmorde und Selbstmordversuche in einem landlichen Bevolkerungsgebiet. Materia Medica Norkmark 63, 1970

Daniels RG: Emotional crises imitating television (letter). Lancet 1:856, 1986

Diekstra RFW: A social learning approach to the prediction of suicidal behavior, in Proceedings of the 7th International Conference for Suicide Prevention, Amsterdam, August 27–30, 1973. Edited by Speyer N, Diekstra RFW, van de Loo KJM. Amsterdam, Swets and Zeitlinger, 1974, pp 55–66

Doan M: As "cluster suicides" take toll of teenagers. U.S. News and World Report 97:49–50, November 12, 1984

Durkheim E: Le Suicide: Etude de sociologie. Paris, Alcan, 1897. Translated into German under the title Der Selbstmord. Neuwied, Luchterhand, 1973

Ellis SJ, Walsh S: Soap may seriously damage your health. Lancet 1:686, 1986

Farr W: Report on the mortality of cholera in England in 1848–49. London, H.M.S.O., 1852

Flinn DE, Leonhard CV: Prevalence of suicidal ideation and behavior among basic trainees and college students. Milit Med 137:317–320, 1972

Fowler BP: Emotional crisis imitating television (letter). Lancet 1:1036–1037, 1986

Fox J, Manitowabi D, Ward J: An Indian community with a high suicide rate—5 years after. Can J Psychiatry 29:425–427, 1984

Goldney RD, Katsikitis M: Cohort analysis of suicide rates in Australia. Arch Gen Psychiatry 40:71–74, 1983

Gould MS, Shaffer D: The impact of suicide in television movies. N Engl J Med 315:690–694, 1986

Groffman KM: Lernen am Modell—Experimente und Theorien, in Orientierungen zum padagogischen Handeln. Edited by Seidel G. Gottingen, Hogrefe, 1982, pp 51–71

Grosby K, Rhoe JD, Holland J: Suicide by fire: a contemporary method of political protest. Int J Soc Psychiatry 23:60–69, 1977

Häfner H, Schmidtke A: Do cohort effects influence suicide rates? Arch Gen Psychiatry 42:926–927, 1985

Häfner H, Schmidtke A: Increase of suicide through imitation of fictional suicide on television. Unpublished paper presented at the WPA Symposium Epidemiology and the Prevention of Mental Disorder, Reykjavik, Iceland, September 15–17, 1987

Häfner H, Welz R: Attempted suicide—a contagious behavior? Report by the World Psychiatric Association, Regional Symposium, Hong Kong, May 18–21, 1980

Hankoff LD: An epidemic of attempted suicide. Compr Psychiatry 2:294–298, 1961

Harbauer H: Krisen der Pubertat und Suizid. Medizinische Welt 29:1362–1364, 1978

Heer M, Städeli H: Suizidgefährdung im Spiegel psychologischer Testverfahren. Soz Praventivmed 24:58–69, 1979

Hemenway H: To what extent are suicide and other crimes against the person due to suggestion from the press? Bulletin of the American Academy of Medicine 12:253–263, 1911

Henderson S, Lance GN: Types of attempted suicide (parasuicide). Acta Psychiatr Scand 59:31–39, 1979

Henseler H, Zu H, Wedler H: Fragen über Fernsehsendungen zum Selbstmordproblem. Suizidprophylaxe 2:139–140, 1975

Holinger PC: Suicide in adolescence. Am J Psychiatry 134:1433–1434, 1977

Kayton L, Freed H: Effects of a suicide in a psychiatric hospital. Arch Gen Psychiatry 17:187–194, 1967

Kessler RC, Stipp H: The impact of fictional television suicide stories on U.S. fatalities: a replication. American Journal of Sociology 90:151–167, 1984

Kreitman N, Schreiber M: Parasuicide in young Edinburgh women: 1968–75, in The Suicide Syndrome. Edited by Farmer R, Hirsch S. London, Croom Helm, 1979, pp 54–72

Kreitman N, Smith P, Tan ES: Attempted suicide in social networks. British Journal of Preventive and Social Medicine 23:116–123, 1969

Kreitman N, Smith P, Tan ES: Attempted suicide as language: an empirical study. Br J Psychiatry 116:465–473, 1970

Lindsay JS, Nathan D: 122 families. N Z Med J 80:258, 1974

Matthews PC: Der suizidale Patient. Zeitschrift fur Allgemeinmedizin 56:521–523, 1968

Meichenbaum D: Examination of model characteristics in reducing avoidance behavior. J Pers Soc Psychol 17:298–307, 1971

Michaelis W: Verhalten ohne Aggression? Cologne, Kiepenheuer and Witsch, 1976

Motto JA: Suicide and suggestibility—the role of the press. Am J Psychiatry 124:252–256, 1967

Motto JA: Newspaper influence on suicide. Arch Gen Psychiatry 23:143–148, 1970

Murphy GE, Wetzel RD: Suicide risk by birth cohort in the United States, 1949–1974. Arch Gen Psychiatry 37:519–523, 1980

Murphy GE, Wetzel RD: Family history of suicidal behavior among suicide attempters. J Nerv Ment Dis 170:86–90, 1982

Murphy GE, Wetzel RD, Swallow CS, et al: Who calls the suicide prevention center? A study of 55 persons calling on their own behalf. Am J Psychiatry 126:314–324, 1969

Offer D, Barglow P: Adolescent and young adult self-mutilation incidents in a general psychiatric hospital. Arch Gen Psychiatry 3:194–204, 1960

Olin HS: Management precautions for surviving patients after a ward suicide. Hosp Community Psychiatry 31:348–349, 1980

Ostroff RB, Behrends RW, Kinson L, et al: Adolescent suicides modeled after television movie (letter). Am J Psychiatry 142:989, 1985

Pettifor J, Perry D, Plowman B, et al: Risk factors predicting childhood and adolescent suicide. Journal of Child Care 1:17–49, 1983

Pfeffer CR, Plutchik R, Mizruchi MS: Suicidal and assaultive behavior in children: classification, measurement, and interrelations. Am J Psychiatry 140:154–157, 1983

Phelps E: Neurotic books and newspapers as factors in the mortality of suicide and crime. Journal of Social Medicine 12:264–306, 1911

Phillips DP: The influence of suggestion on suicide: substantive and theoretical implications of the Werther effect. American Sociological Review 39:340–354, 1974

Phillips DP: Airplane accident fatalities increase just after newspaper stories about murder and suicide. Science 201:748–749, 1978

Phillips DP: Airplane accidents, murder, and the mass media: towards a theory of imitation and suggestion. Social Forces 58:1001–1024, 1980

Phillips DP: The impact of fictional television stories on U.S. adult fatalities: new evidence on the effect of the mass media on violence. American Journal of Sociology 87:1340–1359, 1982

Phillips DP: The Werther effect: suicide, and other forms of violence are contagious. The Sciences 7/8:32–39, 1985

Phillips DP, Cartensen LL: Clustering of teenage suicides after television news stories about suicide. N Engl J Med 315:685–689, 1986

Platt S: The aftermath of Angie's overdose: is soap (opera) damaging to your health? Br Med J 294:954–957, 1987a

Platt S: The aftermath of a televised soap opera drug overdose: is there a mass media imitation effect?, in Attitudinal Factors in Suicidal Behaviour and Its Prevention. Edited by Diekstra RFW, Maris RW, Platt S, et al. Amsterdam, Swets and Zeitlinger, 1985b

Pöldinger W: Beurteilung des Suizidrisikos. Munchner Medizinische Wochenschrift 127:833–837, 1984

Popow NM: The present epidemic of school suicides in Russia. Newrol Vestnic 18:312–317, 1911

Rada RT, James W: Urethral insertion of foreign bodies: a report of contagious self-mutilation in a maximum-security hospital. Arch Gen Psychiatry 39:423–429, 1982

Ringel E, Spiel W, Stepan M: Untersuchungen uber kindliche Selbstmordversuche. Prax Kinderpsychol Kinderpsychiatr 4:161–168, 1955

Robbins C, Conroy RC: A cluster of adolescent suicide attempts: is suicide contagious? J Adolesc Health Care 3:253–255, 1983

Rost H: Der Selbstmord in den deutschen Stadten. Schonigh, Paderborn, 1912

Roy A: Suicide in depressives. Compr Psychiatry 24:487–491, 1983a

Roy A: Family history of suicide. Arch Gen Psychiatry 40:971–974, 1983b

Rubinstein DH: Epidemic suicide among Micronesian adolescents. Soc Sci Med 17:657–665, 1983

Sandler DA, Connell PA, Welsh K: Emotional crises imitating television (letter). Lancet 1:856, 1986

Schier E: Suizidales Verhalten im Kindes- und Jugendalter, 1: Teil: Begriffsbestimmungen, Psychodynamik, Einteilungsprinzipien, Statistik. Padiatr Grenzgeb 19:43–53, 1980

Schlieffen H von: Der Suizidversuch. Ph.D. thesis, University of Freiburg, 1969

Schmidtke A, Häfner H: Die Vermittlung von Selbstmordmotivation und Selbstmordhandlung durch fiktive Modelle. Nervenarzt 57:502–510, 1986

Schmidtke A, Häfner H: Are there differential effects in the imitation of suicidal behavior? Unpublished paper presented at the first combined meeting "Suicide and cultural values: national and international aspects" of the American Association of Suicidology and the International Association for Suicide Prevention, San Francisco, May 18, 1987

Schmidtke A, Häfner H: The Werther effect after television films. Psychol Med (in press)

Schmidtke A, Häfner H, Möller HJ, et al: Frequencies and trends in attempted suicide in the Federal Republic of Germany, in Current Issues in Suicidology. Edited by Möller HJ, Schmidtke A, Welz R. Berlin, Springer (in press)

Seiden RH, Spence MC: A tale of two bridges: comparative suicide incidence on the Golden Gate and San Francisco Oakland Bay Bridges. Crisis 3:32–40, 1982

Singer U: Massenselbstmord. Stuttgart, Hippokrates, 1980a

Singer U: Der Massensuizid von Massada bis Guayana, in Suizidgefahr. Edited by Faust V, Wolfersdorf M. Stuttgart, Hippokrates, 1980b, pp 45–55

Solomon MI, Hellon CP: Suicide and age in Alberta, Canada, 1951 to 1971. Arch Gen Psychiatry 37:511–513, 1980

Stepien S: Massenselbstmord—ein vernachlässigter Aspekt in der Suizidforschung, in Bestandsaufnahme der Suizidforschung. Edited by Welz R, Möller J. Regensburg, Roderer, 1980

Stutte ML, Stutte H: Selbstmord und Selbstmordversuch im Kindesalter. Agnes-Karll-Schwester 21:444–446, 1967

Taylor P: Cluster phenomenon of young suicides raises "contagion" theory. Washington Post. March 11, 1984, p A3

Unus Multorum: Kapitel I, in Uber den Selbstmord, insbesondere den Schulerselbstmord. Edited by Vereinsleitung des Wienerpsychoanalytischen vereins. Wiesbaden, Bergmann, 1910, pp. 5–18

Walsh BW, Rosen P: Self-mutilation and contagion: an empirical test. Am J Psychiatry 142:119–231, 1985

Ward JA, Fox J: A suicide epidemic on an Indian reserve. Canadian Psychiatric Association Journal 22:423–426, 1985

Wasserman IM: Imitation and suicide: a reexamination of the Werther effect. American Sociological Review 49:427–436, 1984

Wellhöfer PR: Eistellungen zum Selbstmord. Offentliche Gesundheitswesen 37:379–391, 1975

Welz R: Selbstmordversuche in stadtischen Lebensumwelten. Weinheim, Beltz, 1979

Welz R, Häfner H: Imitation und Kontgiosität bei Selbstmordhandlungen, in Bestandsaufnahme der Suizidforschung. Edited by Welz R, Möller HJ. Regensburg, Roderer, 1984, pp 63–76

Wexler L, Weissman MM, Kasl SV: Suicide attempts 1970–1975: updating a United States study and comparisons with international trends. Br J Psychiatry 132:180–185, 1978

Zumkley H: Motivation und Imitation. Zeitschrift fur Entwicklungsgspsychologie und Padagogische Psychologie 12:223–243, 1980

8

Life Stress and Family Risk Factors for Youth Fatal and Nonfatal Suicidal Behavior

Cynthia R. Pfeffer, M.D.

Family factors and other life stresses are important sources of risk for youth suicide. However, there is a paucity of systematic research on the relation of these factors to suicide. In fact, most studies are about youth nonfatal suicidal behavior. This chapter will review these studies of children, adolescents, and young adults and, whenever possible, data about suicide will be compared to data about nonfatal suicidal tendencies.

LIFE EVENT STRESS FACTORS FOR YOUNG AND OLDER ADULTS

Systematic studies have emphasized the role of stressful life events for risk of suicide and nonfatal suicidal behavior. The Lundby study (Hagnell and Rorsman 1980), a controlled prospective investigation, is one of the few studies that has evaluated stressful life events among victims of suicide and individuals who did not commit suicide. The subjects were drawn from a sample of 3,563 people who were evaluated prospectively in 1947, 1957, and 1972. During this 25-year period, there were 28 people who committed suicide: 23 men and 5 women. Their age at death ranged from under 19 years to over 79 years. The youngest suicide victims were 4 men who were 20 to 29 years old at the time of death. There were two age- and sex-matched control groups. One control sample included 56 normal subjects who were studied prospectively until the time of the suicidal deaths of the index subjects. The other control sample included people who died from natural causes at ages corresponding to the ages at which the index subjects died as a result of suicide.

Prominent life events within the week preceding suicide were significantly more common for the suicide victims than the controls and they included humiliating situations with loss of self-respect, object loss, and acute mental illness. Humiliating circumstances, noted in four individuals, involved being discovered in wrongdoing or a rejection from a desired training program. Object loss involved breaking of an engagement in the case of two men and the sale of family property in the case of one woman. Approximately 93% of the index subjects were experiencing a mental illness at the time of suicidal death. Humiliation and object loss were not evident among the control subjects, although one individual who died of natural causes was an alcoholic.

Notable events occurring within the year preceding the suicide were a change of residence or living conditions, major occupational problems, and object loss. Change of residence was more common for the suicide victims than the normal controls. The suicidal group had significantly more occupational changes than the normal controls. The controls who died of natural causes were not appropriate for this analysis since many did not work because of their illness. Object loss was more prevalent among the suicide victims than the two control groups. Although none of the suicide victims had a relative who died during the year preceding the suicide, other losses such as separation or divorce and loss of property occurred among the suicidal group. There were no deaths of relatives for the control subjects, but loss of property or relationships did occur. The suicide victims experienced more illness within the year preceding their deaths than the normal controls. Approximately 93% of the suicide victims compared to 32% of the normal subjects and 61% of the controls who died from natural causes had an illness during this time period.

In summary, this controlled prospective study of a carefully identified population suggested that victims of suicide, in comparison to age- and sex-matched normal controls and controls who died of natural causes, experienced more acute and recent stressful events. Some of the significant events included illness, object loss, undesirable change of residence, occupational difficulties, and humiliation. Most of these factors were a source of stress for the young as well as the older suicide victims.

Many of the factors in the above study have been found to be factors associated with nonfatal suicidal behavior. For example, Paykel et al. (1975) focused on 53 patients admitted to an emergency hospital service after a suicide attempt and compared them to 53 depressed psychiatric patients who were matched for age, sex, marital status, social class, and race. Another control group included 53 individuals from the general population matched on similar demographic variables. The suicide attempters were predominantly under 30 years old, and the group was 70% female; 77% white; 34% married; 28% single; and 38% separated, divorced, or widowed. They were predominantly from the low-middle social class.

Thirty-two life events were evaluated for the 6-month period preceding either the suicide attempt or the onset of depression for the two psychiatric patient groups or the interview for the general population subjects. The suicide attempters reported four times as many events as the general population subjects and 50% more than the depressives. In the preceding 6 months, the suicide attempters experienced 3.3 events, the depressives experienced 2.1 events, and the general population controls experienced 0.8 events. There was a marked peak in the number of events in the months before the suicide attempt. The general population event rate was constant for each of the 6 months. The depressives had an increased rate of events within 2 months of onset of depression, although the number of events in earlier months was constant and similar to that of the general population.

The suicide attempters, compared with the general population subjects, reported more frequent serious arguments with a spouse, having a new person in the house, serious illness of a family member, serious personal physical illness, and having to appear in court for an offense. These issues are similar, in a general way, to the factors regarding illness, humiliation, change in living circumstances, and object loss reported in the Lundby study (Hagnell and Rorsman 1980). Furthermore, in comparison with the depressed subjects, the suicide attempters experienced more frequent serious arguments with a spouse, serious illness of a family member, and plans to be married. However, a major occupational change was reported less by the suicide attempters than the depressives. Thus, change in living circumstance, illness, and potential object loss were more common among the suicidal than the depressed subjects.

When the events were classified according to general types, the suicide attempters, in comparison with the controls, experienced more undesirable events. These included death of a close family member, separation and/or divorce, marital discord, serious illness of a close family member, and financial problems. Increased arguments with a spouse was the single event reported most frequently by the suicide attempters. The suicidal individuals also experienced more entrance events such as marriage, birth, and a new person in the house. When events were rated by the degree to which the events were regarded by the subjects as upsetting, the suicide attempters rated events with more upsetting intensity. In addition, suicide attempters experienced events as less under their own control than the other two groups of subjects.

In summary, this study emphasized the importance of the relation between a suicidal act and recent stressful life events. There was a significant increase in stressful life events within the month of the suicide attempt. Such a defined peak in frequency of stressful events was not apparent in the control subjects. These investigators postulated that the interaction between stressful life events and coping styles or personalities of the subjects was the critical determinant of the suicidal episodes.

Other reports of adult subjects have suggested that stressful life events enhanced risk for suicidal behavior. Slater and Depue (1981) refined the methodology used by Paykel and associates (1975). They used explicit diagnostic criteria in establishing the diagnosis of primary depressive disorder of the subjects. In addition, they used a matched control group of nonsuicidal subjects with primary depressive disorder. They defined the specific criteria for seriousness of a suicide attempt and identified the onset of depression before the suicide attempt.

Fourteen psychiatrically hospitalized suicide attempters with primary depression were compared to 14 hospitalized nonsuicidal individuals with primary depression. Life events were rated for the year preceding the suicide attempt and were categorized as variables related to physical illness, financial/legal or work challenge, interpersonal disruption, and death. Similar to the results of Paykel and associates (1975), this study found that suicide attempters experienced more events in the year before the suicide attempt and that there was a high rate of events between the onset of the depressive episode and the suicide attempt. Particularly relevant was that loss of a supportive person such as a spouse, an adult family member, or a person with whom the subject had a steady relationship, occurred among the suicide attempters and appeared to precipitate the suicide attempt. This study, therefore, emphasized the important role of loss of social support as a contributor to suicidal risk.

LIFE EVENT STRESS FACTORS FOR YOUTH

A variety of data suggest that there is an association between stressful life events and suicidal behavior among young people. One cultural-epidemiological field survey in Micronesia (Rubinstein 1983) offers insights into the role of major societal-familial change and an epidemic increase in youth suicide. The study, conducted from 1979 to 1981, examined all official reports on suicide obtained from hospital records, death certificates, police reports, and other sources. Data were also gathered by means of semistructured interviews using the psychological autopsy format with youth suicide attempters and the friends of the suicide victims. The results indicated that between 1960 and 1980 there were over 300 suicides and over 300 suicide attempts. This amounted to an eightfold increase in suicide rates for males during this same period. The greatest increase was for males who were 15–24 years old and occurred more frequently in areas of Micronesia in which there was a cultural and family change in the direction of moving away from a traditional subsistence culture to that involving modernized family life.

Characteristically, the male suicide occurred after a trivial confrontation with the parents and appeared to be the result of an angry protest against the parents. It appeared that adolescent male suicides in Micronesia were associated with recent changes in intergenerational relations between adolescents and their parents. The increase in suicide rates was exaggerated by the cultural shift in social and economic lifestyles with its loosening of family and communal social support for older adolescent males.

Relatively few systematic data have been collected on specific life and family events of children and adolescents who commit suicide. The existing studies have used records and/or the psychological autopsy technique to obtain data. Shaffer (1974) reviewed coroner, social service, and medical records to determine characteristics of young adolescent suicide completers. This study of 12- to 14-year-old suicide victims reported that among the 31 youngsters who committed suicide, 7 youths were from families in which there was a divorce. Nevertheless, all but 2 youngsters were living at home with one or both parents. The suicides appeared to be precipitated most frequently by a disciplinary crisis at home or in school. This study, although lacking a comparison group, suggested that family crisis and change may have contributed to the suicides of the youngsters.

In a subsequent and currently ongoing study, using the psychological autopsy technique to interview acquaintances of adolescents who committed suicide, Shaffer (cited in Holden 1986) has found similar factors of family disruption. In comparison with control subjects from the general population, the adolescents who committed suicide had higher levels of family strife involving family loss and psychopathology. Similar results were obtained in another psychological autopsy study of 20 adolescents who committed suicide (Shafii et al. 1985). In comparison to 29% of the 17 normal adolescents, 55% of the suicide victims experienced greater parental absence or emotional abusiveness. These studies highlight the significance of family stress factors for youth suicide risk.

Life events have been associated with the incidence of nonfatal suicidal acts among preadolescents and adolescents. For example, using multivariate analyses, Isherwood et al. (1982) compared 150 youth suicide attempters, 100 adolescents and young adults involved in automobile crashes, and 200 subjects randomly selected from the general population. The results indicated that suicide attempters could be differentiated from the accident victims and control subjects using life-event stress factors, which included undesirable events such as death of a parent, divorce, and problems in the family. Other factors that distinguished the three groups and that were associated with suicide attempts were depression, neuroticism, social isolation, having a rural upbringing, and recent history of taking a prescribed medication.

Evaluation of preadolescents has also yielded data suggestive of the importance of life-event stresses, especially those involving family factors on suicide potential. Cohen-Sandler et al. (1982a) carried out a systematic investigation of multiple life events in relation to nonfatal preadolescent suicidal behavior. Twenty psychiatrically hospitalized 5- to 14-year-old children who made a recent suicide attempt were compared with 21 depressed psychiatrically hospitalized preadolescents and 35 psychiatric inpatients with other symptomatology. The Social Readjustment Scale for Children (Coddington 1972) was used to measure a variety of recent and past life stresses. This study indicated that the suicidal children, compared to the nonsuicidal depressed children and the other children with psychopathology, experienced more and an increasing amount of stress as they matured. This was particularly evident in the year before the hospital admission. By age 4.5 the suicidal children experienced significantly more stresses such as the birth of a sibling and divorce of their parents. By the time the suicidal children were about 9 years old, in contrast to the other children, they were more likely to have experienced the birth of a sibling, the death of a grandparent, parental hospitalization, separation and/or divorce, or remarriage of a parent, another type of family loss because someone moved out of the family or died. This study highlighted the fact that throughout their lives, the suicidal children experienced a greater number of parental separations, divorces, and remarriages than the other two groups of children. The important association between family loss due to parental separation and/or divorce has been reported in other studies of suicidal children and adolescents (Stanley and Barter 1970; Adam et al. 1982; Garfinkel et al. 1982; Kosky 1983; Pfeffer et al. 1984; Myers et al. 1985).

The studies just discussed suggest that life stresses on youth early in their lives are associated with youth suicidal behavior. Recent research suggests that stresses occurring in the prenatal and neonatal periods of one's life have been linked to risk for adolescent suicide. Salk and colleagues (1985) analyzed 46 risk factors from the prenatal, birth, and neonatal records of 52 adolescents who committed suicide before the age of 20 years and compared whether these risk factors also existed in the histories of two samples of control subjects who were matched to each index subject. The youngest suicide victim was 12 years old. Eighty-three percent of the suicide victims were white males and 17% were white females. One control group included individuals who were the closest preceding birth to the index subjects and matched for sex, race, and hospital of birth. The second control group was the closest birth following the birth of the index subjects and was also matched for sex, race, and hospital of birth. Social status was similar for the index subjects and the controls.

The results indicated that there was a significantly greater number of prenatal, birth, and neonatal risk factors for the adolescents who committed suicide than for the controls. There were 4.62 ± 4.96 risk factors for the suicide group in comparison to 3.52 ± 3.72 and 3.67 ± 3.71 for each control group. Three risk factors that were found to be significantly more common in the histories of the suicide victims than the controls were infant respiratory distress for more than 1 hour at birth, no maternal antenatal care before 20 weeks of pregnancy, and chronic disease of the mother during the pregnancy. Eighty-one percent of the suicide victims had one of these risk factors present, 19% had two of these risk factors present, and no suicide victims had a history of three of these risk factors present. This suggests that each of these risk factors acts independently in creating suicide risk. The findings of this study suggest that adverse perinatal conditions increase vulnerability to suicide among adolescents. However, it does not provide information on how this may occur. One hypothesis may be that early adverse stress resulting in parent-child difficulties that are combined with subsequent life-event stresses enhance risk for adolescent suicide. Certainly, this hypothesis as well as other mechanisms, not addressed by this study, warrant investigation.

Those who have studied the relationship between life events and youth suicidal behavior have repeatedly hypothesized that the interaction between adverse life events and the coping skills or personality styles of the suicidal individuals is important. These investigators suggest that suicide or suicidal behavior is an end-point response to adversity and an inability to cope. This situation leads to perceptions of despair, helplessness, hopelessness, and an effort to call attention to a situation that requires immediate relief and change. This viewpoint, which puts emphasis on the relationship between interpersonal and intrapsychic processes, suggests that relief can be obtained by enhancing social support. Topol and Reznikoff (1982) investigated related issues in a study to evaluate the extent of problems, perceptions of peer and family relationships, degree of hopelessness, and locus of control among suicidal adolescents.

Thirty psychiatrically hospitalized adolescent suicide attempters were compared to 35 nonsuicidal psychiatric inpatients and 35 students from the general population. All subjects were 13–19 years old and matched for sex, age, race, and social status. Problems were systematically evaluated by a widely used self-report checklist developed by Mooney and Gordon (1950) for high school students. It quantitates factors related to courtship, sex, marriage, home and family, health, and physical development. Locus of control was measured by the Nowicki-Strickland Locus of Control Scale for Children (Nowicki and Strickland 1973). External locus of control involves the personal belief that outcomes of events are due to outside forces and not to personal factors. Internal locus of control is the personal belief that feelings are contingent on one's own behavior or personality. Hopelessness was evaluated with the Beck Hopelessness Scale (Beck et al. 1974). Perceptions of family and peer relationships were measured by the Van der Veen Family Concept Test (Van der Veen 1965).

The results indicated that in contrast to the control subjects, the adolescents who attempted suicide reported more frequent and serious family and peer problems. In fact, the suicidal adolescents, in comparison to the control subjects, indicated that they were less likely to have a close confidant from whom they could enlist support. Furthermore, in contrast to the control subjects, the suicidal teenagers considered their families to be less well adjusted. Hopelessness was highest for the suicidal group, and the suicide attempters perceived themselves as having greater external locus of control than the other teenagers.

This study indicated that adolescent suicide attempters, when compared with matched controls, experienced more frequent and serious family stress, less social support, a lack of personal control over their environment, and more hopeless feelings about their circumstances. It suggested that there exists an interaction between life-event stresses within the family, difficulties in adequate coping mechanisms, despair, and suicidal risk. These findings indicating that suicidal youngsters perceived parents as unavailable and not supportive are compatible with those reported by Goldney (1985) that suicide attempters often view their parents as indifferent, rejecting, and not supportive of the youngster's independent functioning.

Other investigators of suicidal adolescents have reported on stresses arising from disturbed family backgrounds, family separations, frequent arguments with parents, and difficulties in communicating with parents (Stanley and Barter 1970; Hawton et al. 1982b; Miller et al. 1982; Kosky 1983; Ross et al. 1983; Taylor and Stansfeld 1984). Stresses also noted in the histories of suicidal adolescents were school problems, unemployment and occupational difficulties, and problems with boyfriends and girlfriends (Hawton et al. 1982a, 1982b; Myers et al. 1985; Pfeffer et al. 1988). Finally, another aspect of the role of family involvement is elucidated by the findings of studies of suicide attempter children and adolescents who were treated in psychiatric hospitals (Barter et al. 1968; Cohen-Sandler et al. 1982b). The studies showed that those youngsters who were likely to exhibit repeated suicide attempts were more frequently found to be living out of the family home after psychiatric hospital discharge than former psychiatric inpatient suicide attempters who showed no repeated suicidal behavior. These findings have important implications for the treatment of suicide attempters and suggest that a treatment approach aimed at maintaining family involvement is essential to decrease the potential for risk of youth suicidal behavior.

FAMILY PSYCHIATRIC DISORDERS

Systematic investigations of psychiatric symptoms and disorders among relatives of suicidal children, adolescents, and young adults are not extensive or conclusive. Most studies report on family psychopathology as part of the more general investigation of risk factors for youth suicidal behavior.

Most investigations have focused on the psychological status of the parents. For example, Shafii and associates (1985) reported that among 20 adolescents who committed suicide, 60% had a parent with emotional problems, but 24% of the 17 nonsuicidal adolescent controls had a parent with psychological problems. This report did not elaborate on the types of psychopathology evident but noted that there was no significant difference in parental dependency on drugs or alcohol between the two groups of adolescents. The role of family psychopathology among adolescent suicide victims was initially reported by Shaffer (1974) in an uncontrolled record-review study of 31 young adolescents who committed suicide. Approximately 55% of the families of these youngsters included at least one close relative who had either consulted a psychiatrist or received treatment for emotional problems from their general practitioner. Shaffer found that in 20% of the families a parent or sibling was depressed before the adolescent suicide and that 10% of the families included a parent or sibling who was psychotic before the suicidal death. This avenue of investigation is continued by Shaffer and his colleagues (Holden 1986) in an ongoing study of adolescent suicide. They are presently evaluating the prevalence and characteristics of family psychopathology among these suicidal adolescents in comparison with those among adolescents who attempt suicide and a group of nonsuicidal adolescents selected from the general population.,

Among reports of nonfatal suicidal behavior (Garfinkel et al. 1982), a significantly higher percentage of suicide attempter children and adolescents than nonsuicidal adolescents were noted to have a family history of medical and mental illness. Approximately 51.6% of suicide attempters compared to 16.4% of nonattempters had relatives with a mental illness. In this study of 505 children and adolescents admitted to an emergency service after a suicide attempt, drug and alcohol abuse predominated among the emotional problems of the families. For example, almost 60% of the fathers, 30% of the mothers, and 25% of the siblings were substance abusers. However, these data may not provide a reliable indication of the type and extent of psychopathology of family members because of the retrospective nature of the chart-review procedures used in this study, lack of systematic assessment of the relatives, and the variability in the clinician's assessments and documentation in the emergency room records.

Among other clinical populations, suicidal youngsters, when evaluated for family psychopathology, appear to have a higher prevalence of family emotional problems than nonsuicidal controls. Friedman and associates (1984) compared 16 depressed adolescent psychiatric inpatient suicide attempters with 18 nonsuicidal depressed adolescent psychiatric inpatients. Each parent participated in a semistructured interview following the format of the Schedule for Affective Disorders and Schizophrenia (Endicott and Spitzer 1978). Family histories of psychiatric illness were determined by interviewing the adolescents and their parents with the Family History–Research Diagnostic Criteria methodology (Andreasen et al. 1977).

The results of the data collected with the Family History–Research Diagnostic Criteria indicated that there was no difference in lifetime prevalence of any psychiatric disorder among the parents. More specifically, among these psychiatrically hospitalized adolescents, presence of affective disorders among the parents and/or siblings was not different for the suicide attempters and the nonattempters. Fifty-six percent of the attempters and 39% of the nonattempters had a first-degree relative with an affective disorder. Furthermore, suicide attempts or suicide among first-degree relatives were approximately 12% for both groups of adolescents. However, when chronicity of psychiatric illness was considered, the suicide attempters had a significantly greater history of chronic mental illness among relatives than the nonsuicidal adolescents. Such illnesses were almost exclusively depression and alcohol abuse and occurred significantly more often before age 14 years for the suicidal than the nonsuicidal adolescents.

This study suggested that suicidal depressed adolescents who required psychiatric hospitalization in contrast to nonsuicidal depressed adolescent psychiatric inpatients experienced lengthy episodes of parental psychiatric illness that occurred early in their lives. This study is consistent with others (Stanley and Barter 1970; Cohen-Sandler et al. 1982a; Hawton et al. 1982c; Kosky 1983; Ross et al. 1983) suggesting that suicidal youngsters experience stresses from a variety of family factors early in life.

Another study (Tishler and McKenry 1982) directly evaluated parental psychopathology among suicidal adolescents. It examined 46 adolescents, age 12–14 years, who were evaluated in an emergency service for a suicide attempt. These adolescents were compared to nonsuicidal adolescents matched for sex and social status and admitted to the same emergency service for other complaints. The presence of symptoms of parental psychopathology was evaluated by means of scores rated on the Brief Symptom Inventory–SCL-90 (Derogatis et al. 1973). The scores for the fathers of the suicide attempters, in contrast to the scores for the fathers of the nonsuicidal adolescents, indicated that there was more depression and more use of alcohol. The mothers of the suicide attempters, in contrast to the mothers of the nonsuicidal individuals, had higher scores of anxiety and alcohol use but no difference in depression scores. The scores of depression, alcohol use, and anxiety for the mothers and fathers, although differing for the suicidal and nonsuicidal groups of adolescents, were all within the normal range for the Brief Symptom Inventory rating.

Although other studies (Pfeffer et al. 1979; Cohen-Sandler et al. 1982a; Garfinkel et al. 1982) indicate that parents of suicidal children and adolescents compared with parents of nonsuicidal children and adolescents have more symptomatology of depression and substance abuse, others (Pfeffer et al. 1980; Carlson and Cantwell 1982; Myers et al. 1985) have not found this to be clearly evident. The variability, lack of robustness, and the different findings of various studies may be related to research methodology involving the type and size of the population studied and the techniques used to assess parental psychiatric symptoms, behaviors, and disorders. Few studies used direct interviews of the parents with standardized research instruments to measure psychopathology.

Another interpretation for the variable results of this type of research is that the relation between specific parental psychiatric disorders and youth suicidal behavior is not necessarily strong and that there may be other variables contributing to suicidal risk. In fact, when children and adolescents of depressed parents are evaluated for suicidal risk (Weissman et al. 1984) a low prevalence of suicidal ideas or acts was found among the offspring, ages 6–18 years, of depressed parents. Approximately 6.5% of the 194 offspring with depressed parents reported suicidal ideas, and 0.9% attempted suicide.

In summary, the studies of youth suicidal behavior and parental psychiatric disorders indicate that suicidal youngsters have histories of parents with emotional problems. Although studies indicate variable results, a number of investigations suggest an association between youth suicidal behavior and parental depression and alcoholism. More systematic investigations are needed to more reliably evaluate this association.

FAMILY SUICIDAL BEHAVIOR

A number of studies of adult suicide victims and suicide attempters highlight the fact that suicidal behavior is evident in relatives of these suicidal individuals (Schulsinger et al. 1979; Murphy and Wetzel 1982; Roy 1983; Tsaung 1983; Egeland and Sussex 1985). With regard to youth suicide, Shaffer (1974) reported that among 31 suicide victims who were less than 15 years old, there were relatives who exhibited suicidal behavior in 23% of the cases of youth suicide. Among them, 13% of the youth suicide victims had a history of suicidal behavior in a sibling or a parent, which occurred before the youth suicide. In approximately 10% of the youth suicides, a first-degree relative showed suicidal tendencies after the suicidal death of the youngster. Shaffer reports (Holden 1986) in his ongoing study of youth suicide that at least 33% of the cases had a relative who attempted suicide. Shafii and associates (1985) compared family suicidal behavior of 20 adolescent suicide victims and 17 adolescent comparison subjects. Thirty percent of the adolescent suicide victims, compared to 12% of the controls, had a parent or adult relative with suicidal ideas or acts. Furthermore, as an estimate of the extent of exposure of adolescents to suicidal behavior, the study reported that 50% of the suicide victims had a sibling or friend who attempted or committed suicide. Only 12% of the controls had such a history with regard to a sibling or a friend. Shafii and associates (1985) proposed that "exposure to suicide or suicidal behavior of relatives and friends appears to be a significant factor influencing a vulnerable young person to commit suicide" (p. 1064). It must be recognized that mechanisms other than exposure to suicidal behavior may also contribute to youth suicidal risk, as the next chapter will discuss.

Table 1 indicates the findings of several studies of children and

Table 1. Youth Nonfatal Suicidal Behavior and Family Suicidal Behavior

Study	Suicidal subjects	Nonsuicidal controls	Results of suicidal vs. control	p
Pfeffer et al. 1979	42 Preadolescent psychiatric inpatients	16 Preadolescent psychiatric inpatients	Child suicidal behavior associated with parent suicidal behavior	Sig.
Pfeffer et al. 1980	13 Preadolescent psychiatric outpatients	26 Preadolescent psychiatric outpatients	15 vs. 0%	.05
Garfinkel et al. 1982	443 Adolescents in emergency room	442 Adolescents in emergency room	8.3 vs. 1.1%	.01
Tishler and McKenry 1982	42 Adolescents in emergency room	46 Adolescents in emergency room	Mothers: 34 vs. 9% Fathers: 12 vs. 11%	.05 NS
Pfeffer et al. 1984	12 Preadolescent nonpatients	89 Preadolescent nonpatients	Mother's suicidal ideas associated with child's suicidal ideas	Sig.
Myers et al. 1985	16 Preadolescent psychiatric inpatients	287 Preadolescent psychiatric inpatients	25 vs. 6%	.04

adolescents showing a significant relation between youth nonfatal suicidal behavior and family suicidal behavior.

The two studies (Garfinkel et al. 1982; Tishler and McKenry 1982)
of adolescents were carried out in medical emergency services where
the adolescents were evaluated for suicide attempts. Garfinkel et al.
(1982) examined the emergency room medical records and reported
that of the 443 suicidal adolescents for whom family data were available,
8.3% had a history of suicidal behavior. Suicide occurred in 2.5% of the
family histories of these adolescents. These data were in contrast to
1.1% of the family histories of suicidal behavior among the comparison
group of nonsuicidal adolescents seen in the same emergency room for
other reasons. The study did not indicate, however, what the relation
was between the suicidal family member and the suicidal adolescent.

In the other study of adolescent suicide attempters, Tishler and
McKenry (1982) asked the parents to complete a Brief Symptom Inventory (Derogatis et al. 1973) to measure their suicidal tendencies. Approximately 34% of the mothers of the suicide attempters compared to
9% of the mothers of the nonsuicidal controls reported suicidal ideas.
There was no difference in suicidal ideation among the fathers of the
suicide attempters and the nonsuicidal adolescents. Approximately 12%
of the fathers of both groups of adolescents reported suicidal ideation.
None of the parents of either group of adolescents reported suicide
attempts.

Studies of suicidal preadolescents have been carried out in clinical
and nonclinical samples. Pfeffer and associates (1979, 1980, 1984) evaluated children, ages 6–12 years, in psychiatric inpatient and outpatient
settings and also those randomly selected from schools. In these investigations, an association was found between preadolescent suicidal behavior and parental suicidal behavior. The results were derived from
information obtained during semistructured interviews of the child and
at least one parent. Myers et al. (1985), in a chart-review study of psychiatrically hospitalized preadolescents, found that parental history of the
children with suicidal ideas and/or acts included significantly more
prevalent suicidal behaviors than were found among the parents of
nonsuicidal psychiatric inpatient preadolescents. However, the presence of parental suicidal behavior did not predict the severity of the
child's suicidal behavior.

In summary, research on family patterns of youth suicidal behavior
indicates that there is an association between youth suicidal behavior
and family suicidal behavior. However, previous research has many
methodological limitations; the greatest is in not interviewing relatives
by use of systematic methods to evaluate suicidal behavior.

FAMILY VIOLENT BEHAVIOR

A number of studies of suicidal children and adolescents conclude that family violence, parental arguments, and physical and sexual abuse are associated with suicidal behavior. Shafii and colleagues (1985) in their study of 20 adolescents who committed suicide found that 55% of these youngsters compared to 29% of nonsuicidal peers experienced parental physical and emotional abusiveness. Shaffer's ongoing psychological autopsy study of adolescent suicide victims (Holden 1986) revealed similar results: that adolescent suicide victims have a history of family turmoil beset by violence and abuse.

A number of studies of nonfatal suicidal behavior in children and adolescents, highlighted in Table 2, have documented physical and sexual abuse in the histories of the suicidal youngsters.

The association between physical abuse and youth suicidal behavior has been demonstrated in very young children as well as among adolescents. Rosenthal and Rosenthal (1984) studied 2.5- to 5-year-old preschool children who exhibited suicidal ideas and acts. They compared 16 suicidal preschoolers in outpatient psychiatric treatment with 16 nonsuicidal preschooler psychiatric outpatients who had behavior problems. A significantly greater number of the suicidal children compared to the nonsuicidal children were abused or neglected. In addition, 81% of the suicidal children in contrast to 25% of the nonsuicidal children were unwanted by their parents. The parents of the unwanted children wished they had not had the child and felt burdened by the presence of the youngster. The children of these parents appeared to feel abandoned, despairing, and wished to find someone who would be kind to them. Of note was that 75% of the suicidal preschool children showed no pain or crying when they were injured. Whether this was also a manifestation of their response to being abused or neglected requires further study.

Green (1978) was one of the first investigators to record the relation between preadolescent suicidal behavior and child abuse and neglect. In his study of 60 abused children, 30 neglected children, and 30 nonabused or neglected comparison children, it was determined that approximately 41% of the abused children exhibited self-destructive impulses that included suicidal ideas and acts. This was a significantly greater prevalence of self-destructive tendencies than was found in 17% of the neglected and 7% of the comparison children. Green noted that in most of the cases of self-destructive behavior, this behavior was precipitated by parental beatings, or it occurred after an actual or threatened separation from the parents.

Table 2. Youth Nonfatal Suicidal Behavior and Parental Violence and Abuse

Study	Standardized subjects	Nonsuicidal controls	Results of suicidal vs. control	p
Kosky 1983	20 Preadolescent psychiatric inpatients	50 Preadolescent psychiatric inpatients	60 vs. 4%	.01
Pfeffer et al. 1983	59 Preadolescent psychiatric inpatients and outpatients	43 Preadolescent psychiatric inpatients and outpatients	Suicidal-assaultive children had parents with suicidal and assaultive behavior	.01
Rosenthal and Rosenthal 1984	16 Preschool psychiatric outpatients	16 Preschool psychiatric outpatients	81 vs. 38%	.05
Myers et al. 1985	61 Preadolescent inpatients	287 Preadolescent psychiatric inpatients	36 vs. 16%	.03
Deykin et al. 1985	159 Adolescents in emergency room	318 Adolescents in emergency room	15 vs. 4.4%	.001
Pfeffer et al. 1988	117 Adolescent psychiatric inpatients	83 Adolescent psychiatric inpatients	History of recent physical abuse $r = .162$	.05

Other studies of preadolescents have also reported a relation between parental physical abuse and childhood suicidal behavior (Kosky 1983; Myers et al. 1985). One investigation of preadolescents suggested that the relation between parental violence and childhood suicidal behavior is complex and that it may be associated with particular characteristics of the suicidal child. In that study, Pfeffer and associates (1983) documented that there were subtypes of suicidal preadolescents. One subtype was the suicidal child who showed no assaultive behavior but had good reality testing, significant depressive symptoms, and appeared to be experiencing environmental stress. The other subtype included preadolescents with suicidal and assaultive behaviors. These children were depressed and had poor reality testing. They had parents who exhibited both suicidal and violent behaviors.

Finally, violence and suicidal behavior have been found to be related among adolescents. Deykin et al. (1985) presented the most comprehensive report on adolescent suicide attempts and a history of abuse and neglect. In this study, 159 adolescents, 13–17 years old, who were treated in an emergency service for suicide attempts were compared to 318 nonsuicidal adolescents seen at the same time in the same emergency service. Information about whether the adolescents had a history of abuse or neglect was obtained from the department of social service reports. The results indicated that the adolescent suicide attempters were three to six times more likely to have had contact with the social service department for suspected abuse or neglect before the suicide attempt. Approximately 12% of the suicide attempts could be explained by events requiring social service department involvement, thereby suggesting that a sizable number of suicidal adolescents have experienced parental violence or neglect.

PROCESSES LINKING FAMILY FACTORS AND YOUTH SUICIDAL BEHAVIOR

The research reviewed in this chapter suggests that there is an association between youth suicidal behavior and factors involving stressful family events, parental emotional and physical illness, and parental suicidal and violent behaviors. The research discussed, however, has many limitations involving the circumscribed types of populations of suicidal youngsters studied, the retrospective nature of many studies, and the dearth of data derived from systematic interviews of family members. Nevertheless, the findings of these studies suggest that continued investigation of family risk factors for youth suicidal behavior would be a fruitful endeavor.

Among the issues highlighted in this chapter was the fact that suicidal youngsters have experiences with family risk factors early in their lives, beginning as far back as birth and the preschool years. Furthermore, these family risk factors tend to be chronic. An implication of these results is that research should focus prospectively on following youngsters who have these risk factors in their early histories to determine how such factors enhance risk for suicidal behavior. For example, not all children who have a depressed parent become suicidal (Weissman et al. 1984). Therefore, an important question to be answered is what factors are associated with suicidal risk among children who have depressed parents? One mechanism that could be proposed is that certain characteristics of the parents' depression are associated with suicidal risk in their children. There is, in fact, some evidence to support a hypothesis that chronic and severe depression in parents predicts psychopathological outcome in offspring (Friedman et al. 1984; Keller et al. 1986).

Another issue highlighted by these studies is that a variety of family life-event stresses, as also noted in studies of adult suicidal individuals, are associated with youth suicidal behavior. One type of stress involves loss of social support because of family change caused by death, parental separation, divorce, family moves, additions of relatives to the household, and changes in economic status of the family. Another type of stress is related to problems in parental adaptive functioning that are created by parental psychopathology. These problems may be evident as difficulties in the parent-child interactions. An extreme feature of such problems involves parental physical abuse.

Although not systematically investigated, many of these studies describe, in an anecdotal way, the responses of the suicidal youngsters to these stresses. Suicidal children and adolescents report feelings of despair, hopelessness, rejection, worthlessness, and wishes to escape intolerable circumstances, to find a benevolent and supportive friend or relative, or to escape by totally annihilating themselves. Some adolescents suggest that suicide is a retaliation toward their parents for all of the wrongdoing they perpetrated on the adolescents. While the descriptions of these responses may be accurate portrayals of the feelings and fantasies of suicidal youngsters, they do not sufficiently account for what precipitates a suicidal act.

The studies discussed in this chapter do not directly evaluate the processes or mechanisms leading to suicidal fantasies or acts. Different types of studies are needed to evaluate the mechanisms underlying the relation of family risk factors to youth suicidal behavior. For example, one mechanism that can be studied is whether early loss of social support affects the development of personality characteristics and/or biological systems that then enhance vulnerability to suicidal risk.

Another mechanism may involve the genetic basis of risk for suicidal behavior. In this circumstance, stress involving parent-child discord and loss of social support may work synergistically with an underlying genetic vulnerability. The next chapter will describe research that supports the association between genetic factors and suicidal risk.

From a theoretical perspective, youth suicidal behavior is a multidetermined symptom and, as this chapter noted, family factors are important features of risk. Yet, not all suicidal youngsters experience similar types of family risk factors. In fact, some children with certain family risk factors, such as divorce, may not be suicidal. Thus, it is also necessary that research focus on evaluating the interactions between risk factors and protective factors that act to decrease suicidal risk. Such an orientation is consistent with a theoretical model of risk for suicidal behavior that suggests opposing components that either enhance or decrease risk. For example, a supportive family member who has the capacity to provide empathy, is consistently available, can set limits, and is able to gratify the youngster's individual needs for self-esteem may offer the necessary ingredients to offset other family stresses that may exist. The family factors described in this chapter such as family disorganization, parental psychopathology, and family violence are vectors that enhance suicidal behavior. An understanding of opposing vectors for suicidal risk may illuminate approaches for assessment and intervention for youth who are at risk for suicidal behavior.

IMPLICATIONS FOR CLINICAL PRACTICE

The recognition of family risk factors for youth suicidal behavior is an essential feature in planning intervention and prevention. Thus, youngsters who experience chronic and acute severe family stresses such as the process of an acrimonious parental divorce, the death of a parent, history of chronic parental depression or alcoholism, sexual or physical abuse, and suicidal behavior of family members should be considered potentially at risk for suicidal behavior. These "at risk" youngsters should be screened for other signs of suicidal risk such as depression, suicidal thoughts or acts, and preoccupations with death (Pfeffer 1986). Interventions should focus on enhancing adaptive skills of the youngster, decreasing depression and suicidal tendencies, and modifying family stress. Furthermore, when evaluating a youngster with suicidal behavior, a comprehensive history of psychiatric symptoms, psychiatric disorders, and the nature of family interactions should be obtained. Such an assessment will help the clinician in planning the types of interventions that are relevant.

Treatment aimed to diminish family risk factors is an essential feature of preventing suicidal risk among children and adolescents. Thus, it may be that by treating a severely depressed parent who has a young child, primary suicide prevention may occur. Furthermore, prevention of suicidal behavior may occur if one can identify and involve a family member or friend who can provide social support to a youngster who is in a circumstance where the types of family risk factors described in this chapter are evident.

REFERENCES

Adam KS, Lohrenz JG, Harper D, et al: Early parental loss and suicidal ideation in university studies. Can J Psychiatry 27:275–281, 1982

Andreasen N, Endicott J, Spitzer RL, et al: The family history method using diagnostic criteria: the reliability and validity. Arch Gen Psychiatry 34:1220–1235, 1977

Barter J, Swaback D, Todd D: Adolescent suicide attempts: a follow-up study of hospitalized patients. Arch Gen Psychiatry 19:523–527, 1968

Beck AT, Weissman A, Lester D, et al: The measurement of pessimism: the hopelessness scale. J Consult Clin Psychol 42:861–865, 1974

Carlson GA, Cantwell DP: Suicidal behavior and depression in children and adolescents. J Am Acad Child Psychiatry 21:361–368, 1982

Coddington RD: The significance of life events as etiologic factors in the diseases of children, I: a survey of professional workers. J Psychosom Res 16:7–18, 1972

Cohen-Sandler R, Berman AL, King RA: Life stress and symptomatology: determinants of suicidal behavior in children. J Am Acad Child Psychiatry 21:178–186, 1982a

Cohen-Sandler R, Berman AL, King RA: A follow-up study of hospitalized suicidal children. J Am Acad Child Psychiatry 21:398–403, 1982b

Derogatis LR, Lipman RS, Covi L: The SCL-90: an outpatient psychiatric rating scale—preliminary report. Psychopharmacol Bull 9:13–27, 1973

Deykin EY, Alpert JJ, McNamarra JJ: A pilot study of the effect of exposure to child abuse or neglect on adolescent suicidal behavior. Am J Psychiatry 142:1299–1303, 1985

Egeland JA, Sussex JN: Suicide and family loading for affective disorders. JAMA 254:915–918, 1985

Endicott J, Spitzer R: A diagnostic interview: the Schedule for Affective Disorders and Schizophrenia. Arch Gen Psychiatry 35:837–844, 1978

Friedman RC, Corn R, Hurt SW, et al: Family history of illness in the seriously suicidal adolescent: a life-cycle approach. Am J Orthopsychiatry 54:390–397, 1984

Garfinkel BD, Froese A, Hood J: Suicide attempts in children and adolescents. Am J Psychiatry 39:1257–1261, 1982

Goldney RD: Parental representation in young women who attempt suicide. Acta Psychiatr Scand 72:230–232, 1985

Green AH: Self-destructive behavior in battered children. Am J Psychiatry 135:579–582, 1978

Hagnell O, Rorsman B: Suicide in the Lundby Study: a controlled prospective investigation of stressful life events. Neuropsychobiology 6:319–322, 1980

Hawton K, Cole D, O'Grady M, et al: Motivational aspects of deliberate self-poisoning in adolescents. Br J Psychiatry 141:286–291, 1982a

Hawton K, O'Grady J, Osborn J, et al: Adolescents who take overdoses: their characteristics, problems, and contacts with helping agencies. Br J Psychiatry 140:118–123, 1982b

Hawton K, Osborn M, O'Grady J, et al: Classification of adolescents who take overdoses. Br J Psychiatry 140:124–131, 1982c

Holden C: Youth suicide: new research focuses on a growing social problem. Science 233:839–841, 1986

Isherwood J, Adam KS, Hornblow AR: Life event stress, psychosocial factors, suicide attempt and auto-accident proclivity. J Psychosom Res 26:371–383, 1982

Keller MB, Beardslee WR, Dorer DJ, et al: Impact of severity and chronicity of parental affective illness on adaptive functioning and psychopathology in children. Arch Gen Psychiatry 43:930–937, 1986

Kosky R: Childhood suicidal behavior. J Child Psychol Psychiatry 24:457–468, 1983

Miller ML, Chiles JA, Barnes VE: Suicide attempters within a delinquent population. J Consult Clin Psychol 4:491–498, 1982

Mooney RL, Gordon LV: The Mooney Problem Checklists: Manual, 1950 Revisions. New York, Psychological Corporation, 1950

Murphy GE, Wetzel RD: Family history of suicidal behavior among suicide attempters. J Nerv Ment Dis 170:86–90, 1982

Myers KM, Burke P, McCauley E: Suicidal behavior by hospitalized preadolescent children on a psychiatric unit. J Am Acad Child Psychiatry 24:474–480, 1985

Nowicki S Jr, Strickland BR: A locus of control scale for children. J Consult Clin Psychol 40:148–154, 1973

Paykel ES, Prusoff BA, Myers JK: Suicide attempts and recent life events: a controlled comparison. Arch Gen Psychiatry 32:327–333, 1975

Pfeffer CR: The Suicidal Child. New York, Guilford Press, 1986

Pfeffer CR, Conte HR, Plutchik R, et al: Suicidal behavior in latency-age children: an empirical study. J Am Acad Child Psychiatry 18:679–692, 1979

Pfeffer CR, Conte HR, Plutchik R, et al: Suicidal behavior in latency-age children: an outpatient population. J Am Acad Child Psychiatry 19:703–710, 1980

Pfeffer CR, Plutchik R, Mizruchi MS: Suicidal and assaultive behavior in children: classification, measurement, and interrelations. Am J Psychiatry 140:154–157, 1983

Pfeffer CR, Zuckerman S, Plutchik R, et al: Suicidal behavior in normal school children: a comparison with child psychiatric inpatients. J Am Acad Child Psychiatry 23:416–423, 1984

Pfeffer CR, Newcorn J, Kaplan G, et al: Suicidal behavior in adolescent psychiatric inpatients. J Am Acad Child Adolesc Psychiatry 27:357–361, 1988

Rosenthal PA, Rosenthal S: Suicidal behavior by preschool children. Am J Psychiatry 141:520–525, 1984

Ross MW, Clayer JR, Campbell RL: Parental rearing patterns and suicidal thoughts. Acta Psychiatr Scand 67:429–433, 1983

Roy A: Family history of suicide. Arch Gen Psychiatry 40:971–974, 1983

Rubinstein DH: Epidemic suicide among Micronesian adolescents. Soc Sci Med 17:657–665, 1983

Salk L, Lipsitt LP, Sturner WQ, et al: Relationship to maternal and perinatal conditions to eventual adolescent suicide. Lancet 1:624–627, 1985

Schulsinger F, Kety SS, Rosenthal D, et al: A family study of suicide, in Origin, Prevention and Treatment of Affective Disorders. Edited by Schou M, Stromgren E. New York, Academic Press, 1979

Shaffer D: Suicide in childhood and early adolescence. J Child Psychol Psychiatry 15:275–291, 1974

Shafii M, Carrigan S, Whittinghall JR, et al: Psychological autopsy of completed suicide in children and adolescents. Am J Psychiatry 142:1061–1064, 1985

Slater J, Depue RA: The contribution of environmental events and social support to serious suicide attempts in primary depressive disorder. Journal of Abnormal Psychology 90:275–285, 1981

Stanley EJ, Barter JT: Adolescent suicidal behavior. Am J Orthopsychiatry 40:87–96, 1970

Taylor EA, Stansfeld SA: Children who poison themselves, I: a clinical comparison with psychiatric controls. Br J Psychiatry 145:127–135, 1984

Tishler CL, McKenry PC: Parental negative self and adolescent suicide attempts. J Am Acad Child Psychiatry 21:404–408, 1982

Topol P, Reznikoff M: Perceived peer and family relationships, hopelessness, and locus of control as factors in adolescent suicide attempts. Suicide Life Threat Behav 12:141–150, 1982

Tsaung MT: Risk of suicide in the relatives of schizophrenics, manics, depressives, and controls. J Clin Psychiatry 44:396–400, 1983

Van der Veen F: The parents' concept of the family unit and child adjustment. Journal of Counseling Psychology 12:196–200, 1965

Weissman MM, Prusoff BA, Gammon GD, et al: Psychopathology in the children (ages 6–18) of depressed and normal parents. J Am Acad Child Psychiatry 23:78–84, 1984

9

Genetics and
Suicidal Behavior

Alec Roy, M.B.

Systematic study of suicidal behavior among relatives of suicidal youth is almost nonexistent. Nevertheless, there are five lines of evidence about genetic factors in suicide. This chapter will review the clinical, twin, Iowa-500, Amish, and Copenhagen adoption studies, which provide evidence about genetic factors in suicide. Most of these are studies of suicidal behavior among adults, but it is likely that genetic factors for suicide are similar in both adolescents and adults.

CLINICAL STUDIES

A family history of suicide has been noted to be associated with suicidal behavior at all stages of the life cycle. There are five such studies among adolescents. In 1974 Shaffer reported a comprehensive survey of all 31 suicides among children aged 14 years or younger in England and Wales during the 7 years from 1962 to 1968 (Shaffer 1974). Suicidal behavior in a first-degree relative had occurred in 7 (22.6%) of these 31 youth suicides. In four relatives this suicidal behavior had occurred before the child's suicide, but in three other cases a first-degree relative attempted suicide after the child had committed suicide. There was also a high incidence of depression among the first-degree relatives (20%).

In 1981, Tishler et al. found that 22% of a series of 108 adolescents seen at a children's hospital emergency room after attempting suicide had a history that at least one family member had exhibited suicidal behavior in the past.

Garfinkel et al. (1982) reported a review of the hospital charts of 505 children and adolescents who appeared at the emergency room of the Hospital for Sick Children in Toronto between January 1, 1970, and January 30, 1977, and had deliberately inflicted self-injury with a documented conscious desire to die from the injury. A control group was derived by examining the charts of individuals of the same sex and of a similar age who did not have a history of attempting suicide but who had been admitted at about the same time to the same emergency room. As shown in Table 1, they found that significantly more of the youthful suicide attempters than control counterparts had a family history of suicidal behavior (8.3 vs. 1.1%, $p < .01$).

Garfinkel and associates also used Weissman and Worden's (1972) Risk/Rescue Rating scale to obtain ratings of severity for the adolescents' suicide attempts. Interestingly, they found that significantly more of those who had made serious suicide attempts had a family history of suicide (Table 2).

As found in Shaffer's London study (1974), the suicide attempters in Garfinkel et al.'s study (1982) also had a significant excess of relatives with mental illness and they concluded that: "A strong genetic loading for affective disorder in families of individuals who attempt suicide is supported by our findings of an eight times higher rate of suicide attempts or suicide in the families of the index group and an absence of completed suicide in the families of the controls" (p. 1260). "Attempted suicide is on a continuum with completed suicide, as demonstrated by the finding that there was no family history of completed suicide in the

Table 1. Family History Differences Between Children and Adolescents Who Attempted Suicide and Controls

Family characteristic	Suicide attempters			Controls			Significance		
	Available n	With characteristic n	%	Available n	With characteristic n	%	χ^2	df	p
History of mental illness	442	228	51.6	452	74	16.4	122.3	1	.01
History of suicide	443	37	8.3	442	5	1.1	23.95	2	.01
Suicide attempts		26	5.9		5	1.1			
Completed suicide		11	2.5		0				

Note. Reprinted with permission from Garfinkel B, et al.: Suicide attempts in children and adolescents. Am J Psychiatry 139:1257–1261, 1982. Copyright 1982, the American Psychiatric Association.

Table 2. Variables Discriminating the Severity of 604 Suicide Attempts by Children and Adolescents

	Percent of attempts			Significance		
Variable	Low danger (n =385)	Moderate danger (n =149)	Severe danger (n =70)	χ^2	df	p
Family history of suicide						
Yes	4.6	12.7	16.1			
No	95.4	87.3	83.9	12.67	2	.01

Note. Reprinted with permission from Garfinkel B, et al: Suicide attempts in children and adolescents. Am J Psychiatry 139:1257–1261, 1982. Copyright 1982, the American Psychiatric Association.

control group and that the follow-up mortality rate from suicide in the index group surpassed the death rate for the controls" (p. 1261).

In 1985 Shafii et al. reported data derived from psychological autopsies carried out after lengthy home visits with the families of 20 children and adolescents who had committed suicide in Jefferson County (Louisville), Kentucky, between January 1980 and June 1983. Friends and significant others were also contacted, and three extensive questionnaires were completed. Shafii and associates were able to match 17 of the suicide victims with controls drawn from among the suicide victims' closest friends. These controls, and their families, were interviewed with the same methodology that was used with the families of the suicide victims. Shafii and associates also found that significantly more of the youth suicide victims than controls had a family history of suicide, as shown in Table 3. Again, there was a significant difference between the families of suicide victims and controls for emotional problems in the family. These workers concluded that "exposure to suicide or suicidal behavior of relatives and friends appears to be a significant factor in influencing a vulnerable young person to commit suicide" (p. 1064).

In an ongoing study, Shaffer et al. (1985) are performing extensive psychological autopsies on a consecutive series of youthful suicide victims (under 19 years of age) in New York City. In a preliminary report of the first 52 suicide victims studied, they noted that a substantial number (20, 38%) had a relative who had either committed or attempted suicide. Although cautioning that the family data are complex and are not yet fully explored, Shaffer (1985) considers that this aspect of the youthful suicides may represent an environmental rather than a genetic phenomenon; that they may be imitative acts similar to the recently well-publicized clustering of teenage suicides.

Table 3. Significant Differences Between Children and Adolescents Aged 12–19 Who Committed Suicide and Matched-Pair Control Subjects

Family and environmental variables	Suicide victims ($n = 20$)		Control subjects ($n = 17$)		McNemar test	
					McNemar (df = 1)	p
	n	%	n	%		
Exposure to suicide	13	65	3	18	6.12	< .008
Sibling's or friend's (attempted or completed suicide)	12	60	2	12	6.12	< .008
Parent's or adult relative's (suicidal ideation, threats, attempts, or completed suicide)	6	30	2	12	2.25	NS[a]
Parent's emotional problems	12	60	4	24	5.14	< .02

Note. Reprinted with permission from Shafii M, et al: Psychological autopsy of completed suicide in children and adolescents. Am J Psychiatry 142:1061–1064, 1985. Copyright 1985, the American Psychiatric Association.
[a]$\chi^2 = 3.3$, df = 1, $p < .04$.

Among adults who exhibit suicidal behavior there are also surprisingly few studies about the presence or absence of a family history of suicide. In an early study, Farberow and Simon (1969) reported that among 100 suicide victims in Vienna and Los Angeles, 6 had a parent who had killed himself or herself, a rate more than 88 times the expected rate. Robins et al. (1957) found that 11% of 109 suicide attempters had a family history of suicidal behavior. Murphy et al. (1969) reported that one-third of 55 callers to a suicide prevention center had a family history of suicidal behavior and that this was significantly more likely to be the case if the callers had themselves attempted suicide. Flinn and Leonard (1972) noted that among 480 young nonpsychiatric subjects, those reporting their own suicidal behavior also reported more knowledge about suicidal behavior in others.

More recently, Murphy and Wetzel (1982) systematically interviewed a random sample of all persons seen and admitted during a 1-year period at the St. Louis County Hospital after a suicide attempt. Of the 127 patients in the study, 14% gave a family history of suicide, 24% gave a family history of attempted suicide, and 6% gave a family history of suicide threats. One or more of these family suicidal behaviors was reported by 36% of the suicide attempters. Among suicide attempters with a primary diagnosis of primary affective disorder, 17% had a family history of suicide and 17% had a family history of suicide attempt (Table 4). As individuals with affective disorders comprise a larger proportion of suicides than individuals with personality disorders, Murphy and Wetzel predicted that more of their patients with affective disorders could be expected to present a significant suicide risk in the future.

Table 4. Family History of Suicidal Behavior by Broad Diagnostic Groups

Diagnostic group	n	Percentage with family history of		
		Suicide	Attempt	Any[a]
Personality disorders	56	20	34	46
Primary affective disorder	29	17	17	38
Other diagnoses and none	42	5	17	21
All patients	127	14	24	36

Note. Reprinted with permission from Murphy G, Wetzel R: Family history of suicidal behavior among suicide attempters. J Nerv Ment Dis 170:86–90, 1982. Copyright 1982, the Williams & Wilkins Co., Baltimore.
[a]Any suicidal behavior includes suicide and attempted and threatened suicide.

Therefore, they concluded that a "systematic family history of such behavior coupled with modern clinical diagnosis should prove useful in identifying those attempters at increased risk for suicide" (p. 90).

The first study providing data about how commonly a family history of suicide is found among psychiatric patients was that of Pitts and Winokur (1983). They found that among 748 consecutive patients admitted to a hospital, 37 (4.9%) reported a possible or definite suicide in a first-degree relative. In 25 (68%) of the 37 cases the diagnosis was an affective disorder, and the investigators noted that the statistical probability of this distribution occurring by chance was less than .02. When the probable diagnoses in the cases of the first-degree relatives who committed suicide were considered, in 24 of the 37 patient-relative pairings, both members had affective disorders. Pitts and Winokur estimated that 79% of the suicides of the first-degree relatives were associated with probable affective disorder.

In 1983 Roy reported a study of all the 5,845 psychiatric patients admitted to the Clarke Institute of Psychiatry in Toronto between January 1974 and June 1981 (Roy 1983). There were 243 inpatients with a family history of suicide (4.2%), a percentage very similar to the 4.9% reported by Pitts and Winokur 19 years earlier. The patients with a family history of suicide were compared with the 5,602 inpatients without such a history. As shown in Table 5, a family history of suicide was found to significantly increase the risk for an attempt at suicide in a wide variety of diagnostic groups. Almost one-half (48.6%) of the patients with a family history of suicide had themselves attempted suicide. More than one-half (56.4%) of all the patients with a family history of suicide had a primary diagnosis of an affective disorder, and more than one-third (34.6%) had a recurrent unipolar or bipolar affective disorder.

Recently, Linkowski et al. (1985) investigated past suicidal behavior

Table 5. A Consecutive Series of 5,845 Inpatients Admitted to the Clarke Institute of Psychiatry Between January 1974 and June 1981. Patients, by Diagnostic Group, Who Attempted Suicide Comparing Those with a Family History of Suicide with Those Without Such a History

Diagnostic group	Second- or first-degree relative suicide		No family history of suicide	
	No. (%) who attempted	No. of attempts	No. (%) who attempted	p
Schizophrenia	15/33 (45.4)	28	150/1114 (13.5)	< .0001
Unipolar	13/32 (41.6)	24	50/372 (13.4)	< .0001
Bipolar	22/58 (37.9)	48	56/405 (13.9)	< .0001
Depressive neurosis	26/47 (55.3)	45	221/715 (30.9)	< .0001
Personality disorder	33/48 (68.8)	89	328/1048 (31.3)	< .0001
Alcohol	3/7 (42.9)	3	42/147 (28.5)	NS
Others	6/18 (33.3)	15	378/1801 (21.0)	NS
Total	118/243 (48.6)	252	1225/5602 (21.8)	< .0001

Note. Reprinted with permission from Roy A: Family history of suicide. Arch Gen Psychiatry 40:971–974, 1983.

and family history of suicide among a consecutive series of 713 patients with affective disorder admitted over several years to the psychiatric department of the University of Brussels. They found that 123 (17%) of the depressed patients had a first- or second-degree relative who committed suicide. They also found that a family history of suicide significantly increased the probability of a suicide attempt among the depressed females, especially the risk for a violent suicide attempt. This increased probability is shown in Table 6 for comparisons A, B, and C and for their odds ratios. Among the male depressives, a family history of suicide significantly increased the risk only for a violent suicide attempt, as shown in Table 6 for comparison C and its odds ratio. Linkowski and associates concluded that "A positive family history for violent suicide should be considered as a strong predictor of active suicidal attempting behavior in major depressive illness" (p. 237).

A family history of suicide has also been found significantly more among psychiatric patients who commit suicide (Roy 1982). As manic-depression is the psychiatric diagnosis most commonly found among suicide victims, it is not surprising to find that across the various published series, approximately 10% of manic-depressive patients have a family history of suicide (Roy 1985a, 1985b, 1986a, 1986b).

A family history of suicide has also been noted to be associated with suicidal behavior among individuals in the last stages of the life cycle. Batchelor and Napier (1953) found that among 40 consecutive cases of

Table 6. Significances and Relative Odds Ratios for the Comparisons Tested in Subgroups of Depressive Attempters and Nonattempters

	Comparison*					
	A		B		C	
	M	F	M	F	M	F
Significance of main effect**						
Polarity	NS	0.045	NS	NS	NS	0.021
Family history (FH+)	NS	0.004	NS	0.0003	0.010	0.010
Age	NS	NS	NS	NS	0.050	NS
Relative odds ratio***						
Polarity (BP vs. UP)		0.65				2.43
Family history (FH+ vs. FH−)		2.02		3.53	14.96	2.68
Age (years)						
31–45 vs. 15–30					0.32	
46–60 vs. 31–45					4.92	
> 60 vs. 46–60					2.19	
> 60 vs. 15–30					3.46	
No. of patients	260	453	260	453	66	173

Note. Reproduced with permission from Linkowski P, de Maertelaer V, Mendlewicz J: Suicidal behavior in major depressive illness. Acta Psychiatr Scand 72:233–238, 1985. Copyright 1985, Munksgaard International Publishers Ltd.

* A) Presence versus absence of any suicidal attempts; B) violent versus non-violent attempt plus no suicidal attempt; C) violent versus non-violent attempts. M = males; F = females.

** All interactions between main effects (polarity × FH+, polarity × Age and FH+ × Age) not significant.

*** Given only for statistically significant main effects.

attempted suicide by individuals admitted to a general hospital who were aged 60 years or over, a family history of suicide was present in 7 (17%) of the cases.

THE IOWA-500 STUDY

The Iowa-500 Study is a follow-up study of just over 500 psychiatric patients consecutively admitted to the University of Iowa Psychiatric Hospital between 1934 and 1944 (Tsuang 1977, 1978). The 525 patients in the study were chosen because they met certain research criteria. They included 200 schizophrenic, 100 manic, and 225 depressed patients. They were compared with a control group of 160 psychiatrically normal individuals admitted to the University of Iowa Hospital during the same period for appendectomy or herniorrhaphy. Follow-up studies between 1972 and 1976 revealed that 30 of these 685 subjects subsequently committed suicide—29 of the suicides were found among the 525 psychiatric patients and only 1 among the normal controls (5.5 vs.

0.6%) (Tsuang 1978). This finding is impressive evidence for the close association of suicide with psychiatric disorder.

The Iowa-500 Study has yielded other informative data (Tsuang and Woolson 1978), and Tsuang (1983) has recently reported the development of this study in another important direction. He and his associates followed up not only the psychiatric patients and controls but also their first-degree relatives. The first-degree relatives were interviewed, and Tsuang was interested in the answers to four questions that are relevant to the possible role of genetic factors in suicide. These questions were:

1. Are relatives of patients with schizophrenia and affective disorders subject to higher risk of suicide than relatives of nonpsychiatric control patients?
2. Are relatives of patients with schizophrenia and affective disorders who committed suicide subject to higher risk of suicide than relatives of patients who did not commit suicide?
3. Is the risk of suicide among relatives of schizophrenic patients different from that for relatives of manic and depressed patients?
4. Are the suicide risks different for male and female relatives of patients from different diagnosis categories?

The first-degree relatives of the psychiatric patients were found to have a risk of suicide almost eight times greater than the risk in relatives of normal controls. When only deceased relatives were considered, the relatives of psychiatric patients were found to have a risk of suicide almost six times greater than the risk among the deceased relatives of the controls (Table 7).

Among the first-degree relatives of the psychiatric patients, those who were the relatives of 1 of the 29 patients in the Iowa-500 Study who committed suicide themselves had a four times greater risk of committing suicide compared with the relatives of the patients who did not commit suicide. Among the deceased relatives the suicide risk was three times greater, as shown in Table 8.

Next, the individual psychiatric diagnoses were examined. The risk of suicide was significantly greater among the first-degree relatives of depressed patients than it was among the relatives of either schizophrenic or manic patients. When the relatives of patients who committed suicide were compared, the suicide risk was even higher, but it was equally high among the relatives of both depressed and manic patients. These features are shown in Table 9.

The suicide risk was also examined separately for the male and female relatives of psychiatric patients. As noted in Table 10, in general

Table 7. Risk of Suicide Among Relatives of Patients and Controls

| Subjects | Relatives[a] | | | | |
| | | Suicide | | | |
	n	*n*	%	BZ	MR (%) ± SE
Patients (*n* = 510)					
All relatives	3,947	55	1.4	2,348	2.3 ± 0.3[b]
Deceased relatives	2,294	55	2.4	1,338	4.1 ± 0.5[b]
Controls (*n* = 153)					
All relatives	1,403	2	0.1	672	0.3 ± 0.2
Deceased relatives	589	2	0.3	305	0.7 ± 0.5

Note. n = number of first-degree relatives. Risk of suicide among relatives was computed using age-adjusted numbers of subjects exposed to the risk of suicide based on suicide statistics from the Iowa general population. Reprinted with permission from Tsuang MT: Risk of suicide in the relatives of schizophrenics, manics, depressives, and controls. J Clin Psychiatry 44:396–400, 1983. Copyright 1983, Physicians Postgraduate Press, Inc.
  [a] BZ = Bezugsziffer (age-adjusted size of the sample); MR = Morbidity risk.
  [b] *p* < .01 (comparison of patients with controls).

Table 8. Risk of Suicide Among Relatives of Patients with and Without Suicide

| Subjects | Relatives | | | | |
| | | Suicides | | | |
	n	*n*	%	BZ	MR (%) ± SE
Suicide (*n* = 29)					
All relatives	193	9	4.7	114	7.9 ± 2.5[a]
Deceased relatives	136	9	6.6	78	11.5 ± 3.6[a]
No suicide (*n* = 481)					
All relatives	3,754	46	1.2	2,234	2.1 ± 0.3
Deceased relatives	2,158	46	2.1	1,259	3.7 ± 0.5

Note. n = number of first-degree relatives; BZ = Bezugsziffer (age-adjusted size of the sample); MR = Morbidity risk. Reprinted with permission from Tsuang MT: Risk of suicide in the relatives of schizophrenics, manics, depressives, and controls. J Clin Psychiatry 44:396–400, 1983. Copyright 1983, Physicians Postgraduate Press, Inc.
  [a] *p* < .05 (comparison of suicide with no suicide).

the suicide risk was higher for male first-degree relatives than it was for female first-degree relatives.

Thus, the follow-up of first-degree relatives of the subjects in the Iowa-500 Study is an important study that demonstrates there are genetic factors in suicide. The main findings are summarized in Table 11 and indicate that there is a high risk of suicide among schizophrenic and affective disorder patients. They also suggest that relatives of patients

Table 9. Risk of Suicide Among Living and Dead Relatives of Schizophrenics, Manics, and Depressives with Suicide and Without Suicide

Patients		Relatives			
		Suicides			
	n	n	%	BZ	MR (%) ± SE
Schizophrenia (S)					
Suicide ($n = 8$)	41	0	0.0	23	0.0 ± 0.0
No suicide ($n = 187$)	1,159	9	0.8	723	1.2 ± 0.4
Total ($n = 195$)	1,200	9	0.8	746	1.2 ± 0.4
Mania (M)					
Suicide ($n = 6$)	53	3	5.7	32	9.4 ± 5.2
No suicide ($n = 86$)	748	4	0.5	426	0.9 ± 0.5
Total ($n = 92$)	801	7	0.9	458	1.5 ± 0.6
Depression (D)					
Suicide ($n = 15$)	99	6	6.1	59	10.2 ± 3.9
No suicide ($n = 208$)	1,847	33	1.8	1,085	3.0 ± 0.5
Total ($n = 223$)	1,946	39	2.0	1,144	3.4 ± 0.5

Note. Significant comparisons are as follows: Suicide, S vs. M ($p < .10$), S vs. D ($p < .01$); no suicide, S vs. D ($p < .01$), M vs. D ($p < .01$); and Total S vs. D ($p < .01$); M vs. D ($p < .05$). n = number of first degree relatives; BZ = Bezugsziffer (age-adjusted size of the sample); MR = Morbidity risk. Reprinted with permission from Tsuang MT: Risk of suicide in the relatives of schizophrenics, manics, depressives, and controls. J Clin Psychiatry 44:396–400, 1983. Copyright 1983, Physicians Postgraduate Press, Inc.

Table 10. Risk of Suicide Among Relatives of Schizophrenics, Manics, and Depressives by Sex

Diagnostic group		Relatives[a]			
		Suicides			
	n	n	%	BZ	MR (%) ± SE
Schizophrenia					
Male relatives	601	9	1.5	359	2.5 ± 0.8[a]
Female relatives	590	0	0.0	394	0.0 ± 0.0
Mania					
Male relatives	395	5	1.3	221	2.3 ± 1.0
Female relatives	390	2	0.5	238	0.8 ± 0.6
Depression					
Male relatives	994	30	3.0	587	5.1 ± 0.9[a]
Female relatives	921	9	1.0	568	1.6 ± 0.5

Note. n = number of first-degree relatives; BZ = Bezugsziffer (age-adjusted size of the sample); MR = Morbidity risk. Reprinted with permission from Tsuang MT: Risk of suicide in the relatives of schizophrenics, manics, depressives, and controls. J Clin Psychiatry 44:396–400, 1983. Copyright 1983, Physicians Postgraduate Press, Inc.

[a] $p < .01$ (comparison of males and females).

Table 11. Summary of Morbidity Risks of Suicide in Patients and Relatives

Diagnostic group	Patients			Relatives			Relatives of suicides		
	n	BZ	MR%	*n*	BZ	MR%	*n*	BZ	MR%
Schizophrenia	8	125	6.4	9	746	1.2	0	23	0.0
Mania	6	62	9.7	7	458	1.5	3	32	9.4
Depression	15	173	8.7	39	1,144	3.4	6	59	10.2
Control	1	97	1.0	2	672	0.3	0	7	0.0

Note. *n* = number of subjects who committed suicide; BZ = Bezugsziffer (age-adjusted size of the sample); MR = Morbidity risk. Reprinted with permission from Tsuang MT: Risk of suicide in the relatives of schizophrenics, manics, depressives, and controls. J Clin Psychiatry 44:396–400, 1983. Copyright 1983, Physicians Postgraduate Press, Inc.

with affective disorders have a high morbidity risk and that the relatives of patients who had an affective disorder and committed suicide are at highest risk.

TWIN STUDIES

Compelling evidence for the genetic transmission of manic-depression and schizophrenia is that the concordance rate for these psychiatric disorders is substantially higher among identical twins, who share the same genes, than it is among fraternal twins, who share only 50% of their genes (Kallman and Anastasio 1947). Thus, if the propensity to commit suicide was genetically transmitted, concordance for suicide should be found more frequently among identical than fraternal twins. This was well stated by Kallman and Anastasio (1947):

> If hereditary factors play a decisive role, we should find a concordant tendency to suicide more frequently in one-egg than in two-egg pairs regardless of ordinary differences in environment. If the main emphasis is placed on certain constellations of non-genetic factors, concordance should be expected in some twin pairs of either type, who shared the same environment and responded to a similar degree of distress with the same type of psychosis. (p. 54)

Kallman and associates had collected 2,500 twin index cases from mental institutions, tuberculosis hospitals, old age homes, and other parts of the population of New York State. In 1947, he reported that among this clinical material there were 11 twin pairs where one twin was known to have committed suicide. Three of the 11 twin pairs were monozygotic, and 8 were dizygotic. In none of the 11 twin pairs had the other twin committed suicide (Kallman and Anastasio 1947; Kallman et al. 1949). This negative finding led them to conclude that "there is no statistical evidence for the popular notion that the tendency to commit suicide recurs in certain families as the result of a special hereditary trait or of a particular type of genetically determined personality deviation" (Kallman et al. 1949, p. 126).

However, 20 years later, in 1947, Haberlandt (1965, 1967) pooled the accumulated data from twin studies from different countries. By then 149 sets of twins had been reported where one twin was known to have committed suicide. Among these twin pairs there were 9 sets of twins where both twins had committed suicide. All of the 9 twin pairs were identical twins; there was no set of fraternal twins concordant for suicide.

Four of the 9 monozygotic twin sets concordant for suicide came from the Danish Psychiatric Twin Register, and their case histories revealed that in three cases the twins were also concordant for manic-depressive disorder (Juel-Nielsen and Videbech 1970). In another of the 9 monozygotic twins sets the twins were also concordant for schizophrenia. Since Haberlandt's review, Zair (1981) has reported a 10th pair of identical twins who both committed suicide. Again there was an association with affective disorder, as both twins had killed themselves during a depressive episode, and both of their parents and a grandmother had also been treated for depression.

Approximately 1 in 250 births is an identical twin, and between 0.5 and 1% of all deaths among the general population are due to suicide. Thus, it is somewhat surprising that only 10 pairs of monozygotic twins concordant for suicide have been reported in the 173 years since the first report of suicide in twins (Williams 1918). Also, in 5 of the 10 twin pairs, the twins were also concordant for either depression or schizophrenia. Thus, although twin data provide evidence for the genetic transmission of suicide, the evidence may be partly confounded by the issue of the genetic transmission of psychiatric disorders themselves.

THE AMISH STUDY

In 1985 Egeland and Sussex made their first report on the suicide data obtained from the study of affective disorders among the Old Order Amish community of Lancaster County in southeastern Pennsylvania (Egeland and Sussex 1985). This is a continuing study into the genetics and course of illness of the affective disorders among this population (Egeland and Hostetter 1983). Suicide research among the Amish is of great interest for several reasons. They are an Anabaptist, nonviolent, pacifist society where there are no violent crimes and where there has been no known murder. Alcohol is prohibited and there is no alcoholism. Also, they are a wealthy farming community among whom there is no unemployment. Their strong religious beliefs foster a tightly knit community, and three generations commonly live together under the same roof. Family life is valued and divorce is prohibited. Social isolation is rare, and the cohesive nature of their community offers social support for individuals who encounter stress or adverse life events. Thus, several of the important social risk factors for suicide among individuals in the general population such as unemployment, divided or separated marital status, social isolation, and alcoholism are not commonly found among these Amish (Robins et al. 1959; Dorpat and Ripley 1960; Barraclough et al. 1974; Murphy and Robins 1967). This means that genetic factors for suicide may play a larger part in suicides occurring among the Amish.

Not surprisingly, suicide is a relatively rare event among this group of Amish. In fact, Egeland and Sussex were only able to find 26 suicides between 1880 and 1980. Over these 100 years, the suicide rates among the Amish have consistently been substantially lower than the rates for the rest of the United States.

Egeland and Sussex's team used the Schedule for Affective Disorders and Schizophrenia–Lifetime Version (SADS-L). They conducted an average of six interviews, with various family members, for each of the 26 suicide victims. A five-member psychiatric board used the Research Diagnostic Criteria (RDC) to make a psychiatric diagnosis based on these interviews and supplemented by information from other sources. The first important finding of the study was that 24 of the 26 suicide victims met RDC criteria for a major affective disorder. Eight had bipolar I, 4 had bipolar II, and 12 had unipolar affective disorder. A further case met the diagnostic criteria for a minor depression. Furthermore, most of the suicide victims had a heavy family loading for affective disorders. For example, among the 8 bipolar I suicide victims, the morbidity risk for affective disorders among their 110 first-degree relatives was 29% compared with the 1–4% found among the general population.

The second finding of the study was that almost three-fourths of the 26 suicide victims were found to cluster in four family pedigrees, each of which contained a heavy loading for affective disorders and suicide. For example, in one family pedigree with a very heavy loading for affective disorders, there have been 7 suicides. All 7 suicide victims were found among individuals with definite affective disorder. In a second pedigree, also with a heavy loading for affective disorders, there have been 6 suicides—5 of which were found among individuals with definite affective disorder.

Interestingly, the converse was not true, as there were other family pedigrees with heavy loadings for affective disorder but without suicides. It is also of note that the morbidity risk for affective disorders among 170 first-degree relatives in other bipolar I pedigrees without suicide was, similar to that found in bipolar pedigrees with suicide, also in the 20% range. Thus, in this study a familial loading for affective disorders was not in itself a predictor for suicide.

The third finding of the study was that only 6 (23%) of the 26 suicide victims had received any psychiatric treatment despite the fact that 24 of them had severe affective disorders whose natural history is usually that of recurrent episodes. The other 20 suicide victims either had never received any medical treatment for their psychiatric disorder, or they were seeing a family doctor at the time that they committed suicide, or they were planning to seek help for themselves.

Egeland and Sussex (1985) concluded that "Our study of suicides among the Amish replicates findings that indicate an increased suicidal risk for patients with a diagnosis of major affective disorder and a strong family history of suicide" (p. 918). "Bipolar and unipolar illness conveys a high risk as a diagnostic pattern in pedigrees. The number not receiving adequate treatment for manic-depressive illness (among the suicides) supports the common belief that intervention for these patients at risk is recommended" (p. 918). The authors also say of intervention that, "It appears most warranted in those families in which there is a family history of suicide. The clustering of suicides in Amish pedigrees follows the distribution of affective illness in the kinship and suggests the role of inheritance" (p. 918).

DANISH-AMERICAN ADOPTION STUDIES

The strongest evidence that we have for the presence of genetic factors in suicide comes from the adoption studies carried out in Denmark by Schulsinger and associates (1979). The strength of the adoption strategy is that it is one of the best ways to tease apart "nature" and "nurture" issues, because individuals separated at birth, or shortly afterward, share their genes but no subsequent environmental experiences with their biological relatives. In contrast, adoptees share their environmental experiences through childhood and adolescence with their adopting relatives, but they share no genes with them.

The Psykologisk Institute has a register of the 5,483 adoptions that occurred in greater Copenhagen between 1924 and 1947. A screening of the registers of causes of death revealed that 57 of these adoptees eventually committed suicide. They were matched with adopted controls for sex, age, social class of the adopting parents, and time spent both with their biological relatives and in institutions before being adopted. Searches of the causes of death revealed that 12 of the 269 biological relatives of these 57 adopted suicide victims had themselves committed suicide compared with only 2 of the 269 biological relatives of the 57 adopted controls. This is a highly significant difference for suicide between the two groups of relatives (Table 12). None of the adopting relatives of either the suicide or control group had committed suicide.

These striking results are of additional interest because the suicides were largely independent of the presence of psychiatric disorder. Schulsinger and co-workers (1979) also investigated whether the names of the 12 biological relatives who committed suicide appeared on the psychiatric case registers. They found that 6 of these biological suicide relatives had had no contact with the psychiatric services, and they presumably did not suffer from one of the major psychiatric disorders commonly found among suicide victims—manic depression, schizophrenia, or alcoholism—as these are chronic disorders with frequent relapses usually requiring psychiatric hospitalization. Schulsinger and associates (1979) therefore proposed that there may be a genetic predisposition for suicide independent of, or additive to, the major psychiatric disorders associated with suicide.

Wender and associates (1986) went on to study another group of the Danish adoptees. These were the 71 adoptees identified by the psychiatric case register as having suffered from an affective disorder. They were matched with 71 control adoptees without affective disorder. The results of this study showed that significantly more of the biological relatives of the adoptees with affective disorder than the biological relatives of the control counterparts had committed suicide. Thus, this study too demonstrates that there is a genetic component to suicide, as highlighted in Table 13.

Of further interest in this study was the examination of the adoptee suicide victims and their biological relatives by the type of affective disorder suffered by the suicide victim. This revealed that it was particularly the adoptee suicide victims with the diagnosis of "affect reaction" who had significantly more biological relatives who had committed suicide compared with the controls (Table 14). The diagnosis of "affect

Table 12. Incidence of Suicide in the Relatives of Adoptees Who Committed Suicide and Their Controls

Adoptees	Biological relatives	Adoptive relatives
57 Adoptees who died by suicide	12/269 (4.5%)	0/148 (0%)
57 Matched control adoptees	2/269 (0.7%)	0/150 (0%)
	$p < .01$	

Note. Reprinted with permission from Kety S: Genetic factors in suicide, in Suicide. Edited by Roy A. Baltimore, Williams & Wilkins, 1986. Copyright 1986, the Williams & Wilkins Co., Baltimore.

Table 13. Incidence of Suicide in the Relatives of Adoptees Who Have Suffered a Depressive Illness and Their Controls

Adoptees	Biological relatives	Adoptive relatives
71 Adoptees with depression	15/407 (3.7%)	1/187 (0.5%)
71 Matched control adoptees	1/360 (0.3%) $p < .01$	2/171 (1.2%)

Note. Reprinted with permission from Kety S: Genetic factors in suicide, in Suicide. Edited by Roy A. Baltimore, Williams & Wilkins, 1986. Copyright 1986, the Williams & Wilkins Co., Baltimore.

Table 14. Incidence of Suicide in the Biological Relatives of Depressive and Control Adoptees

Diagnosis in adoptee	Incidence of suicide in biological relatives	Significance
Affective reaction	5/66 (7.6%)	$p < .0004*$
Neurotic depression	3/127 (2.4%)	$p < .056$
Bipolar depression	4/75 (5.3%)	$p < .0036$
Unipolar depression	3/139 (2.2%)	$p < .067$
No mental illness	1/360 (0.3%)	

Note. Reprinted with permission from Kety S: Genetic factors in suicide, in Suicide. Edited by Roy A. Baltimore, Williams & Wilkins, 1986. Copyright 1986, the Williams & Wilkins Co., Baltimore.
*Compared with biological relatives of control adoptees with no known history of mental illness.

reaction" is used in Denmark to describe an individual who has affective symptoms accompanying a situational crisis—often an impulsive suicide attempt. These findings led Kety (1986) to suggest that a genetic factor in suicide may be an inability to control impulsive behavior, which has its effect independent of, or additive to, psychiatric disorder. Psychiatric disorders, or environmental stress, may serve as potentiating mechanisms which foster or trigger the impulsive behavior, directing it toward a suicidal outcome.

Kety (1986) also noted that there has been much recent work on the biology of impulsivity and that disturbances in central serotonin systems have been described in relation to suicidal behavior in personality disordered individuals and in patients with various other psychiatric disorders. In this regard, it is noteworthy that Buchsbaum et al. (1976) found that significantly more college students with low levels of the enzyme monoamine oxidase (MAO) in their blood platelets had a family history of suicidal behavior compared with students with high platelet MAO levels. This enzyme is concerned with the metabolism of serotonin. Furthermore, there is some evidence that lithium may be useful in impulsive and aggressive individuals (Shard et al. 1976). Kety (1986) also suggested that controlled trials of drugs acting on the central serotonin system might be informative among patients who exhibit suicidal behaviors.

SUMMARY

Suicide, like so many other symptoms and disorders, tends to run in families. The question is, what is being transmitted? No doubt in some youthful suicide victims what is transmitted is not a genetic factor but a psychological factor. The family member who has committed suicide may serve as a role model to identify with, and the option of committing suicide becomes one possible "solution" to intolerable psychological pain. However, the family, twin, and adoption studies reviewed here show that there are genetic factors in suicide. In many suicide victims these will be genetic factors involved in the genetic transmission of manic depression, schizophrenia, and alcoholism—the psychiatric disorders most commonly associated with suicide. However, the Copenhagen adoption studies strongly suggest there may be a genetic factor for suicide independent of, or additive to, the genetic transmission of psychiatric disorder. Interestingly, support for this possibility comes from the recent Amish studies, which showed that suicide was much more likely to occur when an individual had genetic vulnerabilities both to suicide and to affective illness.

There is a possible practical implication for the prevention of youth suicide arising from this review. It is that an adolescent who develops a depressive episode, or who exhibits suicidal behavior, and who has a family history of suicide might be considered to be at increased risk of committing suicide. Such a youngster warrants intervention that will aim to decrease the depression and suicidal behavior. Furthermore, a clinician should determine the extent of suicidal behavior and the types of psychiatric problems and disorders that exist among the relatives. It also may be necessary to treat a relative such as a parent or sibling, to diminish their suicidal inclinations. It would also be important to discuss with the adolescent and parents the family constellation of psychopathology and the risks that may exist for suicidal behavior. In so doing, early warning signs of suicidal behavior may be identified and immediate intervention obtained. Furthermore, it would be important for the clinician to follow such a youngster closely over time, particularly with a view to determining whether the adolescent is developing a recurrent affective disorder and suicidal behavior for which psychotherapy and/or psychopharmacological intervention again might be appropriate.

REFERENCES

Barraclough B, Bunch J, Nelson B, et al: A hundred cases of suicide: clinical aspects. Br J Psychiatry 125:355–373, 1974

Batchelor I, Napier M: Attempted suicide in old age. Br Med J 2:1186–1190, 1953

Buchsbaum M, Coursey R, Murphy D: The biochemical high-risk paradigm: behavioral and familial correlates of low platelet monoamine oxidase activity. Science 191:339–341, 1976

Dorpat T, Ripley H: A study of suicide in the Seattle area. Compr Psychiatry 1:349–359, 1960

Egeland JA, Hostetter AM: Amish study, I: affective disorders among the Amish, 1976–1980. Am J Psychiatry 140:56–61, 1983

Egeland J, Sussex J: Suicide and family loading for affective disorders. JAMA 254:915–918, 1985

Farberow N, Simon M: Suicide in Los Angeles and Vienna: an intercultural study of two cities. Public Health Rep 84:389–403, 1969

Flinn D, Leonard C: Prevalence of suicidal ideation and behavior among basic trainees and college students. Milit Med 137:317–320, 1972

Garfinkel B, Froese A, Hood J: Suicide attempts in children and adolescents. Am J Psychiatry 139:1257–1261, 1982

Haberlandt W: Der suizid als genetisches problem (zwillings and familien analyse). Anthropol Anz 29:65–89, 1965

Haberlandt W: Aportacion a la genetica del suicido. Folia Clin Int 17:319–322, 1967

Juel-Nielsen N, Videbech T: A twin study of suicide. Acta Genet Med Gemellol 19:307–310, 1970

Kallman F, Anastasio M: Twin studies on the psychopathology of suicide. J Nerv Ment Dis 105:40–55, 1947

Kallman F, DePorte J, Deporte E, et al: Suicide in twins and only children. Am J Hum Genet 2:113–126, 1949

Kety S: Genetic factors in suicide, in Suicide. Edited by Roy A. Baltimore, Williams & Wilkins, 1986

Linkowski P, de Maertelaer V, Mendlewicz J: Suicidal behavior in major depressive illness. Acta Psychiatr Scand 72:233–238, 1985

Murphy G, Robins E: Social factors in suicide. JAMA 199:303–308, 1967

Murphy G, Wetzel R: Family history of suicidal behavior among suicide attempters. J Nerv Ment Dis 170:86–90, 1982

Murphy G, Wetzel R, Swallow C, et al: Who calls the suicide prevention center: a study of 55 persons calling on their own behalf. Am J Psychiatry 126:314–324, 1969

Pitts F, Winokur G: Affective disorder, Part 3: diagnostic correlates and incidence of suicide. Journal of Mental Disease 40:971–974, 1983

Robins E, Schmidt E, O'Neal P: Some interrelations of social factors and clinical diagnosis in attempted suicide. Am J Psychiatry 114:221–231, 1957

Robins E, Murphy G, Wilkinson R, et al: Some clinical observations in the prevention of suicide based on a study of 134 successful suicides. Am J Public Health 49:888–889, 1959

Roy A: Risk factors for suicide in psychiatric patients. Arch Gen Psychiatry 39:1089–1095, 1982

Roy A: Family history of suicide. Arch Gen Psychiatry 40:971–974, 1983

Roy A: Family history of suicide in manic-depressive patients. J Affective Disord 8:187–189, 1985a

Roy A: Family history of suicide in affective disorder patients. J Clin Psychiatry 46:317–319, 1985b

Roy A: Genetics of suicide: psychobiology of suicidal behavior. Ann NY Acad Sci 97–105, 1986a

Roy A: Genetic factors in suicide. Psychopharmacol Bull 22:666–668, 1986b

Schulsinger R, Kety S, Rosenthal D, et al: A family study of suicide, in Origins, Prevention and Treatment of Affective Disorders. Edited by Schou M, Stromgren E. New York, Academic Press, 1979, pp 277–287

Shaffer D: Suicide in childhood and early adolescence. J Child Psychol Psychiatry 5:275–291, 1974

Shaffer D: Quoted in Clinical Psychiatry News, 1985

Shaffer D, Gould M, Trautman P: Suicidal behavior in children and young adults. Unpublished paper presented at the Conference on Psychobiology of Suicidal Behavior, New York Academy of Sciences, New York, September 18–20, 1985

Shafii M, Carrigan S, Whittinghill R, et al: Psychological autopsy of completed suicides in children and adolescents. Am J Psychiatry 142:1061–1064, 1985

Shard M, Marini J, Bridges C, et al: The effect of lithium on impulsive aggressive behavior in man. Am J Psychiatry 133:1409–1413, 1976

Tishler C, McKenry P, Morgan K: Adolescent suicide attempts: some significant factors. Suicide Life Threat Behav 11:86–92, 1981

Tsuang MT: Genetic factors in suicide. Diseases of the Nervous System 38:498–501, 1977

Tsuang MT: Suicide in schizophrenics, manics, depressives, and surgical controls: a comparison with general population suicide mortality. Arch Gen Psychiatry 35:153–155, 1978

Tsuang MT: Risk of suicide in the relatives of schizophrenics, manics, depressives and controls. J Clin Psychiatry 44:396–400, 1983

Tsuang MT, Woolson RF: Excess mortality in schizophrenia and affective disorders: do suicide and accidental deaths solely account for this excess? Arch Gen Psychiatry 35:1181–1185, 1978

Weissman A, Worden J: Risk-rescue rating in suicide assessment. Arch Gen Psychiatry 26:553–560, 1972

Wender P, Kety S, Rosenthal D, et al: Psychiatric disorders in the biological and adoptive families of adopted individuals with affective disorders. Arch Gen Psychiatry 43:923–929, 1986

Williams S: Cit Lowenberg, 1941; 1918

Zair K: A suicidal family. Br J Psychiatry 189:68–69, 1981

10

Biological Correlates of Suicidal Behavior in Youth

J. John Mann, M.D.
Michael D. DeMeo, M.D.
John G. Keilp, M.A.
P. Anne McBride, M.D.

Suicidal behavior and suicide have traditionally been understood to be an extreme response to depression. More recently this view has been modified for three reasons: 1) the risk for suicide is at least partly genetically determined (Roy 1986), 2) an association has been identified between impaired serotonergic function and violent suicide attempts or completed suicide (Mann and Stanley 1986), and 3) severity of depression correlates weakly with suicide (Linehan 1986).

Suicide is not a common event even among high-risk groups such as those suffering from a depressive illness. This raises the question, why is suicide rare and what distinguishes those who suicide from the majority who do not? An explanation may lie in a genetically determined biological vulnerability. Biological studies that have addressed this possibility will be reviewed with an emphasis on findings in youth suicide.

There is controversy over whether there are discontinuous or continuous patterns of suicidal behavior; nevertheless, these patterns of behavior may be subdivided into: 1) ideation, 2) parasuicide or suicide gesture, 3) failed suicide, and 4) completed suicide. The frequency of each of the categories appears to vary across the life span.

Age is a major predictor of the type of suicidal behavior. In general,

This work was partly supported by PHS grant MH-40210 and an Irma T. Hirschl Trust Research Scientist award to Dr. Mann. Renée Azima-Heller assisted in the preparation of the material. The manuscript was expertly typed by Isadora Johnson.

parasuicide is estimated to be 10 times more common than failed or completed suicide, but the relative proportion of parasuicide is much greater in adolescents and younger adults compared with middle and older age groups (Linehan 1986). A central question that a prospective control study will have to answer is whether preadolescents and adolescents who attempt suicide or experience suicidal ideation are the same group who as adults are at greatest risk for attempting or completing suicide. A second question that remains unanswered is, what determines the age-related difference in the proportion of parasuicide to failed or completed suicide between these populations? Age-related modifications in both external and internal psychosocial factors that contribute to suicide risk and the response to such stress factors as well as differences in biological factors may be accounted for by these age-related differences in suicidal behavior.

In the consideration of the biological correlates of suicidal behavior, a distinction should therefore be made between trait-dependent correlates and state-dependent correlates. Trait-dependent biological indices will be similar at different ages or modified slowly by aging effects and therefore are apparent whenever the subject is tested. Such biological traits must be the result of genetic factors or early life effects. The evidence for a genetic risk factor for suicide will be discussed below. The state-dependent biological correlates would only be present at or around the time of the suicide attempt.

EVIDENCE FOR A GENETICALLY DETERMINED RISK FACTOR FOR SUICIDE

The evidence supporting the presence of a genetically determined risk factor for suicide is very clear in adult populations and has been recently reviewed (Roy 1986). Twin studies have demonstrated a higher rate of concordance for suicidal behavior in monozygotic versus dizygotic twins (Haberlandt 1965, 1967). Rates of suicide are significantly elevated in the families of suicide victims (Roy 1986). An important study was carried out among the Amish community in Pennsylvania (Egeland and Sussex 1985). This group is characterized by very strong family ties and a religious commitment that creates a powerful aversion to all forms of violence, including suicide. All of the 26 suicides that had taken place in the last 100 years had been among members of only four families. These families also had a significantly higher rate of affective disorders, indicating a link between suicide and affective disorders. However, the presence of high rates of affective disorders in other families in the absence of any suicides indicates there may be a separate pattern of inheritance for suicide compared with affective disorders or that there may be a genetically determined lower suicide risk form of affective disorder.

The question of nature versus nurture is best addressed by adoption studies. The Copenhagen adoption study found that there was an increased suicide rate in the biological families of 57 adoptees who had suicided (Schulsinger et al. 1979) compared to 57 matched living adoptees. This finding was true for biological families of adoptees with or without a history of a psychiatric illness (about one-half had no known mental illness). This suggests that the risk for suicide was at least partly genetic.

A consequence of the finding of a genetically determined risk factor for suicide is that there may be a detectable biological trait that is the phenotypic expression of that genotype. The pattern of genetic transmission remains to be worked out, but that question can be resolved in parallel with the identification of the biological correlates of suicide.

STRATEGIES OF RESEARCH INTO THE BIOLOGY OF SUICIDAL BEHAVIOR

Two major strategies have been employed in the search for biological correlates of suicidal behavior: 1) studies of postmortem brain tissue from suicide victims and 2) studies of biological indices in suicide attempters. Each strategy has its advantages and disadvantages. Postmortem studies are able to examine the brain itself, but they permit sampling at only one point in time, namely at the time of death of the individual. Moreover, it is usually not possible to get detailed clinical information including a current mental status examination. Studies of patients who have recently attempted suicide are indirect because it is not possible to directly sample the brain, but they do permit repeated sampling and a detailed clinical evaluation.

Three types of clinical studies have been carried out in suicide attempters: 1) assays of monoamines and their metabolites in cerebrospinal fluid (CSF), 2) neuroendocrine challenge tests, and 3) peripheral nervous system function and assay of monoamine elements in peripheral blood cells and platelets.

It is remarkable, particularly in light of the degree to which public attention has focused on the rate of youth suicide (which rose dramatically in the 1960s and 1970s), that there are no published studies that have examined the biology of youth suicide or youth suicide attempters. Therefore, by necessity this chapter describes findings in adult populations.

In the absence of any direct studies of youth suicide, wherever possible the data available on younger adults (aged 18–25 years) have been abstracted from the literature for comparison purposes with subjects over 25 years of age.

Postmortem Brain Studies

As indicated above, the findings of these studies inform us about completed suicide. The relationship of these findings to attempted suicide remains to be determined. As we have reviewed elsewhere (Mann et al. 1986a), levels of serotonin (5-HT) and its metabolite 5-hydroxyindoleacetic acid (5-HIAA) appear to be slightly lower in the brain stem of suicide victims (Shaw et al. 1967; Bourne et al. 1968; Pare et al. 1969; Lloyd et al. 1974; Beskow et al. 1976). Most studies have not found any differences between suicide victims and controls in 5-HT or 5-HIAA in cortical tissue (Beskow et al. 1976; Stanley et al. 1983; Korpi et al. 1986). However, transmitter or metabolite levels may not reflect levels of actual neuronal activity. For that purpose, measurement of receptor binding indices may be more useful. For example, decreasing serotonergic activity by lesioning the 5-HT neurons in the brain stem results in a compensatory increase in postsynaptic 5-HT_2 receptors and a loss of presynaptic imipramine binding sites, which are associated with the 5-HT uptake site on 5-HT nerve terminals (Langer et al. 1980; Brunello et al. 1982).

Conversely, increasing the intrasynaptic levels of 5-HT exposed to the receptor results in downregulation of 5-HT_2 but not 5-HT_1 receptors (Wirz-Justice et al. 1978; Peroutka and Snyder 1979, 1980).

Several laboratories have now reported a decrease in imipramine binding (presynaptic) in the brains of suicide victims (Stanley et al. 1982; Perry et al. 1983; Crow et al. 1984; Paul et al. 1987), although others have not replicated this finding (Meyerson et al. 1982). In general, the control group has been drawn from patients without a known psychiatric illness dying from causes other than suicide.

A comparison of the difference in imipramine binding between suicide victims and controls in the study of Stanley and colleagues (Stanley et al. 1982) revealed that under 25 years of age the suicide group had 65% of the control group level of imipramine binding compared to 53% of control values for the over 25-year-old suicide group. Although the number of subjects in each cell was small, these data do not suggest an age effect. The degree of difference in imipramine binding appeared to be just as great in the younger group as in the older group. Perry and colleagues (Perry et al. 1983) found a decrease in imipramine binding in a study population of patients with an affective disorder that were aged 78 years compared with controls, suggesting that this biochemical difference may span a very wide age range. There are studies that confirm this finding in the middle age range (Paul et al. 1987) as well as others that do not in a suicide group with a mean age of 42.5 years (Cheatham et al. 1987).

An increase in 5-HT$_2$ binding sites (postsynaptic) has been reported in the frontal cortex of suicide victims (Stanley and Mann 1983; Mann et al. 1986b; Meltzer et al. 1987). The effect is specific for the 5-HT$_2$ receptor subtype because no change in 5-HT$_1$ binding has been found (Mann et al. 1986b). These receptor changes are consistent with reduced presynaptic serotonergic activity and compensatory postsynaptic supersensitivity or upregulation. The average age of the suicide group in our studies over the last 2 years has been 39 years.

With regard to the increase in 5-HT$_2$ receptor binding in the prefrontal cortex in suicide victims, this finding in suicide has been less extensively studied. An important observation has been that of a significant age-related loss of 5-HT$_2$ binding sites noted in both postmortem and positron emission tomography (PET) studies (Mann et al. 1985). Thus, while there is little evidence of an age-related effect on presynaptic serotonergic indices, the age-related loss of postsynaptic 5-HT$_2$ receptors appears to begin at least as early as the second decade of life, and we cannot rule out an earlier effect. This is shown in Figure 1.

It is the 5-HT$_2$, not the 5-HT$_1$ receptor population, that is upregulated in the brains of suicide victims (Mann et al. 1986b) and perhaps depressed patients (Ferrier et al. 1986) and downregulated by 5-HT reuptake inhibitor antidepressants (Wirz-Justice et al. 1978; Peroutka and Snyder 1980). This demonstrates the biochemical specificity of the changes in suicide, which involve only the 5-HT$_2$ receptor subtype. Therefore, it may be highly significant for the different forms of suicidal behavior at different ages that this focal receptor population declines by about 50% between the ages of 15 and 70 years. Perhaps the ability to compensate for impaired serotonergic activity declines with age, resulting in a greater probability that when suicidal behavior occurs, it is more likely to be a failed suicide attempt or a completed suicide rather than a gesture or parasuicide.

In comparing the difference in 5-HT$_2$ receptor binding in the prefrontal cortex between suicide victims and controls, we found a 73% increase over control values in the under 25-year-old suicide group and a 37% increase in the over 25-year-old suicide group. Although the numbers of subjects studied were too few to permit meaningful statistics, the possibility that suicide in younger patients is associated with a more pronounced biochemical deficit than in older subjects is important and demands investigation.

Other receptor populations have been studied, including the β-adrenergic, muscarinic cholinergic, GABA-minergic benzodiazepine,

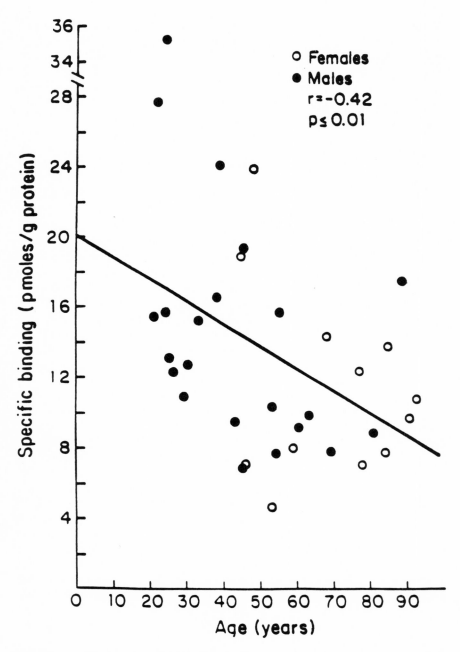

Figure 1. Relationship between age and postmortem serotonin-2 receptor binding to human frontal cortex (0.2nM ^{3}H-spiroperidol).

α_1- and α_2-adrenergic. Too few data are available to comment on most of these receptor populations with two exceptions. There appears to be an increase in β-adrenergic binding in the prefrontal cortex in suicide victims compared with controls (Zanko and Bigeon 1983; Mann et al. 1986b). This may or may not be secondary to the postulated decrease in serotonergic activity. There is no change in the number of muscarinic cholinergic receptors (Stanley 1984; Kaufman et al. 1984). If the contrast is made between the brains of suicide victims and controls under the age of 25 years (Stanley 1984), there were 15% fewer receptors in the suicide group, whereas over the age of 25 years there were 11% more receptors. These differences are not statistically significant but are a reminder of the need to go beyond controlling for age effects and to begin to study age effects.

In summary, although the data are very preliminary, it appears that the differences observed in 5-HT receptor number in the prefrontal cortex of suicide victims compared with controls may be present to at least the same degree in suicide victims below the age of 25 years compared with suicide victims above 25 years of age. Thus, biological factors contributing to suicide risk may be at least as significant for youth suicide as they are for suicide in older individuals.

Studies of the Biology of Suicide Attempters

The studies in vivo are of suicide attempters. That there does not appear to be a biological difference between youth and older suicide victims is perhaps not surprising since both groups have suicided. However, that may not apply to suicide attempters. As indicated above, there is a range of behaviors that characterize suicide attempts, and the distribution of these behavioral patterns changes with age. We have characterized suicidal behavior in 48 patients under and over the age of 25 years. This age cutoff was chosen because this chapter could only describe biological findings from published studies and all of these focused on adult suicide. Biological effects in youth suicide attempters versus older adults have therefore been inferred by comparing the 18- to 25-year-olds with those attempters over 25 years of age.

When suicidal behavior was categorical, divided into failed suicide and parasuicide (and mixed) groups, there was a significantly higher rate of failed suicide in the older group (54 versus 11%) and parasuicide in the younger groups (89 versus 36%). Therefore, if we hypothesize biological and clinical similarities between the failed suicide group and completed suicide group, then a corollary of this hypothesis would be that parasuicides (which predominate in youth) may not be associated with the same biological differences from control subjects that are found in failed suicides (which predominate in older suicide attempters). An alternative hypothesis is that the low 5-HT trait may result in different forms of suicidal behavior at different ages. The available data, limited as they are, will be examined in order to address these two alternatives.

Cerebrospinal fluid studies.   Asberg and colleagues (1976) studied patients with a major depressive disorder and found that CSF levels of 5-HIAA were bimodally distributed, namely, a group with lower levels of 5-HIAA and a group with higher levels of 5-HIAA. The low 5-HIAA group had made more total suicide attempts and more violent suicide attempts but the two groups did not differ with respect to overall severity of depression. Subsequently most studies have confirmed this finding and extended it. It now appears that lower levels of CSF 5-HIAA appear to be associated with suicidal acts in disorders other than affective disorders including schizophrenia and personality disorders (Asberg et al. 1986).

Depressive disorders.   Several studies have now found reduced levels of CSF 5-HIAA in patients with affective disorders principally of the unipolar subtype who have attempted suicide compared to nonattempters (Asberg et al. 1976; Agren 1980; Van Praag 1982; Montgomery and Montgomery 1982; Palanappian et al. 1983; Banki et al. 1984; Perez de los Cobos et al. 1984). Other studies involving bipolar patients have not confirmed this finding (Roy-Byrne et al. 1983; Berrettini et al. 1986). It is possible that part of the explanation for this discrepancy may lie in the fact that bipolar disorder is itself associated with a 5-HT deficiency, which may account for the higher rate of suicide in this disorder as well as obscure any potential additional 5-HT deficit due to a separate suicide risk factor.

Schizophrenia.   The findings with respect to CSF 5-HIAA are less clear in schizophrenia. Three laboratories found lower levels of 5-HIAA in attempters compared with nonattempters (Van Praag 1983; Ninan et al. 1984; Stanley et al. 1986), and two laboratories failed to replicate these findings (Roy 1985; Pickar et al. 1986). Korpi and colleagues (1986) did not find lower levels of 5-HT in brain samples from schizophrenic suicide victims compared to controls, but they did find such an effect in depressed suicide victims. Thus, the important theoretical point that lower CSF 5-HIAA may be an indicator of suicide risk that is generalizable across diagnostic boundaries is not fully supported by the findings in schizophrenia.

Personality disorders.   Another category of patients with an increased risk of suicide is those with personality disorders. Three laboratories have reported evidence of lower levels of CSF 5-HIAA in suicide attempters with personality disorders compared with controls (Brown et al. 1979, 1982; Traskman et al. 1981; Linnoila et al. 1983). The findings raise the interesting question as to what core personality traits may correlate with 5-HT indices and/or suicide risk.

Impulsivity and aggressivity have both been postulated to be correlated with 5-HT (Brown et al. 1979, 1982; Linnoila et al. 1983; Cocarro et al. 1987). Brown and colleagues (1979, 1982) reported a positive correlation between aggressivity and suicidal behavior. The same group reported a negative correlation between 5-HIAA levels and aggressivity and suicidal behavior.

The fenfluramine challenge test assesses the functional integrity of the brain serotonergic system by releasing endogenous stores of 5-HT from the nerve terminals and thereby indirectly activating 5-HT receptors. Thus, it tests both pre- and postsynaptic components of the serotonergic system. Cocarro and colleagues (1987) and our own laboratory have found evidence of a negative correlation between prolactin response due to 5-HT release by fenfluramine and certain indices of aggressivity such as a past history of physical fights, assaultiveness, and disciplinary problems at work or at school. These results suggest a link between aggressivity traits and reduced brain serotonergic responses.

Aggressive behaviors are a component of many conditions. We and others have reported an age-related decline in aggressivity (Keilp et al. 1987) and yet there is an increase in the seriousness of suicidal behavior with increasing age as we have indicated above. Thus, the psychobiological effects of aging may result in two different clinical syndromes. Youth suicide attempters are characterized by greater aggressivity and impulsivity and less lethal methods. Older attempters appear to be less aggressive and impulsive and use more lethal means. Within a limited age range there is a positive correlation between aggressivity and suicidal behavior (Brown et al. 1979, 1982) and both correlated negatively with 5-HIAA levels. A comparison of older and younger patients using a cross-sectional study design indicates that there are substantial age-related alterations in the levels of both aggressivity (decreases) and the seriousness of the suicidal behavior (increases) and both are related to serotonergic function. The significant age-related changes in the serotonergic system may therefore play a role in the different patterns of suicidal behavior in younger compared to older persons. Nevertheless, it is possible that factors beyond the serotonergic system (biologic, social, and psychological) are also responsible for these age-related differences. The role of impulsivity is less clear, but Linnoila and colleagues (1983) found that impulsive homicide as opposed to premeditated homicide was associated with lower levels of 5-HIAA compared to controls.

NEUROENDOCRINE STUDIES

Transmitter Specific Studies

The major focus of this strategy has been on the serotonergic system. Blunted serotonergic neuroendocrine responses have been reported in patients with major depressive disorder as assessed by the prolactin response to the 5-HT precursor L-tryptophan (Henninger et al. 1984). L-tryptophan causes a rise in brain 5-HT and 5-HIAA and presumably when administered acutely results in the release of higher levels of 5-HT. Depressed patients show less of a prolactin response to L-tryptophan. However, administration of 5-hydroxytryptophan, another 5-HT precursor, has been reported to cause greater cortisol release in patients who had made a suicide attempt compared to those without a history of an attempt (Meltzer et al. 1984). Subsequently, Meltzer and colleagues (1987) also found a supersensitive cortisol response using the experimental drug MK212, which activates 5-HT receptors directly. Therefore, these data are consistent with the presence of 5-HT receptor supersensitivity in the brains of the suicide attempter group. Such a finding could be explained by an increase in the number of 5-HT$_2$ receptors in subjects who have attempted suicide as we have already reported occurs in the brains of suicide victims.

The question arises as to whether overall serotonergically mediated responses are blunted in suicide attempters despite the apparent increase in receptor supersensitivity (which presumably occurs as a compensatory response to reduced or impaired presynaptic serotonergic function). The use of fenfluramine-induced prolactin release as described above addresses this question. We studied patients with major and minor depression using the fenfluramine challenge test (DeMeo et al. 1987). There was a significant decline in prolactin responses in normal subjects beyond the age of 30 years. This finding was consistent with our observation of an age-related loss of 5-HT receptors in the brain. Younger depressed patients (teens and twenties) have a blunted prolactin response compared with healthy controls. This blunted response correlated with assaultiveness and evidence of borderline personality traits but not with severity of depression or suicidal behavior. Older subjects had lesser degrees of aggressivity or borderline personality traits, and these correlations with prolactin response were not significant. Cocarro and colleagues (1987) found a negative correlation between peak prolactin response and aggressivity and suicidality in a study of male patients with personality disorders and without a depressive disorder. Thus, it appears that the blunted prolactin response to fenfluramine may be a correlate of certain personality traits and suicidal behavior apart from any possible relationship to depressive illness. Moreover, these biochemical correlates may only be apparent in younger individuals, in whom aggressivity is more pronounced than in older subjects.

Transmitter-Nonspecific Neuroendocrine Challenge Studies

The best known of transmitter-nonspecific challenge tests is the dexamethasone suppression test (DST). This test has been employed as an index of hypothalamic-pituitary-adrenal-cortical (HYPAC) axis function. In this test, a positive (abnormal) result is evidence of a failure of dexamethasone to suppress cortisol levels to a sufficient degree (<5 $\mu g/dl$) for a sufficient period of time (24 hours). Failure to meet these criteria may be termed dexamethasone resistance. Cortisol secretory patterns and levels are two other important indices of HYPAC function.

An association between both hypercortisolemia and resistance to dexamethasone suppression of cortisol levels has been reported with melancholia (Carroll et al. 1981a). These abnormalities are apparently not present in nonmelancholic depressive disorders.

Controversy exists as to whether there is a relationship between suicidal behavior or risk and either hypercortisolemia or dexamethasone resistance. The balance of the data is beginning to indicate that HYPAC dysfunction does not have a specific relationship with suicidal behavior.

Early reports suggested increased cortisol secretion may be associated with suicidal behavior. Increased levels of 24-hour urinary 17-hydrocorticosteroids or urinary free cortisol were found in suicidal patients or in patients who subsequently committed suicide (Bunney and Fawcett 1965; Bunney et al. 1969; Ostroff et al. 1982). In contrast, normal or low levels of urinary cortisol were reported by others in patients who had attempted or completed suicide (Levy and Hensen 1969; Krieger 1970). Two recent large studies found no correlation between plasma cortisol levels and suicidal behavior (Kocsis et al. 1986).

Dexamethasone resistance is not clearly correlated with suicidal behavior. A higher rate of dexamethasone resistance in attempters has been reported by some studies (Carroll et al. 1981b; Targum et al. 1983; Banki et al. 1983) but three other studies did not report this finding (Van

Waltere et al. 1983; Kocsis et al. 1986). It is of note that dexamethasone resistance is comparable to control levels in young patients with mild to moderate nonmelancholic depressive disorder and in those with personality disorders such as borderline personality disorder (Carroll et al. 1981b). HYPAC abnormalities are associated with melancholia. There is no clear specific relationship proven with suicidal behavior at this stage.

Peripheral Blood Studies

Several indices of monoamine system components have been studied in platelets from suicidal subjects: platelet monoamine oxidase (MAO) activity, platelet imipramine binding, platelet 5-HT uptake, platelet 5-HT_2 receptors, and platelet 5-HT content. Results of these studies have been reviewed elsewhere (Mann and Stanley 1986) and only the salient points will be summarized here.

Platelet MAO activity appears to be lower in normal volunteers with a family history of suicide (Buchsbaum et al. 1979; Gottfries et al. 1980) but platelet MAO activity is not altered in suicide attempters (Oreland et al. 1981; Meltzer and Arora 1986) and nor is brain MAO activity directly correlated with suicidal behavior (Mann and Stanley 1984).

Platelet 5-HT uptake kinetics (V_{max} and K_D) have been studied extensively in affective disorders (Meltzer et al. 1981). Maximal 5-HT uptake rate or V_{max} is reduced in melancholic but not in nonmelancholic depression (Meltzer et al. 1981). There is one report of a positive correlation between K_m (affinity) and the score on the Hamilton Depression Suicide Subscale (Meltzer and Arora 1986), which suggests that more suicidal patients have reduced 5-HT uptake affinity. However, we found no difference in V_{max} or K_m in a sample of drug-free melancholic patients who had attempted suicide compared to nonattempters (Mann et al., unpublished data).

Although the number (B_{max}) of imipramine binding sites appears to be reduced in the brain of suicide victims (Stanley et al. 1982; Perry et al. 1983; Crow et al. 1984; Paul et al. 1987), no difference in B_{max} has been found in platelets of attempters compared to nonattempters (Meltzer and Arora 1986). However, an increased K_D (lower affinity) has been reported (Meltzer and Arora 1986). Platelet 5-HT content does not seem to be correlated with suicidal behavior (Meltzer and Arora 1986).

We have developed a method for assaying 5-HT_2 receptors on human platelets (McBride et al. 1983). We found an increased number of 5-HT_2 receptors in suicide attempters compared with nonattempters (McBride et al. 1987). Platelet 5-HT_2 receptor number was greater in patients making more lethal suicide attempts. Young (<24 years old) attempters (who also used less lethal methods) had significantly fewer platelet 5-HT$_2$ receptors than older suicide attempters who used more lethal methods. This was not an effect of age since aging in normal subjects is associated with a possible age-related loss of platelet 5-HT$_2$ receptors. More lethal suicide attempts were therefore correlated with more platelet 5-HT$_2$ receptors. Thus, an increase in platelet 5-HT$_2$ receptor binding in suicide attempters who used more lethal methods is parallel to the observations of increases in brain 5-HT$_2$ receptor number in the prefrontal cortex of suicide completers. This platelet 5-HT$_2$ receptor biological difference in young suicide attempters compared to older attempters correlates with the lethality of the attempt. It suggests that biological factors may at least partly explain different forms of suicidal behavior in older and younger subjects.

CONCLUSION

There are important clinical differences between younger and older patients in the nature of the suicide attempt and the associated psychopathology. There is an association between impaired or altered serotonergic function and suicidal behavior. This association is present in young suicide completers as well as in older suicide completers. Neuroendocrine tests of serotonergic function and platelet 5-HT$_2$ receptor indices differ in younger versus older patients and may partly explain differences in the proportion of more lethal suicidal attempts at different ages.

Studies are required to test the hypothesis that in contrast to suicide attempts using means of low lethality, more lethal suicide attempts and suicide are correlated with decreased serotonergic function across the entire life span. A short-term goal involves the specific study of the relationship of serotonergic indices to suicidal behavior in pre- and postpubertal children so as to provide a basis for comparison with studies in adult populations. Ideally such studies should be prospective and longitudinal in high-risk populations but initially should be cross-sectional. Such a hypothesis, if confirmed, would provide a means for both detecting individuals at high risk for suicide and developing a treatment strategy that involves increasing serotonergic activity by pharmacological means.

REFERENCES

Agren H: Symptom patterns in unipolar and bipolar depression correlating with monoamine metabolites in the cerebrospinal fluid, II. Psychiatry Res 3:225–236, 1980

Asberg M, Thoren P, Traskman L: Serotonin depression: a biochemical subgroup within the affective disorders? Science 191:478–480, 1976

Asberg M, Nordstrom P, Traskman-Bendz L: Cerebrospinal fluid studies in suicide: an overview, in Psychobiology of Suicidal Behavior, Vol 487. Edited by Mann JJ, Stanley M. New York, Annals of the New York Academy of Sciences, 1986

Banki CM, Arato M, Papp Z, et al: The influence of dexamethasone on cerebrospinal fluid monoamine metabolites and cortisol in psychiatric patients. Pharmacopsychiatria 16:77–81, 1983

Banki CM, Arato M, Papp Z, et al: Biochemical markers in suicidal patients: investigations with cerebrospinal fluid amine metabolites and neuroendocrine tests. J Affective Disord 6:341–350, 1984

Berrettini W, Nurenberger J, Narrow W, et al: Cerebrospinal fluid studies in bipolar patients with and without a history of suicide attempts, in Psychobiology of Suicidal Behavior, Vol 487. Edited by Mann JJ, Stanley M. New York, Annals of the New York Academy of Sciences, 1986

Beskow J, Gottfries OG, Roos BE, et al: Determination of monoamine and monoamine metabolites in the human brain: postmortem studies in a group of suicides and in a control group. Acta Psychiatr Scand 53:7–20, 1976

Bourne HR, Bunney WE Jr, Colburn RW, et al: Noradrenaline, 5-hydroxytryptamine, and 5-hydroxyindoleacetic acid in hindbrains of suicidal patients. Lancet 2:805–808, 1968

Brown GL, Goodwin FK, Ballenger JC, et al: Aggression in human correlates with cerebrospinal fluid amine metabolites. Psychiatry Res 1:131–139, 1979

Brown GL, Ebert MH, Goyer PF: Aggression, suicide, and serotonin: relationships to CSF amine metabolites. Am J Psychiatry 139:741–746, 1982

Brunello N, Chuang DM, Costa E: Different synaptic location of mianserin and imipramine binding sites. Science 215:1112–1115, 1982

Buchsbaum MS, Haier RJ, Murphy DL: Suicide attempts, platelet monoamine oxidase and the average evoked response. Acta Psychiatr Scand 56:69–77, 1979

Bunney WE Jr, Fawcett JA: Possibility of a biochemical test for suicidal potential. Arch Gen Psychiatry 13:232–239, 1965

Bunney WE Jr, Fawcett JA, Davis JM, et al: Further evaluation of urinary 17-hydroxycorticosteroids in suicidal patients. Arch Gen Psychiatry 21:138–150, 1969

Carroll BJ, Feinberg M, Greden JF, et al: A specific laboratory test for the diagnosis of melancholia: standardization, validation and clinical utility. Arch Gen Psychiatry 38:15–22, 1981a

Carroll BJ, Greden JF, Feinberg M: Suicide, neuroendocrine dysfunction and CSF 5-HIAA concentrations in depression, in Recent Advances in Neuropsychopharmacology. Edited by Angrist B. Oxford, Pergamon Press, 1981b

Cheatham SC, Croff JA, Crompton MR, et al: Serotonin and GABA function in depressive suicide victims. Abstract presented at New Directions in Affective Disorders, Jerusalem, Israel, April 25, 1987

Cocarro EF, Siever LJ, Klar H, et al: 5-HT function and history of suicidal behavior. American Psychiatric Association New Research Abstracts, NR158 105, Chicago, IL, 1987

Crow TJ, Cross AJ, Cooper SJ, et al: Neurotransmitter receptors and mono-amine metabolites in the patients with Alzheimer-type dementia and depression and suicides. Neuropharmacology 23:1561–1569, 1984

DeMeo M, McBride PA, Keilp J, et al: Fenfluramine-stimulated prolactin release and age related differences in depressed inpatient versus controls (abstract). Presented at the annual meeting of the Society of Biological Psychiatry (224), Chicago, IL, 1987

Egeland JA, Sussex JN: Suicide and family loading for affective disorders. JAMA 254:915–918, 1985

Ferrier IN, McKeith IG, Cross AJ, et al: Postmortem neurochemical studies in depression, in Psychobiology of Suicidal Behavior, Vol 487. Edited by Mann JJ, Stanley M. New York, Annals of the New York Academy of Sciences, 1986

Gottfries CG, Knorring LV, Oreland L: Platelet monoamine oxidase activity in mental disorders. Neuropsychopharmacology 4:185–192, 1980

Haberlandt W: Der suizid als genetisches problem (zwillings-und familien analyse). Anthropol Anz 29:65–89, 1965

Haberlandt W: Aportacion a la genetica del suicidio. Folia Clinica Intenvenciones 17:319–322, 1967

Henninger GR, Charney DS, Steinberg DE: Serotonergic function in depression. Arch Gen Psychiatry 41:398–402, 1984

Kaufman CA, Gillin JC, Hill B, et al: Muscarinic binding in suicides. Psychiatry Res 12:47–55, 1984

Keilp J, Raduns C, Evans S, et al: Psychopathology in parasuicide and failed suicide. American Psychiatric Association New Research Abstracts, NR45, Chicago, IL, 1987

Kocsis JH, Kennedy S, Brown RP, et al: Neuroendocrine studies in depression: relationship to suicidal behavior, in Psychobiology of Suicidal Behavior, Vol 487. Edited by Mann JJ, Stanley M. New York, Annals of the New York Academy of Sciences, 1986

Korpi ER, Kleinman JE, Goodman SI, et al: Serotonin and 5-hydroxindoleacetic acid concentrations in brains of suicide victims: comparison in chronic schizophrenic patients with suicide as a cause of death. Arch Gen Psychiatry 43:594–600, 1986

Krieger G: Biochemical predictors of suicide. Diseases of the Nervous System 31:478–482, 1970

Langer SZ, Moret C, Raisman R, et al: High affinity [³H]imipramine binding in rat hypothalamus: association with uptake of serotonin but not of norepinephrine. Science 210:1133–1135, 1980

Levy B, Hensen E: Failure of the urinary test for suicidal potential. Arch Gen Psychiatry 20:415–418, 1969

Linehan M: Suicidal people—one population or two? in Psychobiology of Suicidal Behavior, Vol 487. Edited by Mann JJ, Stanley M. New York, Annals of the New York Academy of Sciences, 1986

Linnoila M, Virkkunen M, Scheinin M, et al: Low cerebrospinal fluid 5-hydroxyindoleacetic acid concentrations differentiates impulsive from nonimpulsive violent behavior. Life Sciences 33:2609–2614, 1983

Lloyd KG, Farley IJ, Deck JHN, et al: Serotonin and 5-hydroxyindoleacetic acid in discrete areas of the brainstem of suicide victims and control patients, in

Advances in Biochemical Psychopharmacology, Vol II. New York, Raven Press, 1974

Mann JJ, Stanley M: Postmortem monoamine oxidase enzyme kinetics in the frontal cortex of suicide victims and controls. Acta Psychiatr Scand 69:135–139, 1984

Mann JJ, Stanley M (eds): Psychobiology of Suicidal Behavior, Vol 487. New York, Annals of the New York Academy of Sciences, 1986

Mann JJ, Petito C, Stanley M, et al: Amine receptor binding and monoamine oxidase activity in postmortem brain tissue; effect of age, gender, and postmortem delay, in Clinical and Pharmacological Studies in Psychiatric Disorders. Edited by Burrows GD, Norman TR, Dennerstein L. London, John Libbey, 1985

Mann JJ, McBride PA, Stanley M: Postmortem monoamine receptors and enzyme studies in suicide, in Psychobiology of Suicidal Behavior, Vol 487. Edited by Mann JJ, Stanley M. New York, Annals of the New York Academy of Sciences, 1986a

Mann JJ, Stanley M, McBride PA, et al: Increased serotonin and beta-adrenergic receptor binding in the frontal cortices of suicide victims. Arch Gen Psychiatry 43:954–959, 1986b

McBride PA, Mann JJ, McEwen B, et al: Characterization of serotonin binding sites on human platelets. Life Sciences 33:2033–2041, 1983

McBride PA, Brown RP, DeMeo M, et al: Platelet 5-HT$_2$ receptors: depression and suicide. American Psychiatric Association New Research Abstracts, NR157, Chicago, IL, 1987

Meltzer HY, Arora RC: Platelet markers of suicidality, in Psychobiology of Suicidal Behavior, Vol 487. Edited by Mann JJ, Stanley M. New York, Annals of the New York Academy of Sciences, 1986

Meltzer HY, Arora RC, Baber R, et al: Serotonin uptake in blood platelets of psychiatric patients. Arch Gen Psychiatry 38:1322–1326, 1981

Meltzer HY, Perline R, Tricou BJ, et al: Effect of 5-hydroxytrophan on serum cortisol levels in major affective disorders, II: relation to suicide, psychosis and depressive symptoms. Arch Gen Psychiatry 41:379–387, 1984

Meltzer HY, Nash JF, Ohmori T, et al: Neuroendocrine and biochemical studies of serotonin and dopamine in depression and suicide (abstract S60). International Conference on New Directions in Affective Disorders. Jerusalem, Israel, April 25, 1987

Meyerson LR, Wennogle LP, Abel MS, et al: Human brain receptor alterations in suicide victims. Pharmacology Biochem Behav 17:159–163, 1982

Montgomery SA, Montgomery D: Pharmacological prevention of suicidal behavior. J Affective Disord 4:291–298, 1982

Ninan PT, Van Kammen DP, Scheinin M, et al: CSF 5-hydroxyindoleacetic acid in suicidal schizophrenic patients. Am J Psychiatry 141:566–569, 1984

Oreland L, Wiberg A, Asberg M, et al: Platelet MAO activity and monoamine metabolites in cerebrospinal fluid in depressed and suicidal patients and in healthy controls. Psychiatry Res 4:21–29, 1981

Ostroff R, Giller E, Bonese K, et al: Neuroendocrine risk factors of suicide. Am J Psychiatry 139:1323–1325, 1982

Palanappian V, Ramachandran V, Somasundaram O: Suicidal ideation and biogenic amines in depression. Indian Journal of Psychiatry 25:268–292, 1983

Pare CMB, Yeung DPH, Price K, et al: 5-Hydroxytryptamine, noradrenaline, and dopamine in brainstem, hypothalamus, and caudate nucleus of controls and patients committing suicide by coal-gas poisoning. Lancet 1:131–135, 1969

Paul SM, Rehavi M, Skolnick P, et al: High affinity binding of antidepressants to a biogenic amine transport site in human brain and platelet: studies in depression, in Frontiers of Clinical Neuroscience: Neurobiology of Mood Disorders. Edited by Post RM, Ballenger JC. Baltimore, Williams & Wilkins, 1987

Perez de los Cobos JZ, Lopez-Ibor Alino JJ, Saiz Ruiz J: Correlatos biologicos del suicido y la agesividad en depressiones mayores (con melancolia): 5-HIAA en LCR, DST, y respuesta terpeutica a 5-HT$_2$. Unpublished paper presented to the First Congress of the Spanish Society for Biological Psychiatry, Barcelona, Spain, 1984

Peroutka SL, Snyder SH: Multiple serotonin receptors: differential binding of ^{3}H-hydroxytryptamine, ^{3}H-lysergic acid diethylamide and ^{3}H-spiroperidol. J Mol Pharmacol 16:687–699, 1979

Peroutka SL, Snyder SH: Regulation of serotonin (5-HT$_2$) receptors labeled with [^{3}H]spiroperidol by chronic treatment with antidepressant amitriptyline. Pharmacology Experimental Therapy 215:582–587, 1980

Perry EK, Marshall EF, Blessed G, et al: Decreased imipramine binding in the brains of patients with depressive illness. French Journal of Psychiatry 142:188–192, 1983

Pickar D, Roy A, Breier A, et al: Suicide and aggression in schizophrenia: neurobiologic correlates, in Psychobiology of Suicidal Behavior, Vol 487. Edited by Mann JJ, Stanley M. New York, Annals of the New York Academy of Sciences, 1986

Roy A: Suicide and psychiatric patients. Psychiatr Clin North Am 8:227–241, 1985

Roy A: Genetics of suicide, in Psychobiology of Suicidal Behavior, Vol 487. Edited by Mann JJ, Stanley M. New York, Annals of the New York Academy of Sciences, 1986

Roy-Byrne P, Post RM, Rubinow DR, et al: CSF 5-HIAA and personal and family history of suicide in affectively ill patients: a negative study. Psychiatry Res 10:263–274, 1983

Schulsinger F, Kety S, Rosenthal D, et al: A family study of suicide, in Origins, Prevention and Treatment of Affective Disorders. Edited by Schou M, Stromgren E. New York, Academic Press, 1979

Shaw DM, Camps FE, Eccleston EG: 5-Hydroxytryptamine in the hind-brain of depressive suicides. Br J Psychiatry 113:1407–1411, 1967

Stanley M: Cholinergic receptor binding in the frontal cortex of suicide victims. Am J Psychiatry 141:1432–1436, 1984

Stanley M, Mann JJ: Increased serotonin-2 binding sites in frontal cortex of suicide victims. Lancet 2:214–216, 1983

Stanley M, Virgilio J, Gershon S: Triated imipramine binding sites are decreased in the frontal cortex of suicides. Science 216:1337–1339, 1982

Stanley M, McIntyre I, Gershon S: Alterations in pre- and postsynaptic serotonergic neurons in suicide victims. Psychopharmacol Bull 19:684–687, 1983

Stanley M, Stanley B, Traskman-Bendz L, et al: Depressive symptoms and CSF levels of 5-HIAA in schizophrenic patients who have attempted suicide (abstract). Presented at the annual meeting of the American College of Neuropsychiatry, Washington, DC, December 1986

Targum SD, Rosen L, Capadanno AE: The dexamethasone suppression test in suicidal patients with unipolar depression. Am J Psychiatry 140:877–879, 1983

Traskman L, Asberg M, Bertillsson K, et al: Monoamine metabolites in CSF and suicidal behavior. Arch Gen Psychiatry 38:631–636, 1981

Van Praag HM: Depression and suicide and the metabolism of serotonin in the brain. J Affective Disord 4:275–290, 1982

Van Praag HM: CSF 5-HIAA and suicide in nondepressed schizophrenics. Lancet 2:977–978, 1983

Van Waltere JP, Charles G, Wilmotte J: Test de function a la dexamethasone et suicide. Acta Psychiatr Scand 83:569–578, 1983

Wirz-Justice A, Krauchi K, Lichtsteiner M, et al: Is it possible to modify serotonin receptor sensitivity? Life Sci 23:1249–1254, 1978

Zanko MT, Bigeon A: Increased β-adrenergic receptor binding in human frontal cortex of suicide victims (abstract). Presented at the annual meeting of the Society of Neuroscience, Boston, MA, October 20–25, 1983

11

Developing Strategies
to Prevent Youth Suicide

Mark L. Rosenberg, M.D., M.P.P.
David M. Eddy, M.D., Ph.D.
Robert C. Wolpert, Ph.D.
Eugenia P. Broumas

Youth suicide is an important social problem. In the United States, suicide is the second leading cause of death for persons 15 to 24 years of age. More than 1 in every 1,000 children will commit suicide before reaching the age of 25. This year in the United States, about 1 of each 8,000 youths aged 15 to 24 years will commit suicide, totaling about 5,000 deaths (Centers for Disease Control 1986). For comparison, accidents, the leading cause of death for persons aged 15 to 24 years, will claim about 17,000 youths in this age group; about 7,500 will be murdered; and about 4,800 will die of a specific disease. Suicide rates for certain subpopulations are nearly double the average and seem to be rising.

Many interventions have been proposed to reduce youth suicides. Before committing resources to any of these proposed interventions,

Many people contributed generously with their time and effort in developing the ideas, results, and recommendations in this chapter, and we are grateful for all of their help. The first section of this chapter is drawn from a study prepared for the Secretary's Task Force on Youth Suicide (Eddy et al. 1987). We thank the following people for assistance in developing and answering the questionnaire: Alan Berman, Ph.D., Donald Berwick, M.D., Gerald L. Brown, M.D., Lucy Davidson, M.D., Norman Farberow, Ph.D., Elliot Gershon, M.D., Frederick Goodwin, M.D., Robert Litman, M.D., Howard Miller, Ph.D., Jerome Motto, M.D., Emily Mumford, Ph.D., George E. Murphy, M.D., Cynthia Pfeffer, M.D., David Shaffer, M.D., Morton Silverman, M.D., Jack Smith, M.S., Howard Sudak, M.D., and Robert Yufit, Ph.D. Special thanks to Judy F. Eddy for assistance in preparing the ques-

we would like to know whether they work to actually prevent youth suicide. In addition, because our resources are limited, we would like to know which interventions are the most effective so that we can set priorities among them (as well as among suicide prevention and other social problems) and get the "biggest bang for the buck." Finally, we want a comprehensive approach to the problem that specifies how much of our resources to spend on research, how much on services, where the resources should come from, and who should conduct this effort.

The first part of this chapter describes the use of a model to analyze the effectiveness of six interventions for decreasing youth suicides in the United States. The next part of the chapter describes how this analysis was incorporated into a broad preventive strategy by the Department of Health and Human Services Task Force on Youth Suicide. The final part of this chapter presents a strategy suggested by the Centers for Disease Control for addressing the special problem of youth suicide clusters.

EFFECTIVENESS OF INTERVENTIONS TO PREVENT YOUTH SUICIDE

Estimating the effectiveness of interventions to prevent youth suicide can be extremely difficult because of the many factors that must be considered. First, at least four major types of psychiatric problems can increase the chance a youth will commit suicide: depression, manic-depressive disorders, character disorders characterized by impulsiveness and aggression, and schizophrenia. (In addition, many youths who commit suicide do not display psychiatric symptoms.) Youths with each type of psychiatric problem respond to different interventions in different ways. Second, the proposed interventions have many different mechanisms of action, including prevention (e.g., affective education), early detection (e.g., school-based screening programs or programs to educate families about the symptoms of psychiatric problems), improved treatment, and legal measures such as restricting access to guns. Third, the success of each type of intervention is determined by many unknown variables. For example, estimating the effectiveness of a sui-

tionnaire, for performing the calculations, and for preparing the manuscript. This study was commissioned by the Secretary's Task Force on Youth Suicide. Additional support was provided by the Charles A. Dana Foundation. Marcia Feinleib, Katie Baer, Donna Hiett, Task Force Members, and many other individuals and organizations contributed to the Recommendations of the Secretary's Task Force on Youth Suicide (Department of Health and Human Services 1987). Patrick J. O'Carroll, James A. Mercy, and Lucy E. Davidson helped to formulate the guidelines for community intervention. Lippincott/Harper and Row graciously gave permission to reprint portions of "Estimating the effectiveness of interventions to prevent youth suicide" from *Medical Care*.

cide hotline requires estimating the proportion of potential youth suicide victims who would be inclined to call such a hotline if they had access, the proportion of those who actually have access, the success of the hotline's personnel in thwarting the immediate suicide attempt, and the likelihood that a youth who survives the immediate crisis through the aid of the hotline will not commit suicide at a later time.

Unfortunately, very little empirical research exists that evaluates or compares the effectiveness of different interventions to prevent youth suicide. Policymakers now have little choice but to rely on the subjective judgments of experts. For other health problems, analytic models are effective for soliciting and using knowledge about the cost and effectiveness of a range of interventions to identify the best ways to use limited resources. For cancer control, for example, mathematical models have been used to estimate the effectiveness and costs of a wide variety of prevention, screening, and treatment programs and to set priorities for public programs (World Health Organization 1986). We tried to develop an analogous model for youth suicide to help identify the most cost-effective interventions.

We used a questionnaire to query experts about factors that determine the effectiveness of six major types of proposed interventions for decreasing youth suicides in the United States and then used a model to analyze the effectiveness of those interventions. The interventions examined are the following: 1) affective education, to help youths understand and cope with the types of problems that can lead to suicide; 2) early identification of youths at high risk of committing suicide, to bring them into treatment; 3) school-based screening programs; 4) crisis centers and hotlines; 5) improved training of health care professionals in treating conditions that can lead to suicide; and 6) restriction of access to three main methods of suicide—firearms, medications, and high places.

Methods

To derive preliminary estimates of the effectiveness of different interventions in decreasing suicide, we developed a questionnaire to solicit the subjective judgments of experts in various aspects of the youth suicide problem. To assist the experts, we broke the problem into components and directed the questions at specific factors that could be researched or assessed through the experts' experience.

Specifically, the questionnaire distinguished four major categories of potential youth suicide victims: depressives, manic depressives, "impulse aggressives," and those not manifesting the symptoms of identifiable psychiatric disorders. Many psychiatrists believe the first three categories have much higher suicide rates than the population at large, so individuals in those categories are described as "high risk," whereas those in the fourth category are described as "normal risk." Although persons diagnosed as schizophrenic also have a higher-than-average risk of suicide, we did not ask separate questions about this group because the symptoms necessary to diagnose schizophrenia are frequently not identified before age 25. Additionally, a recent study of almost 200 adolescent suicide victims did not identify a significant number with schizophrenia (D. Shaffer, personal communication, 1986). The effect of each intervention was analyzed for each category separately, and the results were combined.

To structure the questions, the questionnaire used a simple framework that identified the various points at which each intervention would prevent a suicide. This framework is shown in Figure 1.

The framework starts on the left with a potential youth suicide, which we define as a youth who would commit suicide before the age of 25 in the absence of *any* intervention (including current treatment interventions). If a suicide in such a youth is to be prevented, he or she must first be identified as a potential youth suicide victim, he or she must then be offered and accept a treatment, and the treatment must be successful in preventing the suicide. Therefore, the probability that a potential youth suicide victim will actually commit suicide depends on whether the steps of this process are accomplished. A suicide will result from a failure at any step—if the youth is not identified, if the youth does not receive appropriate treatment, or if the treatment fails.

Each of the six interventions we examined affects one or more of the three steps. For example, school-based screening is intended to identify potential youth suicide victims and bring them to treatment. The screening's effectiveness depends on how much it increases the probability that a potential victim of youth suicide will be identified. Education of parents and "gatekeepers" (e.g., persons who come into contact with and talk to suicidal youth, such as health professionals, hairdressers, gym teachers, and bartenders) is also intended to increase the probability that a potentially suicidal youth will be identified and offered treatment.

Figure 1.   Framework identifying points of intervention in youth suicide.

Interventions that aim to improve treatment are intended to decrease the probability that a youth identified as a potential suicide victim will actually commit suicide. At present, not all potentially suicidal youths are offered any treatment, and those who are do not all receive optimal treatment. To analyze this problem, we grouped all possible treatments for each psychological condition into three categories—no treatment, suboptimal treatment, and optimal treatment. One possible treatment intervention involves ensuring that specialists know and offer an optimal treatment for each type of psychiatric problem. Another treatment intervention involves educating other health care professionals (nonspecialists) to refer potentially suicidal youth to appropriate specialists. Such interventions are intended to help ensure that a youth identified as potentially suicidal actually receives optimal treatment.

School-based affective education programs appear on the basic framework at two points. Such programs alert both potential youth suicide victims and their friends to the signs and symptoms preceding a suicide. School-based education programs are intended to increase the probability that potential youth suicide victims will be identified (either by themselves or by their friends) and referred for treatment before committing suicide.

Another more direct result of affective education involves helping potentially suicidal youths and their friends to be more aware of the suicide problem and the steps to correct it and helping them to be more aware of the psychological stresses all youths face. When successful, affective education might itself be a form of treatment. Even without referral to a professional, the self-awareness or the intervention of a friend might prevent a potential youth suicide.

A crisis center also has several effects. The direct effect is that if a potential youth suicide victim contacts a crisis center, he or she might be talked out of committing suicide at that time. The suicidal person might or might not commit suicide at a later time. Secondarily, a potential youth suicide might not only be prevented at that time, but a potential victim might also be brought into a treatment program. These effects would be registered as an increase in the probability that a potential youth suicide victim would be identified and as an increase in the probability that a potential youth suicide victim would receive optimal treatment once identified.

Finally, the effect of interventions designed to restrict access to suicide methods (e.g., guns, drugs, and high places) can be viewed as a form of treatment. Obviously, such interventions do not treat the underlying conditions leading to suicide, but they can prevent an immediate suicidal event. In some cases, restricting access to suicide methods might thwart the suicidal impulse long enough to enable the potential youth suicide victim to pass through a personal crisis and revert to nonsuicidal behavior.

The questionnaire was designed to estimate the effectiveness of interventions by identifying all the important factors that could determine their impact and to focus questions on each specific factor. This approach helps narrow the scope of factors the respondents must consider at one time and helps ensure accurate answers. For example, for an estimate of the overall impact of a crisis center or hotline on reducing the chance that a youth would commit suicide, questions were asked about four topics: 1) the proportion of potential youth suicide victims who would have access to a hotline, 2) the proportion of those with access who would be inclined to call, 3) the proportion of those who call who would have their immediate suicide prevented, and 4) the proportion of these who would not become suicidal again before age 25 either because they changed or because they were brought into a successful treatment program. Thus, the experts were never asked a global question, such as "how much will Intervention A reduce youth suicide," which would require them to consider dozens of factors or venture a wild guess. Rather, they were asked about specific factors one at a time, and the overall effect of each intervention was calculated from their answers about the individual factors, according to the specified framework and the laws of probability theory.

We submitted the questionnaire to 29 individuals identified by the Secretary's Task Force on Youth Suicide. These individuals were not at all intended to be a representative sample of all suicide "experts." Instead, they were selected because they either had many years of experience working on youth suicide prevention, or had expertise on a particular area covered by the questionnaire such as screening, delivering mental health services, or assessing the quality of health services. Fifteen individuals returned the completed questionnaire. Estimates of each intervention's impact were then calculated separately for each of the experts.

Results

The results of the questionnaire are shown in Figures 2 and 3. Figure 2 indicates the estimated effect of various interventions in preventing suicides. For *current* treatment programs, the horizontal axis indicates the proportion of potential youth suicides prevented by existing treatment programs. The experts estimated that 1–39% of potential youth suicides (that would occur in the absence of any treatment) are currently prevented by existing treatment programs. On average, the experts estimated that approximately 10% of youths who would commit

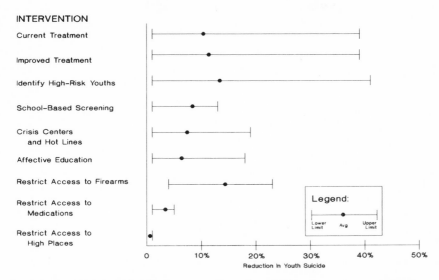

Figure 2. Estimated effectiveness of youth suicide prevention programs. Survey of 15 suicide experts, 1986.

suicide in the absence of any intervention are currently being prevented from committing suicide by existing treatment programs. The median was 6.5%. A 10% reduction in youth suicides would represent approximately 500 suicides prevented each year in the United States.

The experts surveyed expect programs designed to improve the treatment of potential youth suicide victims by health and mental health professionals to decrease youth suicides by 1% to about 39%. The average of the estimates predicted a reduction in potential youth suicide (in addition to the reduction already achieved by current treatment) of 11%. The median was 8%.

Figure 2 also describes the estimated impact of an intervention designed to identify potentially suicidal youth and bring them to treatment, either by making parents more aware of the signs and symptoms of psychiatric problems or by helping gatekeepers (e.g., teachers, barbers, beauticians, bartenders, gym teachers, religious counselors, neighbors, or relatives) identify potential youth suicide victims and bring them to treatment. The experts' answers indicate that such an intervention could reduce the current number of youth suicides by less than 1% to about 41%. The average of the answers was a reduction in youth suicides of about 13%, and the median was 8%.

Screening school-age children was estimated to reduce youth sui-

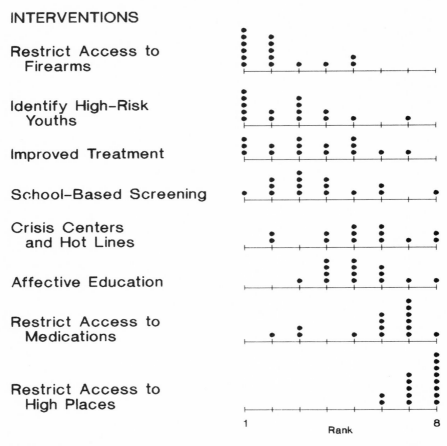

Figure 3. Ranking of interventions to prevent youth suicide estimated by 15 suicide experts.

cides by less than 1% to 13%, with an average and median reduction of 8%.

Crisis centers and hotlines were estimated to reduce youth suicides by less than 1% to 18%. The average of the answers predicted a reduction in youth suicides of about 7%, with a median of 4%.

School-based affective education programs might be expected to reduce youth suicides by less than 1% to 17%. The average of the estimates was a 6% reduction in youth suicides, and the median was 4%.

The last set of interventions involves restricting access to various suicide methods, such as firearms, medications, and high places (e.g., bridges, towers). Estimating the impact of these interventions was aided by data that indicated that about 62.5% of youth suicides are committed with firearms (approximately 80% of these are handguns); about 6% of youth suicides are due to poisonings by prescription medications (e.g., tranquilizers and psychotropic agents); and about 3% of youth suicides are caused by jumping from high places. About 30% of youth suicides are caused by other means, such as hanging and poisoning by carbon monoxide. Thus, restricting access to any one of these suicide methods could have an impact no greater than the proportion of suicides caused by each of these means. For additional assistance in estimating the impacts of these interventions, we asked the experts to assume that an intervention designed to restrict access to firearms would actually prevent only 50% of potential youth suicide victims from having access to firearms. Similarly, we asked them to assume that a program designed to restrict access to medications would actually restrict access for 75% of potential youth suicide victims, and that a program designed to restrict access to high places would actually restrict access for 25% of potential youth suicides. Thus, the maximum possible impact of interventions to restrict access to firearms, medications, and high places is a suicide reduction of 31%, 4.4%, and 0.7%, respectively. These are overestimates of the maximum possible effect, however, because some potentially suicidal youths who are denied access to their chosen means will choose a different means and will still commit suicide. The experts surveyed estimated that programs designed to restrict access to firearms might reduce the number of youth suicides by 4% to 23%, with an average estimate of about 14% and a median of 16%. Given the fairly small proportion of suicides caused by medication overdose, the expected impact of an intervention to restrict access to medications is understandably small. The respondents estimated that such a program would decrease suicides by less than 1% to 4.4%, with an average of about 3% and a median of 2%. The respondents estimated that the expected impact of an intervention to restrict access to high places would be a reduction in suicides of less than 1%, with the average and median of the answers both less than 1%.

The respondents' answers can be examined for patterns; even if there is a wide variation in the estimated impact of each intervention, there might be agreement on the most promising interventions. Unfortunately, this was not the case. For each intervention, the respondents ranked the intervention first, second, third, and so forth. The only intervention that received a high preference from most of the respondents was restricting access to firearms, and the only intervention that clearly received a low priority was restricting access to high places.

Conclusion

This study has led to several conclusions. First, there is much uncertainty among acknowledged experts about the expected effectiveness of different proposed interventions—clearly indicated by the wide range of estimates among the experts who responded to the questionnaire. In addition, most of the experts stated that their individual estimates were "soft" or uncertain. Furthermore, many of the experts did not respond because of their own uncertainty and reluctance to have their answers misinterpreted as hard data. If the experts who chose not to respond were even less certain about the impact of the interventions, the actual range of uncertainty might be even greater than that shown in the figures.

Second, none of the interventions are expected to represent a "cure" for youth suicides. The medians of the experts' predictions indicate that each of the interventions would reduce suicides by less than 1% to 16%. (A 10% reduction in youth suicides would represent approximately 500 youth suicides prevented each year.) Even if *all* suicide interventions were imposed simultaneously, the expected suicide reduction would be less than 50% (their sum) and possibly as low as 15% (if the same individuals responded to each intervention).

However, even if none of the interventions could be considered a "cure," some still might be cost-effective public health programs, depending on the costs of the interventions, a factor not examined in this study. Calculating the costs for saving a life through different suicide prevention interventions and comparing those with the costs of other selected health interventions would be useful. For example, in 1981 the Medicare end-stage renal disease program provided kidney dialysis facilities for approximately 64,000 enrollees, at a cost of approximately $23,000 per year of life (Eggers 1984); the National Heart, Lung, and Blood Institute estimates that between 17,000 and 35,000 victims of end-stage heart disease would benefit from heart transplants each year, at an average cost of about $50,000 per transplant, leading to median life extension of 5 years (Casscells 1986). In the absence of available donor hearts, left ventricular assist devices provide about the same life extension at a cost of about $150,000 per recipient (National Institutes of Health Working Group 1985). For liver transplantation, the cost per patient surviving 1 year exceeds $230,000 (Task Force on Liver Transplantation in Massachusetts 1983). At the other end of the spectrum, the cost of adding a year of life through immunization against measles ranges from $480 to $2,100, and the cost of averting a death through oral rehydration therapy can be as low as $100 (H.V. Fineberg, personal communication, 1987). Screening women over 30 years of age every 3 years for cervical cancer delivers an additional year of life expectancy for approximately $1,000. [Screening annually instead of every 3 years delivers an additional year of life expectancy for approximately $100,000 (Eddy, unpublished data.)]

Third, there is no clear "winner" among the proposed interventions. Not only are the averages of all the answers close, but the differences among the averages for each intervention are very small when compared with the range of uncertainty expressed about each intervention. This wide uncertainty about each intervention (represented graphically in the figures) makes it meaningless to attempt finely tuned comparisons among the different interventions, except on the basis of cost. For example, if two interventions are estimated to have approximately the same effect, but one costs 100 times more than the other, clearly the less costly intervention would be preferred. As a group, the experts thought the most effective intervention was to limit access to firearms, but they varied widely in their choices of the six proposed interventions they believed would be most effective.

Fourth, most of the information needed to plan effective interventions has not yet been collected or compiled. Thus the experts cannot accurately select which interventions will be the most effective or cost-effective at this time. Definitive answers cannot be obtained by polling experts or soliciting their opinions, nor can Congressional hearings or special commissions, which rely on expert opinion, be expected to provide the answers. At this time, arriving at reliable answers will require further research. Perhaps the study's most important conclusion is that a great need exists for additional empirical evidence and for rigorous analysis of the factors that control the effectiveness of different interventions.

Recommendations

Rigorous planning is needed before proceeding with interventions. Because of the great uncertainty about both the effectiveness and costs of different proposed interventions, it is currently not appropriate to implement any large-scale interventions. Insufficient resources exist to undertake all of the possible large-scale interventions, and insufficient data are available to intelligently choose among them. Not only is there no rational basis for choosing which interventions would be most effective or efficient, but implementing any large-scale activity could commit resources prematurely to inappropriate interventions and could falsely convey that our information base is stronger than it is.

Because of the social importance and visibility of youth suicide, there might still be great social pressure to undertake *some* activities before adequately assessing which interventions would be most effective. If so, it will be important to recognize the source of the urgency and to design the intervention specifically to address that objective. For example, if increasing public awareness of the problem and demonstrating society's concern are considered important, then interventions should be selected that achieve those objectives. Furthermore, among the possible set of interventions that achieve those objectives, those with the lowest cost should be given priority. Interventions that are expected to have benefits in addition to achieving reduced youth suicide rates should also be emphasized. For example, an intervention designed to prevent youth suicides by supporting families through life crises might not only prevent youth suicides but could prevent other problem behaviors, such as substance abuse and interpersonal violence.

Developing a rational strategy for preventing youth suicides will require that we learn more about the potential effectiveness and costs of each proposed intervention. This knowledge is best obtained through a program of carefully coordinated and directed research.

First, the work introduced in this paper must be expanded. Some expert respondents in our survey have suggested that additional interventions be considered and identified. The evidence about each intervention should be made available to expert panels, and the panelists should discuss the data in the light of their experience to reach a consensus about the factors that determine the effectiveness of each intervention. "Consensus" estimates for the effectiveness of the interventions can then be calculated.

Second, experts can describe the factors that determine the effectiveness of different interventions and identify those factors about which there is greatest uncertainty. Many of those factors could be examined with short-term, low-cost, empirical research. For example, with retrospective research, investigators can identify the proportion of youth suicide victims who had been identified as being at high risk for suicide before their deaths. This type of information would greatly improve estimates of the potential impact of interventions designed to improve identification of high-risk youths. If this research showed that all youths who committed suicide had previously been identified as being at high risk, a new intervention designed to increase the identification of high-risk youths would have no additional value. Through research, the proportion of youth suicide victims who were already under medical treatment and the proportion of those who were receiving optimal treatment could be identified. This information would improve estimates of the value of professional education programs. Researchers can identify the proportion of youth suicides that occur in clusters to help estimate the effectiveness of forming special teams to offer intensive suicide-prevention services in high schools where a suicide has occurred. The results of this type of short-term research could then be used to set preliminary priorities and to design pilot programs.

Research is also needed on the cost of various interventions. Some information on program costs already exists, but more cost information is needed. Ongoing and new intervention research should routinely address cost aspects.

Longer term research will eventually be required to evaluate the pilot programs. With this research, information could be collected both on operational characteristics of an intervention (such as the yield of previously unidentified high-risk youths identified through a school-based screening program) and on its long-term effectiveness in actually reducing youth suicides. However, because of the low incidence of suicides, very large sample sizes or large community programs will be required to derive meaningful estimates of the effectiveness of different interventions.

Given the urgency of the youth suicide problem, we recommend a strategy of

1. Analyzing the available information.
2. Conducting short-term research to gather empirical data for estimating both the effectiveness and cost of different interventions.
3. Analyzing the results of that research to set preliminary priorities.
4. Designing pilot projects to evaluate the most promising interventions.
5. Evaluating the pilot projects to plan large-scale interventions.

REPORT OF THE SECRETARY'S TASK FORCE ON YOUTH SUICIDE

This analysis and these recommendations were incorporated into the recommendations of the Secretary's Task Force on Youth Suicide. The establishment of this task force was prompted by the recognition that the suicide rate for young people between the ages of 15 and 24 years of age had almost tripled from 1950 to 1980. By 1983, suicide had become the second leading cause of death for young people in this age group (Rosenberg et al. 1987b). The sharp increase in youth suicide rates prompted the Secretary of Health and Human Services to organize a task force to investigate this pressing problem.

The major functions of the task force were to review, assess, and consolidate the available information about suicide; provide forums for communication among health care professionals, educators, researchers, social service workers, and families; and coordinate suicide activities among federal agencies, Congress, state and local governments, private agencies, and professional organizations.

The task force was also charged with recommending activities to address the problem. The task force apportioned these various tasks to three work groups, one on risk factors, another on preventive interventions, and a third on strategies and recommendations. The third work group focused on the subject of this chapter, developing a strategy for the prevention of youth suicide and encompassing this strategy in its recommendations.

In formulating these recommendations, the task force had four objectives. The first objective was to review the findings of task force work groups on risk factors and prevention; use these findings to construct a variety of youth suicide prevention strategies by targeting specific interventions to subpopulations with specific risk factors; evaluate these strategies in terms of cost and effectiveness; and, finally, recommend the most appropriate and cost-effective ones.

The second objective was to present a comprehensive set of recommendations to the Secretary that would address the most urgent needs for research and prevention; reflect input from a diverse set of disciplines, interest groups, and experts in the field; be clear, practical, and few in number; address ways to include many different sectors (such as business, education, health, and mental health); and not require a large expenditure of government funds.

The third objective was to develop an implementation plan to indicate how a wide range of sectors and organizations could all be active participants in implementing the recommendations. These sectors included public health, mental health, health services, education, business and philanthropy, media and entertainment, criminal justice and legal systems, religion, social services, and family; the organizations included government and nongovernment groups.

Finally, the fourth objective was to build a consensus in the suicide prevention communities using the process of developing the recommendations to bring together separate sources of support: the suicide prevention center movement and the "medical community"; lay persons and health professionals; service providers and the research community; and even within the research community, to bring together the biological and psychosocial camps.

The work group constructed preliminary recommendations by reviewing all the papers commissioned by the task force, including the papers on risk factors and on prevention. In addition, recommendations were solicited from all participants at the national conferences on risk factors and prevention. Over 700 experts and participants in youth suicide prevention attended these conferences and more than 200 individuals submitted recommendations. From these sources, the work group compiled a set of preliminary recommendations which were reviewed and revised by the task force. These preliminary recommendations were distributed just prior to the National Conference on Strategies for the Prevention of Youth Suicide. At a day-long invitational meeting, groups composed of experts in specific areas of suicide prevention worked together with representatives of more than 90 different local and national organizations that could play important roles in implementing these recommendations. Each working group was asked to rank the priority of the recommendations for their sector, list the steps essential to implementing each recommendation, identify who should do each step, and present a rough timetable and set of measurable objectives for monitoring progress on each objective. The collected set of recommendations and the implementation plan for each objective, a 120-page document, were distributed for discussion the next day at the National Conference on Strategies for the Prevention of Youth Suicide. These recommendations were further refined, and the 47 recommendations from the conference were combined into 6 final recommendations for the task force.

1. Develop Accurate, Timely, and Valid Data on Suicide and Attempted Suicide

We must develop uniform definitions for suicide and special programs (called "surveillance systems") at the state and local levels to identify and report suicides and suicide attempts more consistently, objectively, and completely. Standardized criteria for determining suicide as a cause of death should be implemented by death certifiers. These procedures may also provide the means to detect unusual patterns, or "clusters," of suicides and help to identify methods to prevent such suicides.

2. Conduct Multidisciplinary Research to Determine and Evaluate the Risk Factors for Suicide

It is important to identify the many psychological, sociological, and biological factors that contribute to an increased likelihood of suicide among youth. Well-planned, coordinated, and adequately funded efforts will help elucidate the causes of suicide, facilitate the identification of youth at greatest risk, and help in targeting intervention and preventive services for young people.

Because the risk factors for suicide are very diverse, we believe that suicide research can be enriched by interdisciplinary efforts that combine, for example, educators, biologists, sociologists, and psychiatrists in research projects.

3. Evaluate the Effectiveness and Cost of Interventions to Prevent Suicide

Little is known about the effectiveness of the many suicide prevention and intervention programs that have sprung up since the 1970s. We need to know more about the kinds of interventions that work and for whom and under what circumstances they work.

We need to evaluate suicide prevention centers, telephone hotlines, school-based intervention and education programs, and peer support groups as well as programs targeted to specific groups. These include programs that enhance the ability of gatekeepers (people who are in frequent contact with youngsters) to recognize the warning signs of potentially suicidal youth and programs that improve early identification and treatment of depression by health care professionals. We also need to evaluate specific treatment modalities for suicide attempters and programs that give emotional support to people who have survived another's suicide.

Because firearms are the most frequently used method for committing suicide, we must assess whether programs limiting access to this lethal means of suicide, especially to persons known to be at high risk, have an overall effect on suicide rates.

4. Support the Delivery of Suicide Prevention Services

While the physical needs of young people who come to health care facilities are usually well attended to, other personal, school, or family problems that may place an adolescent at risk for suicide are frequently not recognized by many health care providers.

Physicians, nurses, and others in health care settings, e.g., emergency rooms, general medical clinics, health maintenance organizations, and prenatal clinics, should be alert about the risk factors for suicide among youth, have the ability to identify those in danger, and have the resources to refer them to appropriate mental health care. Emergency room personnel, for example, should refer adolescents for psychological evaluation when suicide attempts are suspected. In addition, more health care professionals are needed who specialize in psychological problems of youth.

Because its roots lie in many different social, health, and educational problems experienced by youth, suicide cannot be dealt with in isolation from other self-destructive behaviors. Suicide prevention activities should be integrated into broader health promotion programs and health care delivery services directed at preventing other self-destructive behaviors, such as alcohol and substance abuse, teen pregnancy, and interpersonal violence.

These improvements in services will require cooperation among health service, social service, and juvenile justice agencies. They will also require easing the legal and financial barriers that inhibit young people from obtaining appropriate health and mental health care.

Finally, technical assistance for communities in which suicides have occurred should be made more widely available. State and local public health departments are the most appropriate agencies for providing assistance in developing response plans that will reduce the chances of further suicides in the community.

5. Inform and Educate the Public and Health Service Providers About Current Knowledge in the Prevention, Diagnosis, and Treatment of Suicide Among Youth

We must both promote public awareness of youth suicide and provide necessary training for health care professionals in suicide prevention. Developing special programs to improve the ability of gatekeepers to recognize clues to suicide, training school system personnel to assess suicidal risk in young people, and encouraging them to refer high-risk youngsters to appropriate care are important aspects of suicide education. Moreover, we must make every effort to disseminate information on youthful suicide and suicide attempts to interested individuals and organizations through resource centers or information clearinghouses.

6. Involve Both Public and Private Sectors in the Prevention of Youth Suicide

No simple, universally effective intervention will solve the problem of suicide. Preventing youth suicide will require the efforts of all sectors of the community—public and private—implemented at the national, state, and local levels.

Businesses should provide and encourage employees to use employee assistance programs when a family member is at risk for suicide. Foundations and corporations should increase their support for programs to prevent youth suicide. The media and entertainment industry should cooperate in efforts to investigate whether television and other media affect suicidal behavior of young people. Youth services should include primary prevention programs directed toward disadvantaged, socially isolated, and other underserved youth. Religious counselors should be aware of the indicators for suicidal risk and resources from which young people can get help. Legal means should be investigated for ways to limit access to means of suicide and ways to alleviate liability concerns of mental health professionals who treat suicidal youth.

The criminal justice system should educate personnel to recognize the high risk of suicide during periods of incarceration and provide mental health services for identifying and treating suicidal individuals. States should encourage social services in the public and private sectors to develop comprehensive, preventive approaches for families with youth at high risk for suicide, substance abuse, and interpersonal violence. Programs should be developed to strengthen families and enable them to support their youth through life crises.

The factors contributing to youth suicide are complex and defy simplistic solutions. These recommendations are not likely to be accomplished by short-term efforts, but will require a variety of long-term, ongoing, prevention activities and intervention approaches.

A PROGRAM FOR PUBLIC HEALTH AND COMMUNITY AGENCIES

Although suicide has not traditionally been considered a public health problem, the Department of Health and Human Services and the Public Health Service have placed a high priority on developing effective public health approaches to youth suicide prevention. This priority reflects recent changes in the patterns of suicide in this country, and a traditional public health focus on preventing those health problems that take a large toll in terms of lives and potential years of life lost.

Recent attention has also focused on clusters of suicides among young people. These are suicides that are both grouped together in a particular place (such as a community or school district) and occur within a relatively short period of time. Suicide clusters have been known to occur for many years, and apparent clusters of suicides have been reported from many areas of the United States (Davidson and Gould 1987). Unlike clusters of measles or smallpox, however, clusters of suicides are not a reportable condition so we do not now know how frequently they occur, what proportion of all youth suicides might occur in clusters, or whether the frequency of suicide clusters has increased in recent years. One explanation for why clusters occur involves the notion of "contagion," the idea that suicide may spread among some young people who are "exposed" to suicide either directly or indirectly. Direct exposure may occur through a friend's or classmate's suicide; indirect exposure to suicide may occur through news reports, books, movies, or discussions. Although our understanding of suicide contagion is incomplete, there is evidence that suggests indirect exposure to suicide through print and broadcast media might lead some susceptible individuals to commit suicide (Gould and Shaffer 1986; Phillips and Carstensen 1986). Either exposure may lead a susceptible youth to commit suicide, perhaps imitating or copying the initial suicide by choosing a similar method and setting. Individuals may be affected by exposure to a suicide in proportion to the degree they identify with or feel themselves similar to the initial suicide victim.

At the same time that suicide among youth is being recognized as a serious public health problem, questions are being raised about the effectiveness of traditional approaches to suicide prevention. The traditional mental health approach to suicide prevention was based on the notion that the typical person at risk for suicide was an older, clinically depressed, male. In that approach, suicide would be prevented by identifying older, depressed males and treating their depression. However, recent evidence suggests that not only are most suicide victims now young, but in addition, most do not meet traditional medical criteria for a diagnosis of depression. The other widespread approach to suicide prevention has been made through suicide prevention centers or crisis intervention units. But, as we have noted previously, the effectiveness of these and other preventive services or educational efforts has not yet been fully evaluated.

Public Health Interventions

While much more basic research needs to be done and all of the approaches to youth suicide prevention urgently need to be evaluated, several basic principles of preventive health may be usefully applied to this area. The Centers for Disease Control have suggested an interim approach for how a community might respond to the problem (Rosenberg et al. 1987a). These suggestions do not constitute a proven effective intervention; rather, they reflect the state of our current thinking, and they will be modified as we learn more about the problem. A plan for how the community might respond to a young person's suicide should be developed. The knowledge that the subject has been discussed and a plan prepared can, in and of itself, relieve the sense of panic and fear that might otherwise terrify school or community officials. Since there is no proven effective intervention plan, each community should prepare its own response, taking into account its own needs and resources. It may be easier to prepare a reasonable plan *before* one or more suicides occur in the community, because communities are frequently barraged by so-called suicide experts after youth suicides have occurred. These "experts" frequently have strongly held beliefs about what kind of program would be most effective in preventing more youth suicides. For example, some experts advocate "blitzing" the community with discussions and information about suicide directed at children, school staff, parents, and the community at large. Other experts counsel a diametrically opposite approach, that of keeping things quiet, drawing as little attention as possible to the deaths and to the topic of suicide. They argue that more attention drawn to the subject will only increase the risk of "contagion" and result in additional youth suicides. In fact, since neither approach has been adequately evaluated, the community should develop its own approach, aware of the current state of knowledge, and draw up its plan under noncrisis conditions.

First, the plan should include a procedure for identifying young people considered at high risk of suicide. These people might be identified by teachers, guidance counselors, parents, peers, police, mental health professionals, and hospital emergency room personnel. Persons thought to be at high risk include close friends of the persons who committed suicide, young people with a history of suicide threats or attempts or a family history of suicide attempts or suicide, young people with serious drug abuse or alcohol problems, young people with a history of serious emotional problems, people who may be likely to identify with the deceased, and young people who may be socially isolated or without emotional supports. The plan should specify clear and simple procedures for referring these young people at high risk. Listings of mental health services and providers should be widely available.

Second, the plan should identify and assess community resources: Who is available to work with school authorities (such as local or state mental health and public health officials)? Who is available to counsel high-risk students (therapists, psychologists, psychiatrists, guidance counselors)? Who can counsel the surviving family members? If a crisis should occur, which individuals or representatives should serve on a coordinating task force (such as the mayor or administrator, superintendent of schools, PTA president, mental health clinic director)? Is there an existing facility that could provide immediate crisis counseling through a 24-hour hotline and walk-in clinic?

Third, the plan should identify an individual who will act as a spokesperson for the school or community. This individual should be responsible for handling all interactions with the media and for providing accurate and timely information to concerned parents and community members. This is an extremely important function and it is important to obtain and sustain community support for this coordinated approach to the media. The plan should also identify responsible individuals at organizations such as schools, hospitals, and police agencies.

Accurate information is important because active rumors are incendiary. There are no clear-cut guidelines for media coverage of suicide because we do not yet know the effects of different types of media coverage on subsequent youth suicides. There will inevitably be media interest in presenting the information about youth suicides to the public. Besides the risk of "contagion," unguided media coverage can contribute to dividing a community against itself. Inevitably, during a community response to a crisis there will be individuals who disagree with the response that a teacher, school system, or a task force has chosen to adopt: Individuals tend to look for someone to blame for what went wrong. These are normal feelings that can be directly addressed and resolved. But these feelings can become inflamed and newspaper reports can be inflammatory if the dissatisfied individuals start using the media to wage their battles. In addition, media representatives can be inordinately intrusive upon the lives of shocked and grieving students and parents. Some school authorities, for example, might want to protect students from unreasonable requests for interviews by barring reporters from school grounds. In addition, media coverage during a crisis is rarely considered and balanced to the extent that the community might wish; after the crisis, when there is a greater likelihood of accurate in-depth coverage, the reporter or publisher may no longer be interested in this issue.

Finally, the plan should acknowledge the importance of not romanticizing in any way the young person or his or her tragic death. Activities that might be seen as romanticizing the suicide might increase the likelihood of other young people committing suicide through the mechanism of identification or through imitation. Unfortunately, during the period of acute mourning and grief, when the community is under maximal stress, most individuals tend to describe and remember the good qualities of the deceased. They are reluctant to attribute serious problems to the individual who committed suicide either because of denial or guilt, or out of respect. What emerges, then, during the immediate crisis period is a romanticized portrait of the individual(s) who committed suicide. This is frequently the account carried by the media. Wakes and elaborate funerals can perpetuate this romantic view of the individual. In appropriate cases, it may be helpful to acknowledge that the deceased was someone who had very serious problems that set him or her apart from most other young people. For example, if a young person had serious problems related to alcohol abuse or serious mental illness, it would be important to stress that this problem set the suicidal individual apart from most other kids, and that this problem had better solutions than suicide.

SUMMARY

This chapter first described the use of a model to analyze the effectiveness of six interventions for decreasing youth suicides in the United States. Using a questionnaire to query experts about factors that determine the effectiveness of these interventions, our study indicated a wide range of uncertainty about each intervention's effectiveness, and the range of uncertainty among experts about any particular intervention exceeded the differences among the best estimates for each intervention. The study also indicated that no single intervention, or even all six interventions combined, could be considered a "cure" for youth suicides. Additional empirical research about the factors that determine the effectiveness of youth suicide prevention programs, followed by careful analysis, is needed before large-scale programs are launched.

The importance of evaluating the effectiveness of different interventions was stressed in the Report of the Secretary's Task Force on Youth Suicide. The task force developed a comprehensive report that includes recommendations to:

1. Develop accurate, timely, and valid data on suicide and attempted suicide.
2. Conduct multidisciplinary research to determine and evaluate the risk factors for suicide.
3. Evaluate the effectiveness and cost of interventions to prevent suicide.
4. Support the delivery of suicide prevention services.
5. Inform and educate the public and health service providers about current knowledge in the prevention, diagnosis, and treatment of suicide among youth.
6. Involve both public and private sectors in the prevention of youth suicide.

Youth suicides that are clustered within a limited period of time and a defined geographic space require special attention because exposure to such suicides may put additional susceptible young people at high risk for subsequent suicides.

The final section of this chapter presented a strategy for a community-based response to the problem of youth suicide and youth suicide clusters. This strategy highlights the importance of a planned response that includes a procedure for identifying young people at high risk of suicide, identifies and assesses community counseling resources, identifies a community spokesperson, and provides guidance for dealing with youth suicides in a way that does not romanticize the young victims or their tragic deaths.

REFERENCES

Casscells W: Heart transplantation: recent policy developments. N Engl J Med 315:1365–1368, 1986

Centers for Disease Control: Youth Suicide in the United States, 1970–1980. Atlanta, GA, Centers for Disease Control, November 1986

Davidson L, Gould MS: Contagion and Media. Washington, DC, Task Force on Youth Suicide, Department of Health and Human Services, 1987

Department of Health and Human Services: Report of the Secretary's Task Force on Youth Suicide, Vol I: Recommendations. Washington, DC, Department of Health and Human Services, 1987

Eddy DM, Wolpert RL, Rosenberg ML: Estimating the Effectiveness of Interventions to Prevent Youth Suicides: Report of the Secretary's Task Force on Youth Suicide, Vol. IV. Washington, DC, Department of Health and Human Services, 1987

Eggers PW: Trends in medical reimbursement for end-stage renal disease: 1974–1979. Health Care Financing Review 6:31–38, 1984

Gould MS, Shaffer D: The impact of suicide in television movies. N Engl J Med 315:690–694, 1986

National Institutes of Health Working Group on Mechanical Circulatory Support of the National Heart, Lung, and Blood Institute: Artificial Heart and Assist Devices: Directions, Needs, Costs, Societal and Ethical Issues. Bethesda, MD, National Institutes of Health, May 1985

Phillips DP, Carstensen LL: Clustering of teenage suicides after television news stories about suicide. N Engl J Med 315:690–694, 1986

Rosenberg ML, O'Carroll PJ, Mercy JA, et al: Community prevention of youth suicide: an epidemiologic basis and public health approach. Unpublished paper presented at the annual meeting of the American Psychiatric Association, Chicago, IL, May 8, 1987a

Rosenberg ML, Smith JC, Davidson LE, et al: The emergence of youth suicide: an epidemiologic analysis and public health perspective. Annu Rev Public Health 8:417–440, 1987b

Task Force on Liver Transplantation in Massachusetts: Final Report. Boston, MA, Massachusetts Department of Health, May 1983

World Health Organization: The use of quantitative methods in planning national cancer control programmes. Bull WHO 64:683–693, 1986

Epilogue:
Implications for Research and Clinical Practice

Cynthia R. Pfeffer, M.D.

Each of the chapters in this volume suggests that there are many issues that require systematic research. In addition, the studies presented have numerous implications for clinical practice.

Mohammad Shafii comprehensively described the psychological autopsy method and comparison groups to study adolescent suicide. Such an approach is an important method for elucidating factors that may help to solve the unanswered question of whether youth suicide attempters are a distinct group from youth suicide victims. Risk factors for youth suicide that were identified in psychological autopsy investigations can be studied additionally by means of prospective research designs with high-risk youth groups to determine the predictive validity of these factors. Furthermore, knowledge of these empirically derived youth suicide risk factors can guide clinicians to focus their diagnostic assessments demarcating the severity, duration, and the interactions among these risk factors.

The study conducted by Harry M. Hoberman and Barry D. Garfinkel added to and complemented the results of Dr. Shafii's work. They used a larger sample obtained from medical examiner records of adolescents who committed suicide and found that there has been a change in features associated with youth suicide in recent times. Therefore, clinicians should appreciate that there may be period effects that influence factors associated with youth suicide. As a result, clinicians need to maintain up-to-date knowledge about youth suicide so that assessments and interventions will have maximum efficacy. These psychological autopsy studies also suggested that adolescents at risk for suicide have identifiable psychiatric symptoms and psychiatric disorders. Early identification and intervention to reduce morbidity resulting from symptoms of these disorders will be beneficial to prevent risk for youth suicide.

Based on the results of the research presented in this volume, a model for youth suicidal risk can be developed that involves the relative contributions from factors associated with psychiatric, constitutional, and ecological components. Alec Roy presented several lines of evidence from diverse research methodologies with psychiatric patients, a community sample, twins, and adoptees to suggest that, in adults, suicidal behavior has a genetic basis for transmission. However, whether suicidal behavior aggregates in families of children and adolescents who have suicidal tendencies has not been studied empirically. Nevertheless, an important clinical implication is that systematic and comprehensive inquiry about suicidal ideation, nonfatal suicidal acts, and suicide among relatives of every child or adolescent undergoing a mental health assessment is warranted to help identify those youth who may be at risk for suicidal behavior. In fact, although not empirically studied, it may be that treatment offered to a suicidal relative may be an important method for preventing risk of youth suicidal behavior.

J. John Mann, Michael D. DeMeo, John G. Keilp, and P. Anne McBride, in their extensive overview of biological factors associated with suicide, highlighted the important role of the regulation of serotonin functioning but also pointed out the paucity of research on this issue among suicidal children and adolescents. Although there are presently no clear practical clinical implications of these findings, future research may develop a biological risk profile of youth who are vulnerable to display suicidal behavior. Such studies may lead also to suggestions about biological approaches for intervention of suicidal youth that makes use of serotonergic stimulating medication. Such treatment may raise the biological threshold for suicidal risk and thereby provide a means of forestalling a suicidal act.

Ecological components were described in several chapters written by Cynthia R. Pfeffer on environmental stress; Paul C. Holinger on large population studies suggesting period effects; Gerald L. Klerman describing cohort effects for youth suicide; Lucy E. Davidson on youth suicide clusters; David P. Phillips, Lundie L. Carstensen, and Daniel J. Paight on news reports of suicidal behavior; and Heinz Häfner and Armin Schmidtke on imitative effects of fictional media stories of youth suicide. These reports identified significant issues in which controversy and unanswered questions abound and for which additional research is needed. From a clinical perspective, the assessment of child and adolescent suicidal risk should include questions related to experiences with and knowledge about individuals with suicidal tendencies. A clinician should determine whether a youngster recently heard about suicidal behavior through the media, whether a peer experienced recent suicidal tendencies, and whether the youngster has been exposed to a suicidal relative. A clinician should evaluate the meanings and perceptions ascribed by the youngster to these experiences. In addition, the effects of recent and past stresses such as loss of a boyfriend or girlfriend, physical illness, sexual and/or violent abuse, and parental loss through separation/divorce may amplify suicidal risk among youth, according to the chapter presented by Cynthia R. Pfeffer. These experiences should be documented and their impact on the thinking and behavior of a youngster should be evaluated.

Mark L. Rosenberg, David M. Eddy, Robert C. Wolpert, and Eugenia P. Broumas outlined a number of issues that have clinical and public health implications. They highlighted the need to conduct systematic comparative studies of intervention effects for the prevention of suicidal risk. They raised a concern that community and school intervention and prevention programs need to be clearly organized with an important implication that evaluation of the effects of such programs is necessary. Another implication is the need for psychiatrists and other mental health professionals to be involved actively in community efforts to prevent youth suicide and to respond to the needs of a community when a youngster commits suicide.

In conclusion, this book highlights recently acquired empirical knowledge about youth suicide. There are many more aspects of this major mental health problem among youth that require systematic research. Efforts need to be invested in understanding the natural course of suicidal youth, the effects of treatment programs, and the continuities and discontinuities of suicidal behavior among various phases of the life cycle. With regard to clinical practice, efforts need to be supported that advance techniques for early identification and adequate treatment of youth at risk for suicidal behavior. An important facet of this is to develop and maintain continuity in the health care system so that suicidal youth may have better compliance to treatment programs. Finally, it is hoped that the aims of this book, which are to educate clinicians, to stimulate new research, and to enhance and clarify directions for clinical practice, have been achieved.

Index